Thrown Away
Child

D1044494

Thrown Away Child

A True Story of Abuse and Neglect in the Care System

Louise Allen

with Corinne Sweet

**SIMON &
SCHUSTER**

London · New York · Sydney · Toronto · New Delhi

First published in Great Britain by Simon & Schuster UK Ltd, 2017

Copyright © Louise Allen, 2017

The right of Louise Allen to be identified as the author
of this work has been asserted by her in accordance with the
Copyright, Designs and Patents Act, 1988.

9 10 8

Simon & Schuster UK Ltd
1st Floor
222 Gray's Inn Road
London WC1X 8HB

www.simonandschuster.co.uk
www.simonandschuster.com.au
www.simonandschuster.co.in

Simon & Schuster Australia, Sydney
Simon & Schuster India, New Delhi

The author and publishers have made all reasonable efforts to contact
copyright holders for permission, and apologise for any omissions or errors in
the form of credits given. Corrections may be made to future printings

A CIP catalogue record for this book is available from the British Library

Paperback ISBN: 978-1-4711-6674-7
eBook ISBN: 978-1-4711-6675-4

Typeset in Fournier by M Rules
Printed and bound by CPI Group (UK) Ltd, Croydon, CR0 4YY

MIX
Paper | Supporting
responsible forestry
FSC® C171272
FSC
www.fsc.org

To my small but beautiful family

CONTENTS

I

Counting and Corners

One, two, three, four. I'm staring hard at the ceiling, following a long crack in the paint up to the small plastic lightshade. One, two, three, four cracks on the ceiling. I keep counting. I do this all the time. I do this every night, especially while I'm waiting. I do this whenever things are going on, like they are right now. One, two, three four: edges of the door frame, corners of the room. My eyes run along the lines: counting, counting, counting, counting. I am in a tiny dark box room. A plywood partition runs down the centre. One, two, three, four. I know they are in the other half of the room, but I can't see anything, only hear. It happens every night – well, it's only about six o'clock, so it's not properly night, but it is bedtime. No messing. Light comes in through the cracks between the thin pulled curtains. Navy blue. I'm not allowed to sit up and look, so I flatten myself down. Really flat. Hardly breathing. I'm supposed to go to sleep. The bed feels lumpy. I close my eyes tightly. All I can see are orange swirls behind my eyes, purple and blue colours, weird shapes. The shapes are scary but they are also interesting: I follow them, opening and closing my eyes, experimenting. Counting to four at the same time as I blink.

Suddenly I hear the sound of rough material being pulled. She's holding him down. There's a grunt and a whimper. A thick white material strap is fixed to the side of the bed on hooks. I can hear him sobbing quietly behind the partition as she straps him down to the bed in her nightly ritual. I hear her tying and clicking things. I hold my breath. I tighten my body, flattening it even further on the bed, trying to disappear. She is spitting venom at him, and I hear: 'Be quiet, you little bastard.'

One, two, three, four. One, two, three, four. 'Stop whining, will you, or I'll give you something to whine about.' I work my fingers under the thin blanket. I'm cold. I'm always cold. I'm hungry, too. Always hungry. My stomach makes strange growling noises and I try to flatten it down, holding my breath harder, scared she'll hear. I work my fingers harder: pressing thumb to index, to middle, to ring, to little: one, two, three, four.

Thwack! There's the sound of a large woman's hand on young bare skin. 'I'm not changing you now, you little bastard, I've enough work to do.' I hold my breath now, counting faster. William is whimpering very quietly. I know he will be lying in wet clothes now and I'm sure I can smell that stinky sharp odour that wafts around our room at night despite the cold. I'm scared of what comes next and my heart starts to thump. It feels like it's jumping in my chest. When she's done with one, she usually moves on to the next: me. I hold my breath, flatten my body, work my fingers. Please no, please no. I look at the flowery patterns on the wallpaper: faded blue flowers, all tightly packed together in repeating swirls. They make me dizzy. I count one, two, three, four flowers, in little groups of four, with tight little leaves. One, two, three, four. Suddenly a dark shape appears around the partition end – there's a gap between it and the door and I gulp in air as I tense.

'What are you still doing awake, you little bitch?' She moves towards me, and I make out tight, grey wavy hair in the gloom; a sharp nose, beady eyes, a pursed mouth. There's a whiff of vinegar and coal tar soap. She scares me stiff. I'm not breathing, not moving. I'm a board. She's like the demented wicked queen in that film. For a moment I freeze. I'm expecting the hand across the face, and I don't want one. I can hear William moaning next door still, and I know it winds her up. So I'm good. Very good. I blink at her over the top of the thin, rough grey blanket and try to look angelic and appealing. Trying to be small. I can't speak. I'm too scared. I stay still, hardly breathing, flatter by the minute: disappearing into the lumpy mattress. Or so I hope.

Suddenly she is looming over me, thin and beaky, like a pecking bird – her nasty breath on my face, intense and terrifying. There's something in her huge hand. I look at her bushy eyebrows; white and brown spiky slugs. 'Sit up!' she barks, yanking me upright. Suddenly her hand is at my mouth, trying to push something in – it's like a large green jelly bean. She forces it into my mouth: 'Swallow.' I can't. I feel a big dry finger push something through my lips. I half choke. 'C'mon, swallow.' Her other hand goes into her floral pinny pocket and produces a brown bottle – I recognise the cough medicine. She rips the top off. 'Drink. Wash it down.'

I know better than to resist. She often gives me her 'special' medicine. I don't like it; I hate the taste, and it makes me feel weird, but I have no choice. My mouth fills with the gloopy pungent pink stuff and I gag. The pill gets lodged; it's like swallowing a pebble. Finally I manage to swallow it by staying calm and counting – fast: one, two, three, four; one, two, three, four. She doesn't know I'm doing this, but her piercing eyes are on me and she is impatiently screwing the lid back on the bottle. I have to be good and keep calm.

'Lie down, you little bitch.'

I slide down thankfully. I can still hear William, although he's just murmuring now, behind the partition in his sodden smelly pyjamas.

Yank! I suddenly feel the white material strap going across my chest. Yank! She tightens it hard. Click. It's like an iron bar across me. I can't move. I can hardly breathe now, it's so tight, but I know better than to complain. If I want to pee I won't be able to get up, and I'll just have to do it in my old stripy pyjamas and then spend the night lying in wet. I'm beginning to feel a sort of cotton wool feeling in my head and mouth as she moves towards the door of our room.

'Now, I don't want to hear a peep of out you,' she spits towards me with eagle intensity. 'Or you – d'y'hear?' she snaps at William, who is now silent finally. I start counting again, looking at the blurry flowers on the wall. My fingers are trapped by my sides, going numb. I'm pinned to the bed. A strange heaviness comes over me and I'm soon totally gone, sucked into swirling, sickly blackness.

～✖～

This is my life. It has been my life for as long as I can remember. I'm about three or four years old (I don't know exactly when my birthday is, as we never celebrate it. I'm told I was born in 1967, probably in June – it was called the summer of love.) I live in a place called Oxford, in a pleasant-looking house with a garden on the edge of town, near where they make cars, with an orchard out the back. It sounds lovely. In fact, from the outside, it looks lovely – neat and tidy with a little gravel drive. You would never know from looking at the outside what horrible things go on inside. It looks just like the other houses – ordinary, homely and suburban. Yet behind the neat net curtains the life going on in that house – my life – is absolute hell. William's life is also hell. Actually, his is worse. It's been hell for as long as I can remember.

My 'mother' is called Barbara. She is not my 'real' mother, as I was adopted in 1968. Barbara says I was fostered by her and Ian (her husband) when I was just six weeks old. She tells me my real mother threw me away, so she kindly took me in and I should be very grateful. She already had my adopted brother, William, who was also unwanted. 'Mum' tells us we are both very lucky to be with them, the Taylors, as most people wouldn't take in scruffy unwanted children like us. She tells us we have chips on our shoulders, like all thrown away children. I look at my shoulders sometimes, trying to see the chips – does she mean potato chips? I am confused. Often. But I know better than to answer back or question anything because Barbara, or 'Mum', is not to be crossed. Ever. She rules our house with an iron fist in an iron glove.

Ian, or 'Dad', as we call him, is a quiet, shy man and is like a shadow in the background who says and does very little. He seems to obey Barbara totally. We are big trouble. A lot of work. We make her life hell. She tells us this over and over. Of course, what we don't know at the time, and are not to know until a lot later, is that when the Taylors took me in they were already under investigation by the authorities for child cruelty to William, who had been there for two years.

Barbara liked to apply tough discipline. Very tough. William often had black bruises on his face and body, and cuts and weals on his arms, legs and back. It seems that several neighbours reported this to the local authority, but in 1968 there was a shortage of places for children like us. And there were lots of unwanted children. I just thought it was normal to be whacked, slapped and kicked. But we knew we were lucky that Barbara and Ian had found it in their hearts to take in such unwanted, unattractive and unloveable children as us.

Ian worked as an engineer in a local firm, and was good with his hands. However, he didn't have many words and he seldom stood up to Barbara, although the house belonged to his family and he'd actually lived there all his life. Apparently Ian wasn't the marrying kind, was nearly forty, and his family worried about him still being single. When a friend said they knew just the woman for him – Barbara – he was pushed into courting her.

Barbara was also a late starter, and had been a nanny to a local well-to-do family (although she had been brought up in a real old-fashioned workhouse and a convent in London). She had a big family from whom she was now largely estranged. As Ian's family had felt it was time for him to 'settle down', being almost middle-aged and still living at home, he thought, *Why not?* After all, Barbara was seemingly good with children and a housekeeper to boot. It seemed to make sense and was very convenient all round. Once married, in 1960, they decided to try for a child themselves but soon gave up. Either Barbara was too old (she too was nearing forty) or Ian wasn't that interested in having a family – or wasn't quite sure of himself with women.

Whatever, they soon settled into a kind of regular married life. Barbara then started fostering 'unwanted' children to boost their meagre income and to put into practice the no-nonsense nannying skills she had learnt working for middle-class families earlier in her life. She was paid a fairly good weekly amount per child, which was important to Barbara, as she felt she needed to earn her own money. But she was definitely no jolly Mary Poppins, coming herself from the school of hard knocks.

Interestingly, while the newly married couple tried (a bit faint-heartedly) for their own child, Barbara was bored, needed some cash, and decided to do some local childcare. At first she took in a couple of neighbours' children after school for tea for an hour or two. Then she befriended a recently widowed man, Sid, who lived at the end of the road. Barbara had walked her dog regularly with Sid's late wife, Minnie, who had died very suddenly from breast cancer. Sid and Minnie had a six-year-old son, Kevin, and the problem was that Sid was a long-distance lorry driver, not only going off all over the UK, but also to the Continent. His round trips could take up to a week, or even two or three, and Sid was wedded to life on the road. He had no other relatives, and had considered putting Kevin into care.

Barbara came to a casual arrangement with Sid that she and Ian would take Kevin in as a paying guest while his father was on the road. Barbara liked having a project and tried hard to be a proper mum to Kevin, who was very upset at recently losing his own mother, and angry at his dad for being away most of the time. She also wanted to impress Ian that she could be a good mother while they tried for their own baby.

Barbara's own start in life had been tough, and she hadn't had good parenting, but she wanted to help Kevin settle in (and she wanted her own cash). After a while it became clear that when Sid came back from a trip he was always exhausted and needed to sleep. Then, in less than forty-eight hours, he would go off again, and gradually Kevin just slipped into being a permanent member of the Taylor household. Ian just accepted it and got on with his job; he did anything to keep Barbara quiet. When she wanted something she had to have it – and Ian just wanted to keep the peace.

The deal was that Sid would pass Barbara a wedge of cash when he came back from his trips, so Kevin moved into the spare room. After nearly a year, Barbara felt she had got the hang of Kevin – she treated him as well as possible, as if he were her own – and then thought she could up her income by fostering more children with the local authority. At the time there was a glut of unwanted children on the council's books, due to it being the 'swinging sixties', so Barbara and Ian took in little William. To the local authority, Barbara just pretended Kevin was theirs; it was easier that way, and nobody checked. Sid was largely out of the picture by then, and only popped in 'like an uncle' from time to time when he was back. His visits were always brief, and always upset Kevin, who would get very angry afterwards. He gradually stopped popping in and Kevin was fully absorbed into the Taylors.

When William arrived he was a very troubled child, as he had already been handed round several different pairs of foster parents, some of whom had been too tough. He was two, and Barbara found him challenging from the start. She felt William needed a lot of disciplining (unlike her attitude towards Kevin, which was far softer). She took all her bottled-up anger and frustration out on him, while being ultra-understanding with

Kevin, who was often quite provocative. Then, less than a year later, Barbara and Ian were allowed to add me, Louise, a little baby, to her growing family of unwanteds.

Her own baby never appeared, and Barbara was bitter by then that she was probably too old to have a child herself. But she developed an unhealthy split attitude towards her strange brood: she felt sorry for Kevin, and treated him like a little prince; but thought she had to be tough towards William and me, as we were proper unwanteds. Kevin had lost his mum but we were cast-offs. She seemed to worship Kevin, who was a muscly, tough little six-year-old, a bit of a lad. But she mistrusted William and me and disliked us from the start, calling us 'scum'.

For Kevin, nothing was too much trouble. He was cock of the roost when I came on the scene: he always got what he wanted, when he wanted it. In fact, he had the run of the house, being given the biggest bedroom after the master bedroom, with loads of toys and new clothes, paid for by Sid, who seemed relieved to get the lad off his hands. Ian, however, did not seem very interested in Kevin, and spent a lot of time at work or in his shed or watching TV – he generally kept himself apart from things. He definitely wasn't cut out for parenthood. He was like a ghostly shadow in our house. Sometimes it felt like Barbara was married to Kevin rather than Ian.

Another strange thing: our kitchen had padlocks on the cupboards, with a big chain through them, but Kevin had a key and he could unlock and eat food whenever he wanted to. Not like me or William. We had to eat what we were given, when we were given it. Kevin would go into the 'best' front room (which we weren't allowed into) with its magnolia walls and dark, red velvet curtains, and watch TV, eating cereal out of a bowl. Sometimes two bowls, full to the brim. But we weren't allowed to do that. William and I would peek in through the crack in the door, starving hungry and jealous, watching Kevin silently, holding our breath. We would look at each other and nod – sometimes holding hands. We always had to be quiet in case we got into trouble. I knew this from a very early age. As early as I could remember I had to be silent. Be good. Be quiet. Disappear into the cracks in the walls, the lino, the floorboards. Behave. Behave. Behave. But Kevin could be loud, raucous, noisy, galumphing, even violent, and that was fine. He could kick a ball around in the back garden or shout or stomp about and Barbara was fine with that. She'd even laugh. She'd look at him fondly, like she was thinking, *My boy* – although he wasn't 'her boy,' but she sort of pretended like he was. She never said 'my girl' or 'my boy' to me and William – it was always 'little bitch' or 'little bastard'. It also wasn't fair he had new clothes (ours were second hand); he went to school (we often didn't). He didn't have to do chores (we did loads of housework). If he was her prince, we were her paupers.

Barbara was always nice to him, as she wanted to keep in with Sid, who handed over the cash, but horrible to us, who didn't have a parent between us to keep a check on things. She didn't hit Kevin or say rude words to him. She would stroke his hair, smile at him. Sometimes they would cuddle or even play-fight or wrestle on the carpet. They would laugh and roll about together on the floor. We would stand back in the doorway and watch. If she saw us, she'd snap, 'What are you looking at, you little bastards?' and we'd quietly slink away.

Barbara often seemed very nice to people outside of the

house – people she met on the street or who came to the door, like the postman – and when she turned on the charm she was altogether unrecognisable, but to William and me she was harsh all the time. If I was out at the shop I would hear her telling a story about someone who did something terrible to a child and she would shake her head and tut-tut. I would stand there and think, *But you do that to me. You treat us like that.* But I knew better than to say anything. She would hold me hard, with her scrawny fingers digging into my shoulder or wrapped round my arm so tight there would be red fingermarks afterwards. So I would stand there, silently counting: one, two, three, four, pressing my fingers together. Both William and I knew better than to say anything – it wasn't our place to speak. We would look at each other and wink because we knew she was horrible; it was our secret.

Another strange thing I remember from my earliest days with the Taylors is learning to sit on my potty. I must have been about two or three and, as I peed, I felt this terrible burning on my bottom, like it was on fire; as the water rose up and touched me it burned my private bits. I screamed out and tried to stand up. Barbara appeared and pushed me back down on the potty: 'Stay there, you stupid bitch.' Tears were streaming down my face as my thighs and bottom and where I weed were burning with unbelievable pain. I would fear doing a big wee or poo, which made the water rise up. I would tense up, but still she pressed me down on the pink plastic potty, a fierce, grim look on her face: 'Don't you dare move.' Afterwards I'd have large blisters that turned into red sores everywhere, which were painful and running. I would have to sit on the potty for ages, blistered and burning, but after a while I wouldn't cry. I wouldn't be allowed. In any case, there wasn't any point.

Later Barbara would take me to the doctor and shake her head, saying she had 'no idea how I'd got them'. The doctor would look at me with a hard stare, but I would say nothing. I would look at my shoes – the second-hand blue Clarks ones with a T-bar strap. I knew better than to speak. He would put ointment and bandages on my sores, and I still wouldn't cry, but I would fear weeing or pooing for ages after that.

I later saw a big blue bottle of Domestos bleach near the potty. Somehow it got in the potty and I think it was Barbara who put it in. I don't know why. She did this several times, to both William and me, to 'teach us a lesson', but we never said a word to anybody. We didn't understand. We would give each other our special look – we knew what the other was going through. Didn't she want us to learn to use the potty? It was all very confusing.

Sometimes Kevin would watch and snigger from the doorway, making 'ha ha, glad it's you not me' faces and looking very smug to see me in terrible pain.

Barbara could flip. She could seem normal one minute, almost pleasant, and then she would turn. Her pointed face would harden, her eyes would narrow, her lips would purse, and then we'd know we were in for it. A sort of mist would come over her eyes, and I'd feel scared. She would seem remote, dangerous, and I would know to keep quiet. I learnt to please and appease, to be a 'good girl' and live a double life right from the start. If the mist was upon her, and her eyes went funny, she would suddenly grab me and put a chair by the sink.

'Climb it,' she would command. I would inevitably be barefoot and I'd do as I was told. 'Feet in the sink,' she'd bark. I'd know what was coming. I'd hear the kettle bubble and click off.

As the boiling water hit my small feet I would scream, then hold my breath, not wanting to anger her. Instinctively I'd pull my legs back but she'd force them back down.

'Sit. Don't make such a bloody fuss.'

Sometimes she would refill the kettle, boil it again and pour it over my already blistered feet and legs. If I tried to move she would slap my legs until they bled, while holding me down hard with the other hand. I was powerless to get away, so I had to get away in my head – I would go to my special 'Louise place': a cool, calm zone where it was quiet. Sometimes I would gaze at something: a picture on the wall or the garden through the window – it helped to focus on nice things like trees and flowers. Looking at nature helped me breathe. Then I would start counting. Or I'd look at the room and count round things: the edges of the bread bin, the sides of the doorway, the table legs: one, two, three, four. Sometimes, to finish things off, she would get a wooden pole, like a bamboo stick, that she kept handy in the kitchen, and rub my blisters so they were red and bleeding.

By now I was hurting so much I was numb. I couldn't feel any more, or cry. I would sit there, taking it. Waiting for it to end. Only later, in bed, would I feel the searing, stinging pain in my feet and legs and be quiet as a mouse, alongside my equally battered adopted brother. I would hear Ian come in the house and knew he had no idea what had gone on. Or if he did he didn't seem to care, as he never came up to see us, despite my willing him to. William and I would lie there silently or just moaning, side by side, divided by a screen, strapped in and drugged: our life, behind the neat net curtains, was our nasty little secret. It was living hell.

2

Starving the Devil's Child

'You're the devil's child,' Barbara would spit at me as often as she could. 'You're a little bastard born out of wedlock' and 'You've had a touch of the tar brush.' This was to shame me, as I understood these things were bad. Very bad. She disliked me a lot because of them. My hair was dark and silky, my skin was olive and went nut brown in the sun, unlike Barbara, whose hair was wavy, iron grey, and whose skin was pallid and yellowy. I didn't understand about the tar brush; to me brushes were for hair or for painting or for me to sweep up with downstairs.

Barbara said my first foster home hadn't worked out. They hadn't wanted the likes of me, so I'd been left in my pram all day, with a bottle propped up on a towel just out of reach. I didn't thrive. I wasn't held or cuddled, so I cried and cried and cried and the foster parents soon gave me back. They went on holiday and I went to another foster family, who only wanted a baby less than one month old, and I was now six months, so I was given back again. Then I was passed on at nine months, like an unclaimed parcel, to the Taylors, the next fosterers on the list and whose home I was now living in. They already had

Kevin (then six) and William (two) and wanted a baby girl. But all was not right from the start.

'I cannot bear to look at your horrible cold blue eyes,' Barbara would snarl at me. 'They're horrible devil eyes, staring right up at me.'

At the age of three or four I would sometimes tiptoe to the bathroom and peek at my eyes in the mirror. Devil eyes? What were devil eyes? Instead I saw bright-blue eyes, like little blue buttons; like the blue flowers in the garden with the black centres. My favourites. Barbara didn't like to look in them, or hold me, or cuddle me. She seemed to hate me all the time. She never showed me or William any love, affection or care. She only seemed to want to punish us, so she must have been right. I must be the 'devil's child' after all.

In fact, William and I lived a different life from Barbara, Ian and Kevin. We were not allowed to eat when they ate or what they ate and we couldn't sit with them. The kitchen belonged to Barbara and had a door that led onto the garden. It had brown walls and cupboards, a cooker, a fridge, a sink with a drainer and a small plastic table and chairs. The cupboards had big locks with chains running through them and only Barbara and 'the family' could open them. This didn't mean William or me. We weren't allowed to help ourselves to anything; we had to wait and eat what we were given. We were not allowed to complain, or ask. The kitchen never really smelt of food cooking, but of cat food, bleach and vegetables; everything was hidden away. There was no fruit on the table, no bread on the side – everything was out of sight.

At breakfast time, William and I had to sit still at a tiny kiddie table with two baby chairs, and we were given a small bowl of

Ready Brek. It was often cold and a bit lumpy. We ate it very fast and were always hungry afterwards, watching as Kevin had toast and jam. I wanted toast and jam, too, but I learnt not to ask or make a sound. Once I said, 'I want some,' but Barbara's face clouded over and I would feel scared and she would lash out and whack me across the face.

'I want doesn't get.' *Slap*. I was used to this by now. She would casually slap and whack us round the head or across the face as she passed. Her hand was big and hard and it hurt. But I didn't cry. One of Barbara's favourite weapons was her rolled-up newspaper, which she kept in the kitchen. When we were watching Kevin eat, almost drooling, she'd whack us across the head, shoulders or back.

'Sit up straight,' she'd bark. We would sit up straight and watch Kevin eating his toast and jam with relish, spooning on more jam just to show us he could. We said not a word – hating him and fearing Barbara. Kevin would chew on his toast and smile, smug and safe, helping himself to more, triumphant. Meanwhile, Barbara would tell us we were illegitimate and bad or stupid and, with each word, she would swipe us with the newspaper. 'Bad.' *Whack!* 'Stupid.' *Thwack!* 'Bastards.' *Whack!* Each word would be emphasised with a blow from the rolled-up newspaper across the shoulders, legs, arms, bottom, back.

Sometimes she lost her temper so much she forgot to be careful, and I watched her slap William so hard across the face that he fell off his chair. I would wince. He would get kicked, punched, shoved and pushed while I held my breath. I felt, 'Poor William,' but I knew she would turn on me just as quickly, so I would be nice, obedient, silent. Even so, I did get whacked with the paper while being hungry, hungry,

hungry all the time. If I cried, she'd say, 'Look at you, you bloody baby, it's only a newspaper.' I knew there would be no sympathy if she really hurt us, so I learnt to shut up. I learnt to shut down – to go to the Louise place in my head. One, two, three, four.

❦

Both William and I were underweight for our ages, and had been in hospital a few times for not growing properly. 'You're just backward little bastards,' Barbara would say. Indeed, I hadn't sat up until fourteen months, as I had been lying in my cot all day. And I didn't take my first steps until I was two years old. 'You're stupid, that's why,' Barbara would spit. 'Just like that little bugger,' meaning William.

After our small breakfast, which never changed, we never had any food in the day, no snacks or anything like that. But we would see the family go in and eat together round the table at dinnertime. William and I weren't included, so we had to lump it. Our tummies hurt and gurgled with pain. Hungry, hungry, hungry all the time. We would sit on the hard ground in the garden, poking in the earth with a stick, or just sitting and listening to them eating indoors. We could hear the clatter of pans and plates. By teatime we were utterly starving, almost too hungry to eat. We were called in at about five o'clock and would be given the same meal every single day, come rain or shine.

On two baby plates (like dolly plates) Barbara would count out five raisins, then put a dot of salad cream, half a tomato, a handful of crisps, and half a piece of Mother's Pride white bread and butter. That was it: tea. We would gobble it down and have to sit up straight. Meanwhile, Kevin and the family would eat something like chops, potatoes and peas (after we were done), pie and mash or fish and chips. My stomach would feel growly with hunger, a gnawing, uncomfortable feeling. Sometimes I pressed my knee against William's for comfort. I would long for the chops, potatoes and peas, but I would know better than to ask.

Sometimes after tea, and while they were eating, we would wander into the garden and go into the big wooden shed. It was usually locked, but sometimes Ian left it open. I would reach up on tiptoes, push the metal latch and, holding my breath, lift it. Then we would creep in. It was dark and smelt of soil, damp and chemicals, and in the corner was a big brown sack of birdseed. This was what we were after. The first time we saw it William and I looked at each other, silently thinking. I held my breath, really afraid. He was smaller than me, even though he was two years older. He had cuts and bruises all over, almost permanently, and he had brown eyes, freckles and ginger hair, which stuck up like a brush. He moved over to the sack, opened the top and put his hand in, pulling out a handful of seed. He buried his face in it and started eating. I did the same.

It was crunchy, nutty, dry and hard to swallow. It stuck to the roof of my mouth, as it was so gritty, but after a few handfuls the gnawing pain in my tummy eased. We sat on the floor, looking at each other in our secret game, eating the seed in silence, peeking up and down again warily like animals, listening out for movements in the kitchen, which was just up the concrete garden path. There'd be hell to pay if she found out. Then, without a word, William got up and carefully folded the bag top over, so it looked the same as before. I carefully brushed the seeds that had fallen on the ground to the edges of the shed and spread them out. No one would ever know. Ian wouldn't notice, or even care particularly. It was Barbara we were terrified of. And Kevin, her sidekick – he would tell on us if he saw us or suspected anything. Silently we tiptoed to the door, lifted the latch while holding our breath, peeked out to see if it was safe, and then slipped out into the daylight as if nothing had ever happened. It was war, and these were our guerrilla tactics to survive.

❧

Scavenging and stealth became the name of the game. I got to be an expert at covering my tracks. The kitchen had a small open larder at the back, which was cool and dark with a dank smell, and there were some packets and tins in there and shelves with things on. One day I was starving and crept in when Barbara was right down the bottom of the garden. I found a packet of Complan, her favourite night drink, and I opened it very quietly and carefully, holding my breath. I pricked up my ears and waited to hear Barbara's footsteps or biting bark, but meanwhile quickly licked my index finger and dipped it in the box. Quick as a flash I licked my dusty finger and it was malty and sweet tasting, so I dipped and licked, dipped and licked a few times and then, getting scared, shook the box, smoothed all the powder down, closed it carefully and put it back exactly where it had been. I crept out of the larder, hardly breathing, just as I saw Barbara striding up the garden path. I licked my lips carefully, checking for evidence. Phew. None. She was now in the doorway staring at me suspiciously.

'What are you doing in here? Go outside this instant.' At this I smiled my sweetest, most innocent smile.

'Yes, Mum,' I said, and went off down the garden, satisfied. She sensed something was up but I played very innocent.

Another time, Barbara was not at home and Ian had left the butter dish out on the kitchen table. I spied it from the garden through the open door. I tiptoed in and lifted the blue-and-white striped lid – and there was a golden ocean of butter, all soft and shiny. So inviting. I listened carefully. No one was around. I seized my moment and my index finger, my dipper, was licked and in the butter. I quickly scooped out one, two, three fingers full of wonderful, buttery, yellow heaven. And then I stopped. I wouldn't go too far. I'd get found out. So I smoothed it all over. Sculpted it. Made it look perfect. Swallowed. Put the lid on carefully, exactly as it was. Checked my finger for yellowy traces. Not breathing, listening out, I returned to the garden, to exactly where I was before. I was waiting for the swipe of the newspaper, the back of the hand, the shriek of Barbara's sharp cuss. None came. Luckily she was still out, although I always felt that she would somehow be watching or would know.

'I've eyes in the back of my head,' she would tell us. 'Don't think you can get away with anything with me.' But today I had done it. My tummy was happy. My ears and eyes were pricked for any reactions, but this time none came. It was my buttery secret, and I had got away with it. Phew.

My trips to the larder became a way of life, of staying alive. I got very good at being stealthy, quiet and scavenging without leaving a trace. Sometimes there was a new loaf of bread – a wonderful sight and smell – and I developed a way of digging in my fingers, lifting up the crust, pulling out some dough, like a soft white ball of heaven, and stuffing it in my mouth. As I was chewing and savouring I would fold the crust back down and press it carefully to cover my tracks. From the outside it looked completely untouched while I would slink out of the larder swallowing a mouthful of wonderful, melt-in-your-mouth soft bread. Sometimes there was a carton of St. Ivel Five Pints powdered milk, and if it had already been opened I would flip the corner, take a huge slug, swallow and swallow as fast as possible, fold it back and get out of the larder as soon as I could, wiping my mouth with the back of my hand to remove all traces.

I took increasing risks at the age of four and five, and got bolder as I went, but I wasn't always successful. I found a way of sneaking some food from the larder into my knickers, into a pocket or hidden in my cuff, and then take it up to my room. I pulled a little hole in the mattress material underneath where I slept, and popped in there whatever I could scavenge. Sometimes it was a crust, or a biscuit or a bit of cheese. I would fold the material part over it, so it wasn't visible from the outside. I felt I had my own little larder, my own private stash, which I could sneak out later and eat quickly when I was really desperate.

I got bolder and once or twice took small tins of baked beans and sweetcorn out of the larder and hid them in a children's red cardboard suitcase that was in my room. One day Ian came in for a rare visit and he saw the tins out on the carpet.

'Mummy will be cross,' he said, looking pale and terrified himself. 'Take them downstairs now, quickly, and she'll never know. Quick!' Without a word, I scrambled off the floor and slunk like a weasel down the stairs, into the larder and out again, having placed them back on the shelves exactly where I'd found them. My heart was pounding like a sledgehammer and my mouth was dry. That was close.

Then one day I became aware that Barbara was having a woman in the village round for coffee. This was very rare, as we seldom had people to the house. Peeking into the larder, I saw, gleaming on the middle shelf, a big packet of biscuits. Shiny purple paper, snazzy design: a packet of five – FIVE – Club biscuits. I couldn't help myself: I took one out, slipped it up my sleeve and crept upstairs to my room. I hid it under the carpet beneath the bed, right at the corner. I held my breath. I imagined eating it later, sinking my teeth into what I knew was thick dark chocolate and biscuit. Mmmm, the very thought.

Then I heard her coming. Oh no! She'd found out. I could hear her taking the stairs two at a time, thumping the banisters as she went, and I was frozen to the floor. I watched her fling the door open and fly towards me like a demented monster. She bounded up to my face and bent over me, so close I could smell her sour breath, shouting, 'You little thief, give me my biscuits NOW!' I was terrified. She was almost drooling over me. I started crying uncontrollably. I pointed to the corner of the carpet. She lifted up the corner and picked up the biscuit, still wrapped in its shiny purple paper.

Barbara turned and slapped me with the full force of her right arm across the face, and I fell to the floor and hit my head. I lay there sobbing. She walked over to me and kicked my foot, then kicked my side, hissing, 'Thieving little bitch,' then stormed out of the room, biscuit in hand. I cried for some time. It felt like the end of the world. I wiped the back of my hand across my face, and then saw blood on my hand. It had a salty, dark, bitter taste. I looked at the ceiling and counted: one, two, three, four; one, two, three, four; one, two, three, four. Perhaps my luck had begun to run out, or maybe I'd got sloppy. I'd have to be more careful.

~❧~

On Sundays, Barbara did cook Sunday lunch, which usually turned out to be a difficult event. She didn't like cooking and would complain loudly about it. She would bang and crash about in the kitchen. She said she was too hot, and would throw open the doors and windows and swear a lot. Barbara was angry about having to cook, angry with the oven, angry with the food and angry with us. 'Get out from under my feet, you bastards,' she'd shout, and we'd scuttle away.

Her anger included Ian, who was always turfed out of the kitchen. He usually spent Sunday morning cleaning out his work van, which sat on the drive. It was obvious he was staying out of her way. We all did. Ian kept a small Tupperware box in his van, which occasionally had biscuits in it: Garibaldi and Rich Tea. He often had the two front doors wide open, like widespread wings, while he cleaned it out. I would watch from the sidelines and, when he went to get something, I would dart to the Tupperware box and prise it open. If there were two or three biscuits in there, I would sneak one and quickly slip it in my pocket, then close the lid and slide the box back into its place. All before Ian came back, totally unaware.

The biscuit would burn a hole in my pocket. I would put my hand in and then bring my fingers up to my nose and smell that warm, biscuity smell. I relished when I would be able to crumble a bit off and slip it in my mouth, even just the crumbs were marvellous things to melt on the tongue. When dinner was ready, Barbara would shout at us to get Ian: 'Tell Daddy dinner's ready.'

We would run to the drive and tell him, and he would say, 'Oh, ready? Now?' He didn't look that keen. We would look panicked, William and I, as we knew he had to come instantly to appease Barbara. We would give each other a look. I would go back and very quickly get some cutlery and plates out and put them on the big kitchen table – big plates for them; side plates for us on the little kiddie table. We would have tiny bits of roast, like a doll's meal, while they had a whole plateful and seconds. Kevin would look very smug as he ate to his heart's content. He'd taunt us whenever he could.

Then one day I was in the garden, down by the big brown shed with the birdseed, which was now locked more often than not. The day we first got the birdseed (and subsequent days) had been unusual, since then a huge new shiny padlock had now appeared. Maybe Barbara had found traces of the seed; we didn't know. We didn't talk about it. It was all done in silence with looks, nods and gestures.

This day I noticed the padlock was open and I was starving. It was afternoon time and ages till we would get our meagre tea. Barbara would make jam and mincemeat in the autumn and put it in labelled jars on high shelves. I got on an old wooden chair and found a jar of mincemeat, which had already been opened. I got my dipper out and plunged it into the sweet, strong-smelling goo. Once covered, I shoved it in my mouth and – Oh heaven – the fruity, tangy taste was utterly wonderful. I was just swallowing when I became aware of a change in the light and a grating noise. I swung round, terrified: Barbara was standing behind me, her face red with fury.

In two strides she was across the floor. She grabbed my arm, pulled the jar from my other hand and put it back on a high shelf.

'You nasty little thief,' she was spitting, incandescent, as she dragged me hard and fast off the chair and into the garden, pushing me down the end of the footpath. She dragged me along on my knees and by my arm, yanking it overhead. I fell forwards into the flowerbed, full of roses and dahlias, and she kicked me in the side with her brown lace-up shoe.

'You little bitch,' she snarled, and with that she pushed my head face down into the earth. 'Eat dirt, go on, you little thief.' I was shaking uncontrollably now and crying, but she stood astride me, with me hunched on my knees in the flowerbed, face down. 'Eat dirt!' she screamed. So I put my hand in the earth, scraped some out and raised it to my mouth. 'Go on, then. Eat if you're that hungry.'

I licked a bit of dirt from my hand; it was gritty and disgusting. She pushed her foot into my side again and kicked. Suddenly she pulled my hair and yanked my head backwards. She bent her red face over mine and spat: 'Louise, I said EAT, you little bitch. That'll teach you never to steal again, you horrible little girl.'

She made me dig my hand in the dirt and eat a whole load, and as I ate I cried and cried and it dribbled out of my mouth and down my chin and onto my blue gingham summer dress, making everything a dirty mess. It was then that I saw I was also eating cat poo, little sausages of white stuff mixed in the dirt. I fell on my face and sicked it all up, all the dirt, the poo, the mincemeat. Barbara stalked away shouting, 'One day you'll learn that you can't do as you please.' I sat, sobbing, my hands on my knees, a total mess.

'Louise,' she barked from down the garden, now by the chicken run. We had about six chickens in a coop behind chicken wire alongside the back of the house. 'Come and help, you lazy little bitch.'

I got to my feet, stunned, and stumbled up the garden. My side really hurt and I was covered in sick, dirt and dribble. I was still sobbing quietly, but I knew better than to show any more feelings, so I tried to stop myself. I started counting as I walked. Counting, counting, counting. Barbara pointed to big sacks that the hen straw had to go in once they had used it, and I had to hold them open while she forked mess and straw into them. She said not a word to me the whole while, and I just tried to calm myself down, thinking I really had to be more careful in future or I wouldn't survive.

3

Caravan Saviours

The back garden was big, with a chicken run on the left with a long wire fence and, next to that, right at the bottom, an orchard with old apple, pear and plum trees. At the end of the orchard was a piece of land that served as a small traveller site, with a few cream and blue caravans on it, occupied by a mixture of Polish and Irish people. William and I often wandered through the garden, past the shed with the birdseed and mincemeat, past the greenhouse, and then into the orchard beyond. We would stand by a leafy apple tree and watch the travellers: the women had colourful headscarves and aprons, full skirts and crinkled white shirts and looked very old. We crept through the orchard hedge up to the long, cream caravans and were fascinated by their dinky net curtains and plastic flowers. Everything looked very neat and tidy inside.

In one caravan lived an old, thin couple we called 'the robot' and 'the witch' – it made us both giggle. There was another, smaller, pale-blue caravan, set to one side, which belonged to an older Irish man. We watched him come out of his caravan dressed in big brown trousers with braces, an old stripy shirt with no collar, with rolled-up sleeves and a flat cap. He had a crinkly kind face and white hair. He would come out and sit on the step of his caravan and roll up a cigarette and smoke. We would watch him sitting with his cigarette hanging out of his mouth. He'd wave to the Polish people and nod, or just watch the birds. William and I would watch him, half-hiding behind the apple trees. Then we would wander about, picking up fallen fruit and eating the sour flesh, avoiding the worms.

One day we were wandering around the caravans, looking for apples, and we got nearer to the Irishman's blue caravan. We both crept along by the window, which was propped open, and were trying to peek inside when suddenly a hairy arm shot out. We jumped and froze. We were used to being scared and being shouted at, and we supposed we were about to get a beating. William and I were both shaking and wondering how to creep away but were staring at the disembodied arm hanging out the window. We realised there was a nice piece of crusty bread clasped in the strong fingers.

'Take it!' the Irishman whispered hoarsely out the window. William and I looked around, making sure the coast was clear. We didn't want Barbara to find us; there'd be hell to pay. We looked at each other, then back at the hand, and then the crust. 'C'mere wontcha. Take it,' the voice repeated softly. We crept up to the hand like cats, and sniffed. Was it a trick? It smelt like bread. Real bread. Snatch! William grabbed it and broke it roughly in two and we dived into it. Oh, the taste! Yeasty, sweet, soft, divine. No bread had ever tasted anything like this. It was manna from heaven. The hand disappeared and reappeared with another slice, and that too we gobbled down as fast as we could. William and I stood riveted to the ground, amazed at our fortune, as the caravan door opened and out came the familiar figure of the Irishman. He went down a couple of steps and sat down. 'Sean Brannon,' he said warmly.

We just stood and looked at him, licking our lips, feeling our tummies filling – a warm, wonderful, comforting feeling. Sean smiled at us and sucked on his cigarette. We just stared at him and didn't know what to say. Suddenly, afraid of being found out, we turned and ran away. I was scared there would be a terrible price to pay. What if he told Barbara? What if she saw any crumbs or noticed that we were happy? This was too good to be true. But in my heart I knew we would be back again, just as soon as the coast was clear.

After that we began to creep into the orchard and watch the caravans through the hedge even more closely. We would hang around Sean Brannon's caravan and he would come out and always give us a snack with a kindly wink: some bread, some cake, some milk and biscuits. We were like little cats creeping around, scavenging, looking for whatever we could find to keep us going. The people in the caravans had very little, but what they had they shared with us. They were our saviours, and without them we would have starved. The Polish women began to hand us scraps of cake, pie and bread, too. We always wolfed down on the spot whatever we were given, looking over our shoulders like vigilant animals, waiting for a shout or curse from Barbara.

Sean had some cuddly toys in his caravan, and one time he let us choose one each. I got a little black-and-white panda – I called him Tony. William took a tiny bear called Fizz. We couldn't believe how lucky we were. Sometimes Sean would bring out a piece of wood and a knife and whittle a shape, like a boat. We would stand watching, fascinated. He was kind, warm and friendly. We told him our names, and he was now 'Sean' to us. We would watch as he skilfully carved the wood with his knife – a special knife with a knobbly wooden handle – but all the time our ears were pricked and we were ready to run if we were summoned. We knew better than to not respond to Her Mistress's voice.

✥

About this time Kevin began to pick on William a lot more. When I was five, Kevin was eleven, and William was seven. However, William was very small for his age, while Kevin, because he was well fed, was sturdy and strong. Kevin began to play 'games' with William that scared me. One day he got a flick knife and made William stand with his feet apart on the grass. The game was for Kevin to aim the knife to land between William's legs, blade down in the earth, but for it to be near enough for it to be scary. Another version of this was you had to dance about to miss the knife as it flew towards your feet and legs. I was terrified, as Kevin had already briefly tried this with me, and the knife had landed on my foot, giving me a bad cut. When I showed it to Barbara, bleeding profusely, she just said, 'You should be more careful, you stupid girl.'

I watched the 'game' unfold from the relative safety of the kitchen. Kevin was teasing William and threw the knife, which very nearly landed in William's leg, making him jump. Provoked, William shouted something at Kevin, then Barbara, who had been pinning washing on the line, suddenly strode over and picked up William by the T-shirt collar, swung him round a couple of times and hurled him like a discarded rag doll across the grass into the rockery.

William landed badly but scrambled to his feet. Kevin watched all this grinning, shouting, 'Ha ha!' Enraged, William ran into the kitchen and locked the door, which had glass at the top and wood below, like a stable door. By now I was cowering by the larder, speechless, watching the drama unfold. Barbara was loping up the lawn. 'Come back, you little bastard. I'll kill you when I get my hands on you!'

Her face appeared at the backdoor window, florid and furious, her eyes wild with intent. 'Open it!' she spat.

'No!' said William, through the window. I was both impressed and terrified. He was in for it now. He'd said no. You never said no to Barbara, it wasn't allowed. She turned and marched down the lawn, picking up a cricket bat that Kevin had earlier strewn to one side.

Then she marched back to the door where William was still standing at the window, defiantly looking out. Barbara looked like she was going to explode and I thought I would pee myself with fear. Suddenly she raised the bat and screamed, 'I'll kill you!' and smashed the bat into the glass door, shattering it all over William, who was now screaming in terror, as was I.

Glass flew everywhere. Barbara batted and batted, and William was covered in shards of glass. Instinctively I ran up to William, who was cut and bleeding, but he seemed fixed to the ground. I pulled his arm and we ran upstairs to the bathroom. I could hear more glass shattering as Barbara bashed in the rest of it until she was able to open the door from the inside. Then we could hear her thumping upstairs like a marauding monster.

Once in the bathroom we locked the door and cowered by the side of the bath, under the sink. On the landing, outside the door, she was shouting wildly at both of us: 'Open the bloody door, you bloody little bastards! Open the door!' *Bash. Bash. Bash.* She thumped on the door with the bat. We froze, held hands and shivered, heads down, eyes closed tight shut. I started counting furiously. One, two, three, four. One, two, three, four. One, two, three... Barbara was still beating the door. She was slamming the door handle and bashing away. Suddenly it flung open and she threw herself at William, attacking his head, his legs, his arms, with the bat. I was screaming, crying, pleading: 'Don't hit him, don't hit me!'

She pulled me to standing, leant me over the bath, raised my dress, pulled down my knickers and whacked the bat as hard as she could on my bare bottom. William was sobbing uncontrollably in a heap on the floor. She kept whacking me, one, two, three times, and I thought I would die. Then she turned to William and kicked him in the stomach as he lay there, sobbing.

'Take your clothes off,' she raged. 'Both of you. Now!'

Crying and shaking, we undressed as she turned the cold tap on and put the plug in the bath. 'Get in.' I put my toes in the icy water and, although terrified, did as I was told. William followed and we sat down in the freezing bath; the water came up to our chins.

'Stay there, you little bastards,' Barbara spat, then turned and stormed out of the bathroom. William and I sat there, blinking, shivering, terrified, not knowing at all what to do. We knew better than to move. We stared at each other, too frightened to speak. It was probably late afternoon, and we sat in that icy bath watching the evening light come in slowly. I started really shaking, but everything felt numb. I could see William's body turning shades of red and blue, where Barbara had landed her bat. His cuts were bloody streaks. His lips were purple. Were we going to be here for ever? Would we die?

We could hear voices downstairs in the kitchen and the sounds of teatime: plates, chairs, movement. Still we sat in the freezing-cold bath, too terrified to move, no idea what to do. Had she forgotten us? Why didn't Ian come? Would we be here all night? Eventually she came up – it was night now, and it was dark and we were grey shadows in icy water, numb, exhausted, hungry, frightened. 'Get out,' was all she said.

Barely able to move, we clambered stiffly out of the bath, one after the other, and stood dripping and shivering on the lino floor. Barbara told us to get dressed, so we did; we were too scared to do anything but obey. Tears started rolling down my cheeks, but she just barked, 'No snivelling,' and then we went into our tiny box room without our tea or even a drink, and the usual horrific night ritual began all over again.

❧

After an incident like this, nothing was said. There was no sorry, no making up, no nothing. The window was replaced the next day – 'You two just cost me money' – and life went on as before. The only difference was that Barbara seemed more and more horrible to William now, and encouraged Kevin to attack him whenever he wanted to. She never intervened, and in fact seemed to enjoy it, even encourage it. 'I hate the little bugger,' is what I would hear her saying to Kevin, and William became their mutual punchbag.

Ian just turned a blind eye to everything, and lived like a ghost in the house. As he was a quiet man, he was well liked in the village and at work, but he was a blank slate to us. William and I had very few times with him alone, but on some weekends, when Barbara was in a black mood, he would take us out on a job. We would get in his van and it felt like a treat. One day we went to a house next to where Ian grew up in Oxford. It was a lovely old ramshackle place, very untidy inside, with books everywhere. Even the toilet was full of books, newspapers and magazines. I thought Barbara would be furious to see how unclean it all was, as she took bleach to everything.

Iris and John, whose house it was, wanted Ian to mend something, and William and I were sat at a table with a plate of slightly stale chocolate bourbons and custard creams and two full glasses of orange squash. It was heaven. Ian busied himself mending things, and Iris, who told me she was a writer, read the newspaper, asking me what I thought about this and that. I just sat nibbling on the wonderful biscuits, looking at her with saucer eyes. I didn't know what to say but she was kind, like Sean. The radio would be on, with voices talking, and John and Iris would sit together and do a crossword or talk about something. I would stare at them, watching how nice they were with each other, as one made tea in a big old brown teapot and put a greasy cosy over the top. Or the other did some washing up.

We went to see them several times, and I later learnt the woman's name was Iris Murdoch. She would often have a nap and I would watch her lovely, clever face and copy her expressions while she was snoozing. William would be walking round the room, touching things and getting restless, but I loved it there. I sat eating biscuits, sipping squash and felt safe. It was a lovely feeling in their glass conservatory, overlooking a beautiful garden. It was a quiet moment, and a real break from being at home.

When Ian was done, John and Iris would say goodbye very politely and one day John spontaneously picked up a packet of 'mixed seeds' and shook them. He said, 'These are forget-me-nots, Louise, so you'd better *forget me not!*' The grown-ups laughed, and I later understood why it was funny.

～≈～

One day there was going to be a visit from a 'social worker'. We had these strange people come round every so often, and before they arrived Barbara would get even more grumpy and agitated than usual. She would start scrubbing and cleaning furiously, spitting, 'They will never say that I don't have a clean house.' Barbara thought the social workers were just interested in cleanliness. She scoured and cleansed, bashed pots and pans around, and barked at us to scrub ourselves. Our room had to be tidy, which wasn't a problem, as we didn't have any toys or belongings to speak of. In fact it was Barbara who had all the dolls and cuddly toys in her bedroom, not us.

She had a thing about dolls and owned all sorts of old, china and plastic dolls with weird painted faces that she adored. We, of course, were not allowed to play with them. We couldn't even look. We were also not allowed in many of the rooms in the house: certainly not in the living room – with the red velvet curtains and the sideboard and TV – and not in anyone's bedroom, other than our tiny partitioned box room. Barbara was furious, strutting about, swearing, pushing us out of the way: 'Get out from under my feet. I don't want those bloody interfering social workers to see you.'

I was terrified of Barbara but I didn't want to get the same treatment as William, which was horrendous, as he had more beatings than me. So I began to play being extra nice to Mummy. I would flatter her, and try to please and appease her, hoping this would change her mood and her attitude to me, and to us. I thought she must be a very unhappy person as she was always so angry, and I began to make her little gifts. I wanted her to smile, to be nice, to be kind. I wanted to make her happy, to make her like me – and to care.

Before the social worker arrived, I went outside to where the front had recently had more gravel laid by Ian. I noticed some of the stones were really sparkly and shiny, like stars and jewels, and I went and found a little empty box in the wooden shed (it was open for once). I drew all over the box with some colouring pens and picked out some jewel stones of different colours and shapes, arranging them carefully in the box. I went to the kitchen and hung outside, trying to work out Barbara's mood. There was a strong smell of bleach, even outside, as the doors and windows were flung wide open. I hovered in the doorway, trying to find a way to talk to her.

'What is it? Can't you see I'm busy?' she snapped. I felt terrified, but I persevered. 'Mummy,' I started, 'I made you a present…'

She stopped and looked at me, her eyes narrowing, her nose becoming very pointy.

'You been in the shed?'

I felt my face go red. 'Er, yes, sorry, Mummy.'

Her face hardened. 'You're not allowed in there.'

I persisted and offered her the box with my sweetest smile. She bent towards me, opened the box and looked in. A snarl came to her lips. 'That's my new gravel in there. What the bloody hell do you think you're doing, you little thief?'

I felt tears pricking my eyes as I continued to try to look sweetly at her. Surely she could see it was a gift, a present from me? Jewels.

'Put it outside and get out of my way.'

I put it on the window ledge and slunk off, totally crushed. I went down to the chickens and talked to them for a while, and sat on the grass feeling very sad indeed. William was already in the garden kicking stones about and digging for worms. We didn't have toys to play with. Then I heard a car on the gravel and I noticed the social workers arrive. I watched as Barbara turned into another person completely: smiley, charming, chatty. Ian hovered in the background then disappeared. She made a pot of tea and I could see a plate of biscuits being handed around through the open kitchen window. My stomach rumbled. I clocked that for later – I imagined creeping into the larder and finding a crinkly packet of digestives with thick chocolate…

I was daydreaming about biting into a biscuit when I heard the back door open and one of the social workers came across the grass to where William and I were skulking about. Oh, we'd be in trouble now, no doubt. Both of us shrank from her as she approached, and we crawled backwards across the lawn. We'd had a few visits in the past, and I hated them and never understood what they were for or what we were supposed to do. The woman bent down towards us and smiled and seemed quite friendly, but I knew I had to be on my best behaviour or I would get it later.

'What are you doing?' she asked, smiling. I didn't know the answer, so I didn't say anything. Nor did William. It was uncomfortable. We didn't dare look at each other, so we looked down at the grass. Then I remembered and pointed to my colourful box over on the kitchen window ledge and we all went over to it. I opened the lid.

'Oh, aren't you clever finding those?' she said to me. I smiled, gratified. I could see Barbara in the kitchen, watching like a hawk. I could feel her eyes boring into my back and her claws sinking into my shoulders even though she was six feet away. Barbara was still talking to the other social worker behind me. I could hear her explaining that William needed to be tied into bed as he went sleepwalking at night and he might fall through the banisters. I knew this wasn't true, but knew better than to say anything.

Meanwhile my nice lady talked to William and then came back to me and said, 'Thank you for showing me your stones, they're beautiful.' I could feel Barbara tighten behind me.

Later, as the car left the drive, show over, Barbara marched over to the box, picked it up and strode through to the front of the house. I followed her and watched in despair as she tipped the stones back onto the drive. I watched sadly as she trod them into the rest of the gravel, kicking it all about to mix them in. When she turned back to me, her face was bright red. She strode up to me and slapped me hard across the face, first on one side, and then the other, hissing, 'You stupid little bitch.' It stung like mad and I was thrown backwards against the wall, completely confused as to why she was so angry. Now the social workers were gone, the usual angry Barbara had come back – and boy, didn't we know it.

❦

The next weekend Kevin was picking on William again, despite the broken window incident. I was in the back garden, being punished for something. The boys were out the front, by the willow tree, and I could hear Kevin shouting at William, so I crept round the side of the house to the front, worried what might happen to William.

'You're just a cry baby,' Kevin was sneering, which made William angry, so he charged at him, knee height. I hadn't really noticed Barbara, who was hoeing the front flowerbeds, when all of a sudden she turned round, raised her hoe, and hit William right across the head with the soil-encrusted blade. He screamed and fell to the ground, blood pouring out of his jagged head wound. We all stood stunned for a moment, watching William writhing in agony on the lawn. Then Barbara shouted at Kevin: 'Go and get a towel,' and after hovering for a moment, Kevin ran past me, pushing me against the wall violently as he went.

William was rolling on the ground screaming and blood was spurting all over his face. Barbara stood and looked at him, hissing, 'Be quiet!' and 'Stop it!' But poor William was beside himself. Kevin was back with a towel and she bent over and wrapped it roughly round William's head. He was still lying on the ground, with the towel getting redder by the minute.

'Stay with him,' Barbara barked at Kevin, who said nothing, but didn't move. Barbara then brushed roughly past me without a word and I heard her call for an ambulance, using the phone in the hall. I was holding my breath all the time. I didn't know what to do: should I go to William? Stay by the wall? Try and find Ian? Barbara came out and looked at me hard: 'What did you see?' she snapped. I said nothing. I was shaking. She gave up and went over to William and got him to sit up. Barbara sat on the grass and leant William against her. It was the first time

I had ever seen her do something like that. Kevin just stood around looking awkward, hands deep in his pockets.

When the ambulance arrived, I snuck along the path to the edge of the lawn while the two men in uniform got out and said cheerfully, 'Oh, what have we got here? Been gardening have we?' Poor William said nothing. His head was wrapped in the blood-sodden towel, but he was now floppy on the ground. Barbara said nicely that the poor lad had had a nasty accident and had tripped and fallen on the hoe. She'd told him not to play with tools – they were dangerous. But would he listen?

The ambulance man nodded, put William on a red stretcher and carried him into the ambulance. Barbara got up and gestured to me to get in the ambulance along with her, William and Kevin. I was shaking in my shoes. Was William going to die? There was so much blood, and he was so pale I was scared.

Once we got to hospital, William disappeared behind a big screen and the doctor in the white coat came and said it was a deep wound, and he would have to have stitches, a 'tetanus injection' and a big head bandage for at least a week. He would also have to stay the night in hospital to watch for something called 'concussion'. Barbara turned to me and said loudly, in her nice Mummy voice, so the doctor could hear, 'You see, Louise, that's what happens when you don't look where you're going!'

4

Cruelty To All Small Things

Barbara often boasted that she had worked as a nanny most of her life for a very posh Oxford family before she'd married Ian. 'They had nice children,' she would say, pouring bleach down the sink. 'Well-behaved, not like you – you're no good for anything apart from breeding.'

At five years of age I would be given a large block of carbolic or green Fairy soap, a bucket of water and a brush, and told to get down on my knees and scrub. Everything had to be spotless.

'Scrub the floor, come on,' she would snap. 'Or are you stupid and lazy like that slut who gave birth to you?'

My knees would hurt and my hands would get red and sore, but I would scrub and scrub every inch of the brown-speckled kitchen lino. Barbara would constantly drop these dark hints about my 'real' mother, but I knew better than to ask anything.

'You're fat and ugly, like your mother,' she would say, washing down the drainer, her back to me. 'You won't amount to anything.'

I would dip the brush in the hot soapy water and scrub and scrub, thinking, *Where is my mother?* And then, *I thought* you *were my mother?*

Then she would spit, hanging up the tea towel, 'Nobody wants you anyway,' and I would feel a heavy lump in my chest. I'd feel tears pricking, but I would bite them back. If I had a real mother, why had she left me here with this woman I called Mum? Where was she? Why wasn't she here? It was all very confusing.

I would be set to do a pile of ironing. I could hardly reach across the board. The iron was heavy and steam shot up in my face. Barbara would come and inspect my work: 'Do it again, you lazy little bugger.' I duly did it again. I wanted to please her so badly, to get a smile, a cuddle, a 'thank you'. But they never came no matter how hard I pressed shirts or pillowcases, standing on tiptoe. Then I would beat the carpets with her, using funny-shaped things like tennis bats when she hung the rugs over the line, and all the dust would whoosh out and make me cough. I also learnt how to make the beds with special 'hospital corners', which meant pulling the sheets tight and folding them over precisely like an envelope at two bottom corners.

'You're lucky, my girl, to be living in such a beautiful home as this. Not like me – I grew up in a workhouse,' she said under her breath one day. I imagined a dark frightening place, like a haunted house, with big, noisy industrial machines. She also mentioned a convent, and nuns whom she'd feared and respected. She was also constantly saying men were only after one thing.

'Men will use you just like they use all girls like you,' she would say darkly, as we filled the birdseed into pots for the chickens. 'Your mother was a whore, and you look just like her.'

I would be left thinking, *What is a whore and how does she know I look just like her?* But it was impossible to ask anything further, because an answer was a swipe across the face, a punch, a push, a whack with the back of the hand or the rolled-up newspaper, plus: 'I'll send you back if you don't shut up!'

But if Barbara didn't like me, she absolutely hated William. She would shout at him, punch him, kick him, snarl at him, all the time: 'C'mere, you little ginger bastard, I'll show you what for.' When I was about five years old, and William was seven, I would regularly watch him being pulled by his ear or yanked by his arm and dragged across the lawn, kicking and scream-ing, to be locked in the garden shed for hours on end. My heart would thud in my chest whenever I watched this happen. I was treated to 'shed time', too, many times, and I knew that feeling of loneliness and fear inside, holding my knees and licking them for comfort, while counting and wondering if she would forget me altogether or if I would die of starvation.

Later I would creep around the shed when Barbara wasn't looking and peek through the window. There would be William, huddled in a corner, his head on his knees, his arms round his legs. I knew he would be crying. The only compensation was that the birdseed was in there, and I hoped he'd have some. He was usually bruised and bleeding and often had big cuts across his arms and legs from sticks she would use on him. But if I was brave, and Barbara wasn't around, I'd knock on the window and we'd look at each other. I knew I had to be careful, so I'd slip round the shed and down into the orchard, hoping to catch a glimpse of Sean, who always made my heart lift.

If he was there, smoking on his step, I knew I'd get a friendly 'There she is,' and a little plastic cup of milk or orange squash, a chunk of nutty bread or a biscuit. I would sit next to him on the step and quietly listen to him whittling his wood or humming an Irish tune. I just loved being next to him, and even loved smelling his smoke and watching the light twinkling through the apple trees. For once I felt safe. But I knew I couldn't stay there long, as Barbara would notice my absence and there'd be hell to pay.

Apart from helping with the household chores, I also had to feed the chickens. When I was little we had only three, and I gave them names: there was Percy the cockerel and two others, Lucy and Sophie. Percy was a Rhode Island Red and had a wonderful red comb and big red and brown feathers. He was magnificent. The girls were black and white with red combs. Later we acquired some Peking Bantams, with lovely fluffy bottoms. I liked being with the chickens and I would often go and sit in their coop and talk to them. Sometimes their mites fell on me and I would be crawling with them. I had to brush them off quickly, fearful of what Barbara would say. I also had to collect the chicken eggs three times a day, come rain or shine. Some days there would be three eggs, or five, and other times none or just one.

One breakfast time I came down to the kitchen dressed in the old blue nylon dressing gown Barbara had given me, and I sensed something was wrong. Barbara was red in the face and I couldn't see William anywhere.

'What's the matter with you, sour puss?' Barbara snapped at me. I said nothing and went and sat on the dog's chair. Barbara always had dogs – but not for long. She liked poodles, and she had one after the other. They seemed to have very short lives, though. She would be very hard on them, just like she was on us. She would kick and hit them, smack them across the nose and use a choke collar that she would yank all the time when we were out walking them. At that time she had Topsy the Poodle, and the blue fabric kitchen chair was Topsy's. I often sat in it, as it was small. That morning Kevin was heartily tucking into fried eggs, bacon and toast, and Barbara was pouring him orange juice. They smiled at each other, conspiratorially.

'He's been naughty,' Barbara said suddenly, catching my thought.

'William's in the shed, where he belongs,' Kevin spluttered, nearly spitting out his juice. Barbara smirked along with him. I didn't like it. I knew how horrible the shed was. I got up and went to the back door and looked down the garden, thinking about poor William. It was raining hard.

'Where do you think you're going?'

'I'll get the eggs,' I said, 'but I'll get dressed first.' I wanted to get my shoes and clothes on because of the weather. Barbara's face turned sharp. 'No, you'll get them now. But I don't want a speck of dirt on that dressing gown – if there is, I will kill you.'

I wanted to put on my shoes and clothes, but I knew I couldn't go against her. With that, I opened the door and stepped barefoot into the freezing wet garden. I heard her say to Kevin, 'Do you want a couple of sausages with that?' as I closed the door.

I held my dressing gown out of the muddy pools of water and tiptoed down the garden to the left, towards the chickens. This took me near the shed and, hovering at the window, I could hear whimpering. I peeked in and I could see William in his pyjamas, his head curled onto his knees, his arms round his legs. The padlock was closed outside, so I guessed she had locked him in. I turned to look back and could see her watching me out of the kitchen window, so I had to walk on up the muddy grass path to the chicken run at the end of the garden. I looked back at the house and I could see them both watching me now, and laughing.

I would never usually go out in the rain barefoot. The nylon dressing gown was already wet and I could feel the mud squishing between my toes. Splashes of mud were visible on the bottom of my dressing gown. Fear gripped my heart as I reached the chicken run, opened the wire gate and looked for a flat rock to stand on. But everything was muddy and wet. There were stepping-stones from the gate to the coop, and I put a timid toe on each one, hoping I wouldn't slip off into the sea of mud and chicken poo at either side. All the chickens were inside and I finally got to the boxes where they laid their eggs. Chicken poo was squeezing between my toes and I was already a sodden mess. There was only one egg; it was still warm and had two pale feathers stuck to it. I carefully put it in my pocket and then began my slippery trip back up the garden path.

I didn't dare look into the shed again. It was still raining and I was now crying. My dressing gown and feet were splattered with mud and poo and I had only one egg. It was also freezing and my feet and hands were blue with cold. I sploshed them under the garden hose for a minute in a desperate attempt to rinse off the mud, at least from my feet. I knew I'd be for it. I hadn't wanted to go in my dressing gown and bare feet – it wasn't fair. It was then that I saw all the chicken poo stuck to the bottom of my dressing gown hem.

By now I was on the backdoor step and Barbara marched up to it, yanked it open and looked fiercely at me down her pointy nose. I was soaking wet all over, a real sight. I put my hand in my pocket and held out the one egg. She took it with her left hand and whacked me round the face with her right: 'You stupid, filthy little bitch.' She put the egg down on the side and came back, yanking the dressing gown off me. I had a thin nightie on underneath, also wet.

'Get in here!' With that she pulled me roughly by the arm to the larder – my precious place – but there was also a tall blue vinyl stool in there that she used for punishing us.

She bent me over the stool, face down, my stomach pressed on the top, my head dangling one side, my legs the other. I was shivering with cold and fear. *Whack!* There was a rolled-up newspaper across my rear.

'You never think, do you? You just make more work for me.' *Thwack!* The pressure on my stomach made me feel sick. I could feel bile coming up to my throat, and I wanted to spew. *Whack! Whack! Whack!* On my legs, back, head, arms, bottom. Suddenly I was sick – a mixture of fear and whatever was left in my stomach.

'You filthy little bitch. Eat it up.'

I was forced to get down and lick the vomit off the floor. This made me even sicker. I was then pushed back over the stool and left hanging there with the top of it pressing into my stomach with agony, until she was ready to let me go. This seemed a long, long time later, even hours. I was wet, freezing, in pain and as miserable as I could be. My only way out – I started counting: one, two, three, four; one, two, three, four; one, two, three, four. I then thought of poor William in the shed; at least it wasn't just me she hated. I wondered what small thing he had done to anger her this time.

William took most of the heat from Barbara's hatred. She seemed to loathe him more than me and, sadly, he got the worst of her treatment (and Kevin's). He was my partner in crime, though, and we had little ways of surviving that we developed between us, for relief and fun. These ways stayed with me for a long time, and I learnt to build up a repertoire of survival tactics.

Neither Barbara nor Ian was very sociable, and they never had friends to the house apart from Kevin's father or local women for coffee sometimes. Ian worked for a small company, and at Christmas he would be given bottles of alcohol by customers. He would bring the bottles home and put them in the wooden G-Plan sideboard in the best living room – the room William and I weren't allowed to go into. We had both learnt to scavenge food, but we now had a new game: scavenging alcohol.

For some reason one day William and I decided to tiptoe in, pull out the cork from one bottle and have a swig. It was called cherry brandy and it tasted wonderful. We took two slugs each and then put the cork back in. I felt a wonderful hot feeling go down the back of my throat and into my tummy. The taste was weird and strong but I liked it. We spluttered the first time we tried it. We knew neither Barbara nor Ian drank at home, so we didn't think it would be missed. The best part was that it took away the gnawing in our tummies and left us glowing. We topped the bottle up with water if it got too low. The trick was to never take too much. To not be greedy. And to not get caught.

Over time, we also took slugs out of different bottles in turn: sherry, port, whisky, wine. We were always very careful. We cleared up any drops spilt and also put the bottles back exactly where they'd been in the first place. I had learnt, with the larder and also with the birdseed, that things always had to look exactly the same, no giveaway traces, as Barbara had hawk-like eyes that would pick up any clues. Then we would find, also in the cupboard, 'Good Boy Choc Drops' that would be the Christmas treat for the dog. We helped ourselves to these and felt like a prince and princess at the most wonderful party. We would grin as we scoffed a handful of dry chocs. We would do all this very quietly, very secretively, hardly breathing. We would be in and out of the living room, past the red velvet curtains and the knick-knacks on the mantelpiece and window ledge, as soon as we could. We always knew that time was of the essence – we had to go as quick as lightning, but not make any mistakes. It would never do to drop anything. William was clumsier than me, so I had to keep him in check, even though he was older. But we knew that the reward of having a warm, full tummy and a lovely taste in our mouths was worth it. We would also go to bed feeling quite woozy and happy.

We wouldn't give anything away, and we had to be very controlled in everything we did. Plus we would then have our green sweeties and medicine at bedtime, so we had to not give the game away. But it was war. Every day was war, and we had to do whatever we could to stay alive. It was our little secret and something that made us feel better just for a while. However, worse treatment was always just around the corner.

⤜⤛

It was a wonderful relief to start going out of the house to school a few times a week when I was around five. From the start

Barbara never let me go every day; it was maybe two or three times a week, while William attended the local primary school. We walked with Topsy the poodle, and Barbara would whack us and push us all the way. She strode along very quickly in her brown duffle coat and we trotted after her. She would push and kick the poor dog, yanking and shoving it in all directions, swearing all the time, which made me upset.

But I absolutely loved school right from the start. There were bright colours and things to play with. The teachers didn't shout or hit us and every day I got a small bottle of milk, which was rich and creamy and wonderful. There was lunch, too: little carrot sticks and celery, bread and cheese. Also biscuits, fruit and cake – even orange squash. I thought I had gone to heaven. Most of all I loved colouring in. I sat next to a girl who had big teeth and brown plaits, and we coloured in together. I liked colouring outside the lines, which she thought was funny. We laughed. I didn't usually laugh, and I began to get a new, odd, feeling: I was happy.

I had a lovely teacher, Miss Nickerson, who would give me a big piece of paper and set me up with paints and a jam jar of water and brushes. She had blonde curls and a warm smile and would put an old shirt on me, buttoned at the back, and roll up the sleeves. She would clip my hair back and say, warmly, 'Paint, Louise. Go on.' And I would take my brush and dip it in the most fantastic colours: red, blue, green, yellow.

One day Miss Nickerson showed me a magic trick: 'Look, Louise,' she said, sitting down next to me, smelling of perfume. 'If you mix yellow and blue, you get...' She showed me and, as if by magic, a new colour appeared. 'Green!' I said. Wow! It was absolutely fantastic.

Miss Nickerson said, 'You are really good, Louise. Keep painting.' I was so pleased, so happy, that I took my painting home to show Barbara and Ian.

'You've got paint on your skirt,' was all Barbara said. 'What does that place think it's doing creating more work for me to do?'

My painting lay brightly coloured on the kitchen table being completely ignored. When teatime came, I looked around the kitchen for my painting – if Barbara didn't want it I would take it upstairs. When I asked she just said, 'Oh, that, it's in the dustbin, of course.' She had already ripped it up and thrown it away.

Barbara seemed to resent me enjoying anything at all, especially school, so she would keep me home. But I wanted to go to school. I wanted to draw and paint with the nice Mrs Nickerson. But Barbara would tell me I was ill. I wasn't, I was well. I found home horrible and scary. I had loved learning to make green with Miss Nickerson. I liked sitting on the blue carpet in the sun and picking a book off the shelf and leafing through it. I hadn't learnt to read, I didn't know my alphabet and I couldn't write, but I loved drawing and splodging colourful paint onto fresh white paper. It was a joy. I wanted to go to school and I was upset when I couldn't.

I wandered round the garden, kicking the leaves, picking up stones. Barbara's eyes were nearly always on me somehow. I would wander about, looking at the clouds scudding by. I would go and see Sean and pass the time with him for a while, and then wander back in case Barbara noticed. Why couldn't I go to school? It was nice. The grown-ups there were friendly. There was stuff to do, stuff to play with. I began to collect things. I found a little matchbox and put some dead flies inside it. I took the flies and put them in a row inside the box and then hid it in my bedside drawer. I liked seeing them in there, and I wondered if they'd come back to life.

I began to get curious about my body. And one day I also began to collect my own poo. I did a poo and caught it in my hand. It was warm and nice. I would play with it and look at it, and even touch it and squeeze it. It was a bit like clay. I put it on some toilet paper and got another matchbox and put the poo in it, squishing it in. Then I put the matchbox in my pocket and carried it around. I would also put it under my pillow at night, or in other hidey-holes. It was all mine. Then I had another idea, an even better idea. I took some poo, sneaked into Barbara's bedroom, with my heart in my mouth, and squelched it under her bed. I wasn't allowed in her bedroom, so I waited until she was at the bottom of the garden, and I squished the poo right up into the corners of her bed, under the mattress. You could hardly see it. It gave me pleasure somehow, and I wondered if it would smell. I imagined it smelling and Barbara not being able to figure out where it was coming from – and for some reason this made me feel happy again. I wanted her to feel upset. Also, I did the vacuuming in the house, so when the poo finally crumbled onto the floor, I got rid of it easily. No trace.

I also crept into the garage, where Ian kept his van at night, and I did a little steaming poo in the corner and then covered it over with stones. I'd watched the cats in the garden do this – poo and then cover it – so I did the same. He would never find it; he would never know. If he found it, he would think it was a cat, or even Topsy. Even if he did think it was me, he would never 'kill' me like Barbara; he wouldn't do anything. I felt a huge sense pleasure in my secret poo game – for some reason it was my great comfort and joy.

5

Torture and Trauma

I hated having my hair washed, although I also hated being smelly. I didn't have many baths or showers, so I often felt very grimy. However, anything physical that Barbara did with me or William was done with as much roughness as possible. My hair would be washed in the kitchen with Vosene, out of a big green bottle. Barbara would grab me by the arm and bend my head over roughly to check if I needed a wash. It was done brutally and silently, like I was a rag doll. She would pull my hair apart, yanking it from side to side, saying, 'You filthy little bitch, come here. God, you're a mess.' Hair washing happened at the sink, and the water would either be freezing or boiling. She never asked if I was okay, and would never adjust the temperature even if I screamed. I'd just get a kick or a slap and be told to stay still if I didn't want worse.

When I was small I stood on the horrible blue stool that she bent me over to punish me in the larder, and later I just stood by the sink on a kitchen chair or on tiptoe. She would pour a jug of water over my head and then pour on the Vosene, smelling of strong tar, which would go in my eyes and sting terribly ('Don't fuss!'), while she scrubbed and scrubbed, digging her fingers in hard. I would cry and she would hit me with her rolled-up newspaper, or even a wooden pole that she kept in the larder, to shut me up. To finish, she would pour vinegar over my hair and it would go into the cuts on my head that she'd made with her fingernails while washing, and I would shriek.

'Shut up, you silly bitch, it makes your hair shiny.'

After the hair came the neck scrub. A coarse flannel and carbolic soap was scrubbed on my neck until my skin was scarlet. 'Stand still,' she'd bark, and she would crick my neck to one side and then the other and poke in my ears with a matchstick with a bit of cotton wool wrapped round the end as a cheap cotton bud. Out would come wax and she would snarl, 'You dirty little thing, full of oil and grease; you must be a Jew.'

I hadn't then learnt what a Jew was but it was obviously a bad thing. Sometimes she'd poke so deep it would hurt and the matchstick would come out covered in blood and I would scream, so I'd get whacked and whacked with the newspaper until I eventually stopped. Then I counted, counted, counted, and waited for it all to end.

Everything Barbara did with us or to us was painful, humiliating or scary. She had an air gun, and was quite obsessed with it. I had no idea why she had it but it was kept in a kitchen cupboard. Kevin also had an air gun, and he would shoot at squirrels and birds, to Barbara's delight. Sometimes she would set up paper targets on the lawn – little squares of paper on bamboo sticks with round black rings on them – or a person shape drawn on it in black with a bull's-eye centre. Or she'd put old tin cans along a wall. Barbara and Kevin would stand, legs astride, and shoot at the targets, looking like two toy soldiers on the lawn.

One day William and I were in the garden, hovering around the chicken run, while Barbara and Kevin were doing their target practice, when suddenly I heard William shout, 'Run, run!'

I looked up to see Barbara aiming her gun straight at us. She started shooting at us, at me, and I screamed. William and I ran as fast as our little legs could take us, still screaming, to the orchard with Barbara following after us, shooting. I could hear the pellets pinging off the tree trunks. I was petrified and we ran to take cover behind Sean's caravan. I was shaking like a leaf. Sean was on his step, smoking.

'What's the matter?' he asked gently. Both William and I were panting and sobbing, but were even more terrified of giving the game away. We just stood, shivering and shaking, hiding behind Sean's caravan until we felt things were safe. Sean kept asking what was wrong, but I was scared that if I told him what she was doing that she would come and shoot him to shut him up, too, so I didn't say anything. I couldn't bear for Sean to die; he was our only place of safety, our only friend.

However, the shooting game was not over now she had the taste for it. From then on Barbara would jump out – especially in the garden, which had been my lovely safe place of escape until then – with a gun, and pretend to shoot me point blank in the head. She would pull the trigger and I would scream while she would laugh. It was really the only time I ever saw her do a full belly laugh. Terrifying us really seemed to give her great pleasure. She would 'pretend' to shoot me or William as part of her regular game to keep us silent and obedient. I was terrified she might actually do it one day, especially when she got that scary look in her eyes and her nose and face became hard and pointy.

In fact, one night I was awoken by a creaking in our room. It must have been the middle of the night, as I was usually out for the count for the first part of the night due to the special medicine she gave me. When I came to, I was conscious of a big dark shadow over me – Barbara. In her hand, forced against my temple, was a cold, hard object: the gun. I froze with absolute fear. I was tied down as usual, and I began to struggle against the strap, this way and that. Was she going to kill me? Right this minute? The gun moved closer to the side of my head and pressed into my flesh.

Barbara whispered, 'Bang! You're dead,' and clicked the trigger. I held my breath and closed my eyes, searching for the golden swirls and purple colours that I could see when I scrunched my eyes up. Was I dead yet? I wasn't breathing or moving and all was suddenly quiet. Maybe I was dead now. I slowly opened my eyes and she was gone – just like that. I spent the rest of the night wide awake, tied down, counting, counting, counting, lying in a cold, sodden bed, as I had peed myself in sheer animal fear.

❧

Apart from terrifying us daily, and hurting us physically, Barbara was also keen on humiliating us as much as possible, making both of us wear horrible clothes. She would dress me in her horrible old hand-me-down frocks, which were truly hideous. Brown old-lady dresses with orange and yellow flowers, made out of polyester, or even a pale-blue housecoat like cleaners and housewives wore. All my school friends were wearing lovely flowing dresses, cheesecloth shirts and bell-bottom trousers with pretty T-shirts and beads. I looked like a frumpy old lady in second-hand, cut-down clothes and shoes. I wore old smelly anoraks and nasty yellowing cardigans. A shopping trip for me was a visit to the local charity shop, where I would get something very cheap to wear. I also didn't have proper boots or warm shoes in winter. Barbara got me sandals one winter and I froze. I walked to school and back in these shoes and developed horrible chilblains – big red sores all over my feet, which hurt like hell.

Around October time she would say to me, 'This is the chilblain time of the year,' and would put butter on my feet, and two pairs of socks. She would then put a hot-water bottle on them at night and they hurt terribly; they were itchy, swollen and sore. As a consequence, I would have to wear her maroon old-lady slippers to school. My feet were so bloated and wrapped up I could hardly walk. I was humiliated and bullied: 'What has the Evil One done to you now?' Or, 'She's really ugly and you're really ugly – look at your ugly feet.'

Barbara would keep me off school for weeks at a time, telling them I had flu when it was actually the chilblains crippling me. When I put proper shoes on I screamed with pain. It was horrendous, and meanwhile my feet were getting worse and worse. Then one day, when I was off from school with either the 'flu' or the 'chilblains', Barbara made me walk with her and the dog to the local Co-op. It was agony but I was desperate to get out of the house, so I didn't mind. I hobbled along and into the shop, trailing behind her. I had on two pairs of socks, as always, and my feet hurt like hell. I was wearing the usual maroon slippers and I felt terribly aware of people staring at me – I must have looked a real sight for a child.

Next stop was the chemist. We went in and the chemist said,

'Oh, dear, not feeling well today?' to me. Before I could say anything, Barbara piped up, 'Yes, she's got the flu. I'm keeping her off to stop her being infectious.'

I knew this was rubbish, but I played along. I hung back and looked longingly at the things that were on a carousel of products: lovely coloured hairbands and clips. I was never allowed to grow my hair, and I was dying to have a long, swishy ponytail with pretty things in it. I wanted to look like the girl on the BBC test card, with a hairband. Just then I noticed another woman at the counter asking the chemist about the treatment for chilblains, as she had them herself and said she was in awful pain. I was dreaming about having a mauve comb and wide white hairband when I heard Barbara turn to the woman and say, 'Oh, the best thing for chilblains is fresh air. You need to keep your feet cold, stand on a cold floor and let your feet breathe.'

I was amazed and shocked. This was the complete opposite of what Barbara told me all the time. She told me I had to keep my feet very warm, and even heat them up. The woman said to her, 'Yes, I've heard they can really spread if you keep your feet too hot and have changes of temperature from hot to cold.'

'Yes,' said Barbara, all knowledgeable. 'They spread in the heat. You must keep your feet cool and clean.'

I thought about the butter on my feet, that I hadn't been allowed to wash them for a week, about the two pairs of socks, the slippers, the hot-water bottle. And then I knew – she was making me have chilblains. She was actively growing them. I felt very scared standing there eavesdropping as I looked at the sparkly ponytail clips – she was keeping me home by making my feet bad *on purpose*. How could I trust her about anything at all? She was trying to hurt me all the time!

I suddenly remembered another time when she said my knee was deformed and I couldn't walk on it. I was off school for about a month. The strange thing was I did have a lot of aches and pains in my joints (which my teacher had called 'growing pains'), but I also had a lot of bruises and cuts from beatings – from Barbara's own hands, or from Kevin's. No wonder I was in pain. I was often kept off because I looked battered and bruised. So I ended up missing school and I could never seem to catch up, which made me feel very miserable and stupid. I hated being behind all the time, and I hated being in the remedial class – it was so boring. But even though I hated school, I didn't want to stay home all the time, pretending I was ill.

As we left the shop, and I hobbled down the road on my tortured feet, I realised I would have to be very clever indeed to help myself. I would have to do what I thought was best, and not believe Barbara at all from now on. I would have to cool my feet down, and yet make her feel I was doing what she wanted – keeping them warm. I would have to really outwit her. I didn't understand why she wanted to hurt me all the time and damage my health – like boiling my feet when they needed to be cold to get better – but I knew I had to use my head to keep myself safe from now on or I would surely die.

The only good thing in life was school. I loved it. But the downside was that both William and I not only smelt rotten, we also looked ragged in our second-hand, ripped and torn clothes. William nearly always had cuts and bruises on his face, arms and legs, which were really visible, and he was silent and withdrawn most of the time. He was also very small, as he had not grown very much, and he got picked on a lot and was called a little dwarf by the other children. I felt protective of him, although I was two years younger than him. I wanted to look after him.

Neither of us could read or write yet, and William couldn't sit down for very long and was always running all over the place like a wild thing. He was often in trouble with the teachers and I worried he would get us both into trouble, so I kept my head down and played being a 'good girl', just like I did at home. We were both put in the 'backward' class along with children who couldn't sit up, or who had strangely shaped bodies, or couldn't see, hear or talk properly.

For me, one of the most humiliating things was being made to wear Barbara's hand-me-down clothes. She would take one of her old skirts or blouses or dresses and roughly pin or sew it. I looked like a little granny. I felt shy and embarrassed as the other children stared at me and sniggered or whispered. I looked at the other little girls, with clean blonde curls or freckles and brown plaits, who had neat pastel-coloured dresses with Peter Pan collars, and frilly white socks and new shoes. I knew we both looked odd. William and I both looked grimy and stank, too – we had smelly armpits and often smelt of wee from the night regime. I was so ashamed.

Despite this, the most wonderful thing at Vernon Lane Primary for me was the freedom. I was now six and William was eight. Barbara hated the school, of course, because it was nice for us (she hated a lot of things). She nearly always got us there late in the mornings (there was no real reason for this as we lived nearby – it was just another way of making us stick out). I was so embarrassed to arrive at an empty playground and have to tiptoe in. All eyes would turn on me and I would have to go to the form teacher as she marked 'Late' in the school register. Then I would hear more sniggers and comments.

At the end of the day, when the parents came to collect the children, Barbara would separate herself from them. She would sit by an internal door, away from the other parents, ignoring everyone, looking sour. I used to edge my way round the room and down the corridor towards her, hoping other people didn't see how odd she looked in her horrible grey anorak. She refused to talk to the other parents.

As she pushed me along through the playground she would snap, 'This school is disgusting.' I had no idea why or what she meant. 'Too much freedom by half,' she would snip. 'No bloody discipline – they don't know what they're doing. The Head is mad.'

She would say this loudly as we passed the nice head teacher, Mr James, who would smile at us warmly. I would smile shyly back up at him, but Barbara would put her nose in the air and yank me past, with Topsy being towed roughly behind.

I still loved being with the teachers and Miss Nickerson, though. They let us choose what to do: we could sit on the blue carpet and read a book, play musical instruments or sing songs, do painting or make something out of cardboard. There were paper, pens, plasticine, egg boxes, glue, shiny coloured paper, wool and scissors, and we could just be creative and express ourselves. It was heaven on earth. I found all of this wonderful.

After school one day Miss Nickerson tried to show Barbara my painting work. She took Barbara to one of my paintings drying on an easel.

'What's all this then?' snarled Barbara.

'Well,' started Miss Nickerson, smiling first at me, and then at Barbara, although I could see she was quite nervous with Barbara, 'I think you have a very talented girl. She really is a talented little artist.'

I felt my chest open and I filled with pride. Really? Me? This was so wonderful, Miss Nickerson saying something like this to my mother.

'I'd like to put her work into a competition – she would do the school proud.' I could feel my timid confidence blooming.

Barbara's face tightened. 'No,' she said bluntly. 'No, she's stolen some paintings from the other children, brought them home and copied them. How does that make her an artist? She's a little cheat!'

Miss Nickerson's face was, indeed, a picture. She looked like a bomb had dropped. She didn't know what to say. I felt tears prick my eyes and I wanted the floor to open up and let me drop in. My growing confidence popped like a balloon. I felt my knees tremble. How could she talk to my lovely Miss Nickerson this way? We had all copied some American pop artists, so Miss Nickerson tried to change tack.

'Er, well, yes, the children do copy paintings… but look here, Louise's is the best by far in the class.'

'Oh,' Barbara said loudly, 'I hate bloody Americans. They're so loud and arrogant.' At this, Miss Nickerson looked completely at sea.

'No, no,' Barbara insisted loudly, 'she's copied some of the other children. She's cheated. You're a disgusting school if you encourage cheating. I will complain to the council.'

With that, Barbara snatched me away and dragged me out of

the class, hissing, 'You're not staying here, there's no morals. Filthy, nasty, ignorant people.'

Barbara would not stop telling me I was a cheat. She went on and on at me, whacked me across the face when we got home that day, and put me to bed at four in the afternoon, without tea.

'You'll never amount to anything. You're a liar and a cheat,' she said, slamming the door once I was tied down in the afternoon light. For punishment she took my felt-tips and green computer paper I'd got from Ian to draw on and threw them away. She also took my favourite and only toy, Tony, my black-and-white Panda. When I got it back later, he had a big slash down his front and stuffing was coming out of his belly button. I couldn't cry any more. I didn't understand. I just closed my eyes and kept thinking, I didn't cheat. It's not true. Miss Nickerson believes me.

I clung onto the image of her buttoning up my shirt, carefully and kindly, and rolling up my sleeves and encouraging me to dip my brush in the paint and make lovely colourful swirls. I saw her warm smile and her nice blonde curls and smelt her lovely perfume, and thought, *You won't hurt me*. I will be happy. I will paint. Meanwhile, the tears rolled down my cheeks and I looked at the cracks in the ceiling and the blue flowers on the wallpaper, and started counting, yet again.

After this incident Barbara decided it was time for action. Something was afoot. She had to go to meetings about William at the school with the headteacher and social workers. She wasn't happy. He was way behind and in trouble. She would come back from a meeting and furiously throw pots and pans around in the kitchen, and then open the back door and throw them all out in the garden in a heap.

'Of course he's in trouble; he's an unwanted little bastard,' Barbara spat out, reading yet another letter from the Head. 'They have no idea what I have to deal with day in, day out. I hate the little bugger.'

I knew she hated him. He knew she hated him. We all knew. She swiped at him and kicked him and hurt him in myriad ways: he was her punchbag. She let Kevin punch and kick him whenever he wanted to and never said a word. Ian never intervened, either, opting to slope off to the garage or the shed to do woodwork, and never stopped any of Barbara's torture. He was frightened of her himself, and kept his own head down. We were both kept home from school a lot from then on.

'You're staying home, you're not well enough,' she'd say.

But it seemed we were well enough to do the household chores. I was cutting the grass, collecting the eggs, doing the ironing, scrubbing the floors, cleaning the toilet – and all the while longing to be with Miss Nickerson, making a beautiful picture. I wanted to sit on the carpet and read books, or sing round the piano. Instead I was cleaning out the hens' poo or scrubbing dirty shirt collars.

Two major things happened then that changed my life for ever. After the painting incident, Barbara kept me home from school for ages and ages and told me every day that I wasn't well enough to go in. The pining for Miss Nickerson, nice Mr James and my friend with the big teeth, the milk and biscuits and all the lovely food was unbearable now. Then one morning Barbara stood over me at breakfast and said, 'You're going to a new school.'

I burst into tears.

'I don't want any backchat. You need discipline,' was all she said.

I sobbed and sobbed uncontrollably and was sent to my room with a whack across the shoulders with the newspaper.

'Shut up. You'll do as you're told. Beggars can't be choosers.'

I didn't even care; my heart was broken. Barbara soon gave me my new uniform, which was scratchy, grey and horrible. Of course I had second-hand clothes, nothing new.

This new primary school was much further away, near a rough estate. It was a very different kind of school: regimented, strict, unfriendly and tough. The first day there, Barbara dropped me by the back gate and I had to make my way across the playground, terrified. I was stared at by parents and children alike as I walked in with my odd hand-me-down clothes, looking dirty and dishevelled. I must have looked so out of place in my old-lady shoes. Everyone else had Kickers or plimsolls but I had proper women's shoes, brown with a heel and buckle. They were too big and I looked really silly. Barbara knitted my grey and green tie, and I was laughed at. Always different; always sticking out like a sore thumb.

From day one I was picked on by a big boy called Spencer, who followed me around, taunted me and made my life a misery. He cornered me and pushed me up against the wall, wanting to see in my bag. I ducked out from under his arm but he pursued me every day. Barbara was often late coming to pick me up after school, so I would stand in the corner of the playground, waiting, back against the wall by the gate, looking out, feeling utterly lost. She might be a whole hour late. Or more. Spencer would shout across the playground, 'Nobody wants you, then!' and his mates would laugh.

Barbara would eventually appear in her white Ford Escort and shout through the window to 'Get in!' as if I'd been keeping her waiting all that time. There was never any explanation. Worse was to come. Not only was I at a new school that I didn't like at all, but something terrible was about to happen – something of which I had no warning at all.

One morning, while getting up for breakfast, we were both told we were being kept home from school. 'You're ill and you're staying,' is all Barbara said. The usual. I hated my new school, but I hated staying home even more. I wasn't ill, nor was William, but we were told we had to go back to our bedroom. I hated being in there all day, as there was absolutely nothing to do. We looked at each other, made a face and shrugged. We occupied ourselves by playing made-up games of 'mums and dads' – our favourite. Then William got bored and went to lie on the floor, kicking the wall. So I opened my bedside drawer, went over and sat next to him and showed him the dead flies in my matchbox. He always liked to look at them, so he sat up again. We seldom talked but we both knew we were willing the flies to come back to life. He looked at me and we both grinned; it was our little secret.

Then I heard a car on the gravel. The doorbell rang, followed by voices in the hall.

'William, come here,' was shouted up the stairs by Barbara.

He scrambled to his feet and disappeared. I sat for a moment, listening to the voices. I didn't recognise them and couldn't make out what they were saying. I was puzzled and scared. I didn't know what was going on. After a few minutes I took a deep breath, checked the coast was clear, crept out onto the landing and sat huddled at the top of the stairs, my knees under my chin, my arms round my legs. I licked my knees, which was something I often did when I needed to feel better. At the bottom of the stairs, in the hall, I could see Barbara's navy-blue tartan travel bag. I thought she must be going away. That would be fantastic. Peace at last!

The kitchen door was shut and I could hear voices behind it – a woman's high voice and a man's deep voice mixed with the occasional unmistakeable sound of Barbara. But I couldn't hear what they were saying. I knew William had been in trouble at school: he'd had to go to the headmaster's office several times recently, and he wasn't doing well. He could never concentrate and would get up and walk around in class, which annoyed the teachers. Maybe it was something about that?

I bit my lip. I felt I had a huge rock in my stomach, a pebble in my throat. Then the kitchen door opened and there was the top of William's head, his red hair sticking up as always like a giant toothbrush. He was in his school blazer now but I couldn't see his face. There was a woman in a coat standing next to him, and a man next to Barbara. No one was speaking. They all walked towards the front door and went out. The travel bag was gone.

I had a sudden panic. What was happening? I had to know. I was not allowed downstairs into the 'best' front room, with the red velvet curtains, but I tiptoed down as fast as I could, opened the door and crept in. It faced the drive. I snuck to the window. There was a green car parked out front, and I suddenly saw William in the back with his head down, his hands holding his face. The man and the woman were getting in the car. I wanted to scream: 'Noooooo!' What was happening? Where was he going? I put my hands on the window and pressed my nose up against the pane. 'William,' I wanted to scream. 'William, where are you going?' The car was turning now and the indicator was sticking out, a little orange arm, pointing to the right. What was to the right? I racked my brains. That was the way to Oxford.

I didn't hear Barbara come in behind me, as I was crying and sobbing and tears were streaming down my face, palms stuck to the window. She grabbed me by the hair and pulled me away from the window with such violence that I fell back against the dining table and chairs, knocking one over. *Whack!* She slapped me round the face.

'I told you to stay in your room, you little bitch.' I was distraught, beside myself, sobbing hysterically.

'William…' was all I could get out between sobs.

'He's going somewhere you'll go to if you don't do as you're bloody told,' she shouted at me. I looked at her, wild-eyed, absolutely terrified.

'He wasn't your blood, he wasn't your brother, you weren't related, so stop bloody whining.' She stopped and looked at me crying in a heap on the carpet. 'Go to your room. You won't come out until you stop.'

And that was it. William was gone.

6

Cold Comfort Home

My heart is broken. I'm lying on my bed face down, howling into my pillow. I was sent up here hours ago. She's forgotten I'm here and I don't care; I don't care about anything. It's cold and grey outside and there isn't much daylight. But I howl and howl into my pillow, wanting the pain in my stomach to stop. When I stop howling I see William's red toothbrush hair sticking up in the back of the car – his head is down, in his hands. The indicator is sticking out to the right. The car is going, going, going, and there is nothing I can do to stop it. Then he's gone.

She says, 'He's gone.' That's it. I howl again, long, painful groans, but I have to keep the noise down as I know too much noise will bring her up. I don't want that. I don't want to see her ever again. She's evil. Why does she hate us so much, or rather, why does she hate me? She said I would be sent away. I want to be sent away! I want to be with William! If he has gone somewhere else, why can't I go too? I sit up in the murky daylight and look at the dingy net curtains. *Why?* is all my numb brain can think. *Why? Why? Why?* Why didn't they take me too? How could they leave me behind? How could they leave me with her? With them?

I lie back down, facing the ceiling this time. Snot is running down my face. My eyes are swollen and I can hardly breathe with so much crying. I stare at the ceiling and look at the familiar cracks and the same old white plastic lampshade. Everything is the same. But it's not the same. Behind the partition there is silence. I get up slowly and walk to the end of the partition – William's side of the room. It looks horribly empty. I go to the little chest of drawers at the end of the room: an old wooden one with shiny knobs on. I pull open the top drawer. Empty. This had William's worn-out grey socks and grimy white underwear in it. Nothing. The next drawer – his shorts and shirts: empty. I pull the next two out: empty, empty. A huge well of fear opens in my tummy. Where are his little brown shorts? His grey jumper? His funny old brown shoes? Gone, gone, gone.

Where is he, my William? I've known him all my life, six whole years. He's all I've ever had on my side. Tears bubble down my face again but I have to close the drawers quietly and make sure there is no trace. I always have to do that. In my head I'm screaming – why has William gone? Where has he gone? Why am I still here? But I have to keep quiet. Then I remember – and go to his pillow and lift it. There's Fizz, his little bear from Sean. I burst into sobs. I pick up Fizz and hold him to me. He hasn't even got his little friend. Barbara let us keep Fizz and Tony, as they came from Sean – it was unusual that she let us keep them. The became our treasure. But now he hasn't even got Fizz to keep him company, poor William.

I hide Fizz under my mattress, just in case. Then I stumble back down the side of William's bed and round the end of the partition, and then throw myself face down on my bed once more, howling into the sodden pillow again. I am on the edge of a big black hole and I'm falling into it. There is no one out there to help me. My lovely Miss Nickerson has gone. Ian doesn't care. Kevin hates me. William has gone – really gone. I have no one to ask, no one to turn to.

I reach out for Tony the panda, whose guts are still half hanging out. I cuddle him to me. The pathetic sight of him starts me off again. I can bear the physical pain, the torture, the insults, but the knowledge that I have now lost my brother-in-pain and am truly alone – this is truly unbearable. It is the worst day of my whole life.

❧

The day William left I had no food or drink at all. Barbara left me to it but came in at bedtime with her face all pointy and hard and we went through the usual horrible night routine. Only this time I was the main focus of all her nastiness. I didn't care. I was cried out and numb. I felt empty and exhausted. As she forced the big green pill down my throat, I thought, *Good, I don't care*. As she roughly strapped me into bed, I thought, *See if I care*. I actually welcomed the blurry numbness that took over and pulled me into the familiar dark.

The next day I was forced to go to school, the new school I absolutely hated. Now I didn't want to go to school because I didn't want to go without William. As we left the house, late of course, with Topsy being tugged this way and that, I felt numb. I didn't smile. I didn't look at anything. I didn't care. I watched my horrible old-lady shoes walk along the cracked pavement. They didn't belong to me. But when we got to the bottom of the street I looked right. Right was the way I'd seen William go. It was like I might see him somewhere down the road, or a tuft of red hair sticking out of something, like a dustbin. I looked for green cars everywhere. He had to be somewhere. Why had he gone? Where was he?

Barbara just snapped, 'Stop dawdling. Come on, you're going to school, you little bitch.' For emphasis she yanked Topsy's choke collar so hard that the poor animal took right off from the pavement, hit the low wall, bounced and yelped.

'Shut up!' Barbara hissed fiercely, pulling her upright. I saw red appear round the collar. It was unbearable and my tears started again. *Whack!* An open-handed clip right round the head.

'Stop whining,' she sniffed. 'No one wants you, we're doing you a bloody favour.'

School was terrible. Spencer was on at me straight away as I crept in late: 'Oh, here's the smelly little cry baby,' and everyone turned, stared and sniggered. I knew I looked a sight. My face was swollen and puffy from hours of crying, my clothes were messy and smelly and I hadn't eaten or washed. I sat down. All I could think of was William. What was he doing now, this minute? I went into a daydream. The teacher was talking but I couldn't follow. I didn't understand. The whole day went by in a blur. Even at lunchtime I ate something but didn't taste it – unusual for me, who craved school dinners. I didn't sneak a biscuit into my pocket or a plum into my bag. I didn't care today, as William wouldn't be there when I got home. It would just be me… and them.

That thought was like sitting under a giant black cloud. Just me… and them. No William to sit in the shed with, to eat bird-seed with or to huddle with and lick our knees for comfort or visit Sean with. We didn't really talk but we were in the same horrible boat, literally clinging together every day. We always knew where the other one was, and looked out for each other. Who would shout, 'Run! Run!' if they got the guns out now? And now – where was he? Why was I still here, in this horrible, hateful school and in that horrible, hateful house, with people who despised and ignored me?

Barbara was late collecting me, as usual, so I hung around being taunted by my schoolfellows. She was in a bad mood when she arrived, so I said nothing, just followed silently. When we got home she went straight into the garden without a word and got the bonfire going in the silver incinerator bin beside the shed. She was busy stoking the fire with all sorts of things as I wandered out, and it was soon roaring, smoke curling up into the afternoon sky. There were piles of beige folders on the grass next to her feet. Curious, I crept a bit further forward and saw that she was putting photos in the fire. Sparks were flying up and the fire was spitting and hissing as she did so. Her face was set and glowed red in the flames. She looked like a witch.

I crept even nearer and could see a file full of photos of William. Barbara didn't say anything to me, but just kept throwing in paper, photos, anything that came to hand. Then she strode off to get some more wood and I saw my chance. I swooped and picked up two photos of William, just his face, the typical school photos we'd had done at nice Vernon Lane Primary, and I quickly shoved them inside my long grey socks. Barbara would often search me ('What've you got there, you little thief?'), so I knew not to put anything in my school blazer pocket. I quietly turned and tiptoed away.

'What are you doing?' she boomed down the garden. I

jumped, but turned and managed to say, innocently, 'Nothing.'
Then I turned back and went upstairs on heavy little legs and
had to think quickly about where I was going to hide my precious treasure. I could put them in the mattress, where I kept
my food stash. But would the food hurt the photos? I also had
to be quick, as I knew Barbara would think something was up.
She was always suspicious. I opened my bedside drawer, where
I kept the matchbox with the flies that I was trying to bring
back to life.

I put the photos right at the back of the drawer, side on. I
closed the drawer as quietly as I could and just stood there in
the twilight. I had a bit of William. I could still see his face if I
wanted to. I had a warm feeling, if only for a moment. Just the
idea of seeing his brown eyes, shock of red hair and sticky-out
ears made me feel a little better. My tummy wasn't hurting as
much now. Then I tiptoed downstairs, as if I was away too long
Barbara would get annoyed.

As I came into the kitchen, I could see through the window
that she was still busy with her bonfire, poking a stick into it,
stirring it like a witch. Smoke was still curling upwards and the
sky was getting dark. On the kitchen table there was a notebook. I knew Barbara had to keep records for the social workers
about what she did with us and how she spent money. She never
stopped moaning about it. But she usually kept them locked in
the kitchen cupboards.

I saw my chance. I quickly opened the notebook and made
out, in pencil, the last thing she wrote: William's name and a
phone number. I memorised the number and tiptoed upstairs
again, quiet as a mouse, wrote the number down on an old bit
of school paper and stuffed it under my mattress. Then I folded

the material over it, very carefully. I thought that was a safer place. A phone number for William… maybe he was sick or in hospital? With another family? Or a new school? My head was bursting with questions, but I knew I couldn't ask Barbara any of them because I would never get a straight answer if I did.

The next day Barbara marched me home at high speed in stony silence, dragging poor Topsy along, whose nails scratched the pavement the whole way. I knew she was furious and I felt sick. What was it now? When we got home my two precious photos of William were on the kitchen table.

'What do you call this?' she spat out, going red. I said nothing but my tummy fell through the floor. I wanted to wee. 'You're a sneaky little thief,' she screamed. 'And a liar.' With that, she got the box of matches she used for my ears, lit a match and set fire to William's photos. 'No! No!' I cried, the tears starting.

'Get this into your stupid head,' seethed Barbara, as the photos curled up in flames and fell in the sink, a charred mess. 'You will never, ever see him again. You are not to mention him to me or to anyone else. Ever again! Do you hear?'

I was crying uncontrollably now. I just sobbed and sobbed and couldn't stop. Barbara grabbed me by the shoulders with her scrawny fingers and dug them in like talons. She shook me violently, backwards and forwards, with my head wobbling like a jelly on my neck.

'You are a wicked girl! Who cares about you? You are stupid like your mum. No one wants you. Go to your room.'

With that, I was pushed out the door and I stumbled up the endless stairs to my now very lonely, scary room.

᭙

The next few days went by in a blur. I got up, had my tiny bowl of Ready Brek, all alone at my little table now. Kevin taunted me the whole time, calling me a 'cry baby'. He mimicked a sad clown face to me, and then laughed nastily. He was enjoying my misery. Barbara just told me over and over that I was lucky they were good enough to take in the likes of me. Ian said nothing, just went to work as usual or came in and went to the garage. Once at school, I couldn't pay attention. I could hardly follow what was going on. I couldn't read properly, or write. It was terrible – everything, that is, except art, which I loved (although I still missed Miss Nickerson and her warm face and lovely perfume).

I found some scraps of paper and drew Tony and Fizz. When I drew I felt a bit calmer but I also felt very sad. At school I was bullied and taunted by Spencer and his gang, and at home I was bullied and hit by Kevin and Barbara. Ian seemed more absent than ever – always out in his van or watching TV in the best room in the evening. He never came and talked to me about William, or gave me a hug or explained anything. I was just left to my fear and unhappiness.

When the weekend finally came, I feared the long days ahead away from school. I talked to the chickens when I collected the eggs, and then went down to the orchard. I would gaze intensely at the flowers; I loved the red and yellow petals and deep black centres. I watched the bees dipping in and out of them. Suddenly I remembered Sean Brannon. I'd forgotten him in my unhappiness over William. I hovered around the apple trees, kicking the windfalls and leaves. It was chilly, but I waited and watched his little blue caravan through the hedge. Soon his door opened and there he was on the steps in his usual flat cap, soft brown trousers and braces. He was wearing his rough tweed jacket and was rolling a cigarette, as usual.

I ducked through a hole in the hedge and ran towards the caravan but stopped short of the steps. I stood and looked up at him, feeling I might cry. I bit my lip.

'Where's yer little fella?' Sean asked brightly. I burst into tears. I sobbed and sobbed. Sean lit his cigarette, then got up and came over to me. 'Come on, girlie,' he said, and took my hand. I was going up the steps, into the caravan. I'd never been inside it before. I was still crying, but going into the warm narrow house helped me stop for a while. There was a small sink, and narrow orange and brown cupboards and, at one end, a sort of thin bed with a crocheted top and a fold-out table.

'Want some toast?'

I nodded. I couldn't speak. I wiped my face with the back of my hand and sniffed. I stood and watched Sean get a plastic bag with bread in, pull out a slice, put it in the toaster and press it down.

'Take a seat,' he said gently. I stood still, a bit scared. 'Go on,' he said softly. 'It's all right.'

I crept past the cooker with pots and pans on top towards the place with the bed and table. It was nice and bright and jolly. There were lacy curtains at the window and funny little knick-knacks everywhere: little donkeys, dogs and plastic flowers and a big silver cross with Jesus on the wall. Then I smelt the toast.

Sean appeared beside me with a plate with flowers round the edge. On it was hot toast with butter sinking in. He placed a glass of milk beside it. I picked up the toast and bit, and it melted in my mouth. I ate the toast and drank the milk in silence while Sean sat beside me, smoking his cigarette. I liked being there.

It felt safe. I looked at a picture on the wall of green hills and sky and trees.

'Ireland,' Sean said simply. 'County Cork.' I kept chewing. 'More?'

I nodded. Sean repeated the toast and I ate it all up. I felt calmer after the food and we sat for a bit.

'Want to tell me?' he said quietly. I looked at him. He had grey whiskers and a crinkly face. His eyes were kind. I wanted to tell him with all my heart – they've taken William! Help me! Please! Save me! But I couldn't. I wanted to ask Sean if I could stay with him but I feared Barbara. I felt so alone and frightened with everyone in the house. More than anything I didn't want anyone to hurt Sean. So I said nothing. I didn't dare.

Sean let me look at his knick-knacks and talked to me about Ireland – the hills, his home and family. He loved horses, and talked about them. Also horse racing, his favourite pastime. He'd had a lovely wife who'd died long ago in childbirth. I liked imagining the green grass and the leafy trees, the country lanes and farmhouses and the big horses. When I left, after a very long time sitting quietly with him, he just said softly, 'You can come again… whenever you like.'

I felt warm in my tummy, and full, as I tiptoed down the steps. I also felt naughty, but so much happier inside. Sean was my saviour, my only friend. My hero. His kind eyes and hot toast had saved my life. At least he was still there, along with the nice Polish people. One of the women was pegging out clothes on her line, which hung between her cream caravan and an apple tree. She waved and smiled. There was something to cling onto, after all. But how would I survive without my brother-in-torture?

7

Pulling My Hair Out

It's morning. A school day. I'm sitting on my bed in my shabby grey uniform. I pull out my bedside drawer. It's empty, except at the back there's a matchbox with a picture of a black ship on it. I take it out and pull it open: there are six dead flies, all in a little row, lying on a bed of toilet paper. I look at them in detail and notice their wonderful, veined, see-through wings and little black feet curled up under them. They have big eyes, with lots of colours in them. I will remember them, so I can draw them. I close my eyes and squeeze them shut, as hard as I can, and suddenly I see lots of colours: orange, purple, blue, yellow, flashing lights and swirling colours. Like the flies' eyes. There are stars and sparkles and whirls in the colours in my head, and I'm fascinated by them. The colours feel a relief from everything around me; I can watch a lightshow simply by closing my eyes and squeezing. Then I open them. Everything is orange and yellow for a moment, then white, and then I focus. I'm back in the tiny, dingy room and the flies are still lying dead in a row. I close the matchbox and put it carefully in the back of the drawer and push it shut.

Then I put my right hand up to my eyelashes and pull. Hard.

There's a twinge of pain and I do it again. And again. *Ow! Ow!*
But it is somehow soothing to feel the pain. I soon have a little
handful of eyelashes. I look at them – white at one end, right
at the tip, and then running brown to black. They are long.
I run my fingers along my eyelids and can feel some stubbly
bits – I pull, it hurts, but it's kind of satisfying. I feel along my
eyebrows, all stubbly. I pull. *Ow! Ow!* Out they come. They're
thicker, but still black, with a little white tip at the end. Then
my right hand goes up to my head and I twist my dipper finger
round some strands of my hair and yank. *Ow!* That does hurt.
Out it comes. I now have a handful of hair. It's fine and shiny. I
drop it on the carpet and keep going. I can feel a little bald patch
growing on the top of my head where I pull the hair – yank,
yank. I feel around with my fingers to find the next few hairs,
and then the next. I can't stop. Yank, yank, yank. They're on
the floor, lying in a shiny black pile. I feel a bit calmer now, and
I know I have to go down and face 'them'. I collect up the hair
and put it carefully in the bin, putting a bit of paper over the top.
I know I always have to hide things, to be careful, just in case.
But I have one more thing to do on the way.

I creep out of my room, onto the landing, holding my
breath. I stop and listen out – I can hear Barbara's voice in
the kitchen. She's making breakfast for Kevin. Ian has gone
already. I don't always get breakfast now. There are days
when I'm starved completely because I've been bad. I'm given
a dose of bicarbonate of soda in a glass and told to drink it.
I do, without a word. It tastes yuck and makes me feel sick.
I'm hungry, but I'm used to it now. I try not to think about
William any more. When he pops up, I push him to the back
of my mind. There's a numb place like a black hole in my head

where he used to be. I can't think about him. I'm not allowed to talk about him. It's as if he was never here. In my tummy there is a stone. I carry this stone everywhere. A heavy weight. A dull pain. I get moments when I think I see him, when I'm walking to school, or if we ever go to the shops. Every time I walk down the road I automatically look to the right with a sad, heavy feeling and hope that I might see the top of a red head bobbing along the pavement. I look at all green cars – is he there? But he never is. I just cover the hole in my head with an imaginary stone and keep on walking.

I get to the toilet, which is next to the bathroom, and turn the doorknob as quietly as I can. The toilet is green with a black seat. I know the drill. I sit on the seat and feel a poo coming. I catch it carefully in the palm of my hand. It's hot, soft and heavy. It feels comforting. I look at it a moment, wondering at the colour and texture. It has so many colours in it – not just brown. I place it carefully on the toilet paper and mould it into a flattish oblong. I pull up my knickers one-handed, pull the handle and tiptoe out of the toilet and along to the big bedroom. I listen carefully, but there are voices downstairs and I know Ian is out. I hold my breath and creep in, to the end of their double bed. There is a second single bed to one side of the room, stacked up with china dolls and fluffy toys that I'm not allowed to play with. I get down on my knees as fast as I can, on Barbara's side of the bed, and squish my patty of poo right up into the corner of the bed frame, near the head end of the bed. *Squish, squish, squish*. It sticks. I look under. It looks dark and blends in with the wood. My right hand is dirty now, and I tiptoe out of the room as fast as possible, pulling the door to, leaving it as it was, with my left.

I go quickly into the bathroom to wash my hands with carbolic in the green sink. I put the toilet paper rolled up into the bin. I dry my hands and feel my heart racing. Job done.

※

School was as horrible as ever. It was nothing like Vernon Lane. There were rules and it was boring. I was also in the remedial class, as I still couldn't read or write properly, even though I was now seven. I was laughed at for being so behind. One day we were all taken into a big classroom. Mrs Biggs, the Biology teacher, was in her smart blue suit. She had glasses on and dull mousey hair. She told us she was going to explain the 'life cycle' using chickens to show us. I was instantly interested, as I looked after the chickens at home. I never understood before that the eggs I collected, and which we ate, were also the same eggs that made a chick, which then grows into a big chicken. This seemed a fantastic thing. I learnt that it would take about twenty-one days for a chick to hatch from the egg, and that it had to be 'fertilised' to become a chicken. I didn't really understand what 'fertilised' meant, but it sounded wonderful. The teacher said we could all take an egg home – or even more than one – to watch them hatch over Easter, and explained how to look after them, keep them warm and so on. We needed to ask our parents that night for permission.

All the way home I was wondering how I could ask Barbara if I could look after an egg. I'd never asked her for anything and I feared her answer would be the usual 'No'. She was striding along, grim as ever, dragging Topsy and swearing, but I was desperate to have a chick. I tried to think. I knew she liked chickens herself and often drove miles to farms to get new hens.

She was keen to get good layers and frequently tried out different breeds. With Barbara I learnt that I had to play being nice to her if I ever wanted to get something, anything. So I tried hard to be helpful and polite while finding ways of flattering her. I said things like, 'Thank you for my nice tea,' when in fact I was still starving hungry and bored with having the same old thing. Or, 'That looks nice, Mummy,' when she'd hacked the garden plants down in fury. I'd had to forget my heartbreak over William and put a smile on and be a perfect, helpful little girl, saying, 'Yes, Mummy' or 'No, Mummy' to anything she would ask me. It was the only way I could survive.

That evening I offered to style her grey wavy hair. She actually liked this. I hated it but it was part of my campaign. After my usual, tiny dolls' tea, I wandered round the garden rehearsing what I'd say, while Ian, Kevin and Barbara ate their proper tea. I tried to blank out the meat and gravy smells, determined not to be upset. I imagined how I was going to ask her if I could have an egg or two to look after. Then, later, when I was combing her hair and rolling it with curlers, I worked up my courage and told her about the chicken and egg lesson at school. Usually she snapped at me, but she didn't that night, so I carried on telling her, trying to sound casual, about how you can make a chick hatch at home. I finished her hair and she stood up and peered down her sharp nose at me.

'All right,' she said, 'bring one home.'

Was this really Barbara? I was amazed. It worked. She'd never been nice, but I was so excited about the egg, and I'd planned my campaign so well, curling her hair and flattering her, that I'd somehow got her to let me have one.

I felt my heart lift the next day as I walked home with Barbara and Topsy with an egg-box in my hand, carefully guarding five brown speckled eggs. Mrs Bliss had explained that at least one out of the five would probably hatch, and we should take more than one, just in case. I think the idea of free eggs appealed to Barbara. In fact, she prided herself on her egg-hatching and often took a box of six to my headmaster to show off what a good mother she was.

That afternoon, once we were home, to my further amazement Barbara found a cardboard box and put straw in the bottom. Then we put it in the larder, on the lower shelf, and she got a grey angle-poise lamp and put it on, with the light bulb close over the eggs, wrapped in straw. Was this the same Barbara? She still had the same hard look on her face — she never smiled at me or hugged me — but she was letting me do something I really wanted. She had never, ever done anything like this before. I felt I was walking on eggshells myself.

From then on, all I could think about was my eggs — day and night. As soon as I woke up I jumped out of bed and rushed down to see if any of them had hatched. I knew it would take about three weeks, but I was impatient. It seemed like total magic. For once there was something to look forward to. It seemed to take ages and ages, as every morning there was nothing: the eggs sat there, brown, round and glowing in the straw. I couldn't believe the chicks would ever hatch.

Then one morning Barbara called up the stairs: 'The chicks are hatching.' I rushed down the stairs, which were carpeted in swirling brown-and-orange patterned carpet, to the larder, and peeked into the box. I held my breath. There were the five eggs and, on one of the shells, a crack had appeared. As I watched, the crack got bigger and the egg started moving, and suddenly a little yellow beak appeared, chipping its way out of the brown shell. I was utterly amazed. I watched as a little creature pushed its way out of the round shell and fell onto the straw, all soggy and helpless. My heart went out to it. Then the next crack appeared in the next egg, and soon four out of five of the chicks had hatched, one by one. The last one was even more amazing, as the chick that came out had black feathers. I had never seen a totally black chicken, although some of our hens were black and white. The little black chick lay in a panting heap on the straw, its tiny red-rimmed eyes closed, looking soggy and pathetic. My heart leapt. It was the most astonishing sight I had ever seen.

Barbara appeared in the larder doorway. I looked up at her with saucer eyes, and said, 'Mummy, you can have these three chicks, but could I keep the black one?'

She thought for a second and nodded. 'Yes.' I had to blink. She was saying yes. Was this really the same Barbara? I had to be careful not to show too much pleasure. So I said a polite, 'Thank you, Mummy,' like the good girl I was trying to be, but in my heart I was shrieking and yipping with joy at having my little black chick to myself. I decided to call him Lucky, as I felt sure he would bring me lots.

That day, going off to school, I made sure I did everything Barbara asked of me. I wanted to please her even more now she let me keep my Lucky. I tidied up my room, made my bed with hospital corners and helped clear up the kitchen, folding the tea towels exactly how she liked. I swept the floor and helped dry up. After school I rushed to the larder in wonder. Lucky was staggering to his feet, his eyes were opening, and he and the other chicks were beginning to go 'peep, peep, peep'. It was joyful. I carefully picked up Lucky and held his tiny, shaky body, so fragile and tender. His feathers weren't wet now, they were fluffing out into the softest, finest fur. He was beautiful. He had a little beady eye and a tiny yellow beak set against his black fluff, with a white patch on his chest. My heart swelled with pride. My Lucky. My own little chick.

I talked to him all the time. I walked round the kitchen with him cupped in my hands, held to my chest. He was so tiny I wanted to protect him. I had always talked to the chickens in the garden, and now I was telling Lucky about all sorts of things. I told him his name, and that he would have a good life. I told him I loved him, that we would be friends for ever and I would always look after him. After a while I could tell he was getting tired, so I put him back in the box with the other chicks and they all got into a little pile on top of each other and fell asleep. It was adorable. I stood and watched them sleeping, and bent the lamp down nearer, tucking the straw round to make sure they kept nice and warm and snug.

❧

For the first few days after the chicks had hatched I felt I had woken up in another house altogether. The atmosphere was different and Barbara was nicer than I had ever known her. I felt myself relax a little bit. The night routine was still the same, but I was used to that now, and it was 'normal'. She wasn't being so harsh all the time, so I made the mistake of loosening up a bit as each minute of calm went by. Maybe the chicks had made her happy and things would be different from now on. However, after school one day she seemed back to the old Barbara, her face in a tight, vicious point. I could see she was in a very bad mood; it was like grey clouds covering a watery sun.

I checked on the chicks and they were all there peeping away in a furry little heap. I felt a surge of love. From the larder I could hear Barbara crashing about with the kitchen pans, so I thought I should probably get out of the way. I crept into the kitchen and asked sweetly, 'Can I tell Sean about the chicks?' She knew I visited Sean in the caravan, and was often very bad tempered and suspicious about it. I felt if I told her, and was open about visiting him, she would be less angry. She didn't answer, as her back was to me by the stove, so I crept out the back door and down the garden and beyond, glad to get away.

I knocked on Sean's caravan door. He opened the top half and leant out, smiling widely, showing me his yellowing teeth. I started laughing – I always found his big smile and sparkly eyes very comforting. His head popped back in and he opened the bottom half of the door for me to enter.

'I t'ink I cooked the cabbage a little too long,' he said hoarsely, still laughing, and there was steam and smoke coming off his Baby Belling stove and a strong burnt cabbagey smell. His kitchen was about as big as a narrow phone box on its side and I marvelled at him cooking anything in there.

'Want a drink, girlie?' he asked. I nodded. Out came the Kia-Ora orange squash he'd bought just for me. He filled a beaker almost full and put a bit of water in the top, so it was really strong. He asked me if I'd eaten anything and I shook my head. Sean knew I was always hungry. He had a loaf of bread on his drainer, so he got his one and only sharp knife with the knobbly handle and cut off a huge chunk. He opened his little cream fridge, the size of a small cupboard, and spread on a wedge of yellow butter. He then pulled out a cooked ham and sliced me off a big bit and put it on top. Heaven.

'No Irish mustard, I'm afraid,' he joked. I'd never had mustard and didn't know what it was. He always made a joke and it was clear he wouldn't find Irish mustard in Oxford or anywhere at all.

I squeezed onto his sofa, which doubled up as his bed and was covered with knitted cushions, crotched blankets and dog hair, next to the little table and a huge smelly black Labrador, Frida. She was so old she was half blind and could hardly move. The whole caravan smelt of a mixture of old dog and burnt cabbage but I didn't care, as it was cosy, warm and lovely, especially as I sank my teeth into the buttery bread and ham. I told Sean all about Lucky and his brothers and sisters, as he brought a steaming mug of tea over and sat with me. He rolled one of his cigarettes and listened, smiling.

'Ah, that's grand now, isn't it?' is what he said, when I told him I had made him warm and snug in the box. After a while I noticed the light was changing outside and I got a jolt of fear in my stomach. I shouldn't be away too long.

'You should put Lucky in an apron or a pocket,' Sean said, as I went down the steps. 'T'would keep him nice and warm.'

As I walked back through the orchard and over the lawn I considered what he'd said about an apron – I would have to think of something.

All was not well when I got to the kitchen. It was war. Ian and Barbara were standing facing each other and arguing. She had her hands on her hips and he had his hands in his pockets, looking at the floor. I seldom saw him standing up to her. It sounded bad, and although I wanted to see Lucky, I snuck in and crept past. They didn't notice. No tea had been laid for me, and their voices were getting louder all the time. I didn't know what was wrong. I sat up in my room and could hear doors slamming and voices raised. Barbara came in later and did the usual night routine, but I worried about Lucky. Would he be all right with all the shouting and crossness going on? And then I swirled into the usual drugged darkness.

In the morning I lay under the covers, still worried. I wanted to hide away, as I still felt scared about what was going on, but I wanted to see the chicks, especially my lovely Lucky. I got up and went down straight to the chicks – all was well. I topped up their water and stroked their feathers. They were getting bigger by the day. Then I had an idea. Barbara was out in her greenhouse, watering cuttings in little pots. I knocked on the glass of the sliding door. I could see, when she turned, that she was still in a bad mood and that the 'mist' was still upon her, so I'd have to be careful. When she was like this, it was like she was covered by an angry veil.

'What is it?' she snapped. Back to the old Barbara. I asked if now the chicks were bigger they could go in the shed rather than be in the kitchen. The reason was I wanted to spend more time with them, watching them grow, and it was awkward being in the kitchen as so much went on in there. But I put it to her that it would be better for her.

'They'd be out of your way and I'd not be under your feet,' I said.

There was a pause.

'All right,' she said, finally. 'Close the door and get ready for school.'

I didn't mind Spencer pulling my arm back that day or kicking my shins as I waited for Barbara to pick me up. I didn't care that he and his friends called me 'smelly' and 'dirty little cry baby'. I had Lucky at home, and he was my friend.

Once home I carefully carried the chicks in their cardboard box to the shed, which was unlocked. This would mean I could visit them more. Since William had gone, Barbara left the padlock off the shed quite often. It was still used for my punishment, but she preferred putting me over the stool in the kitchen or just whacking me on the head or round the face with the paper. So the shed had become more of a refuge – a place I went to, along with Sean's caravan, to get some peace. I thought of the times in the shed with William, and our birdseed-eating days (which I still did when I was starving), so it felt oddly like the shed was home.

Having set up the chicks, I saw Sean walking down the outside path, on his way to his caravan. I left the shed and ran after him, keen to tell him about Lucky's new home. In his caravan he gave me two presents: one was a Ruffle bar, a wonderful sweet with chocolate covering a raspberry coconut filling. He bought these just for me, and gave me one nearly every time I visited him. The other was a Co-op bag. My eyes widened. A present. I opened it and inside was a yellow gingham apron with big pockets that had embroidered roses on it. It was for Lucky! The pockets were big enough for him to go in without him being squashed.

From then on I would go to the shed in the apron, put Lucky in, and walk him round the garden, morning and evening. I would feed the chickens and change their water and sort out their feed; I would wander round the orchard and talk to him as my bird-child, my brother. He filled a William-sized space in my life as he grew. If I came up to Lucky he would run towards me, flapping his wings and dancing up and down. I was devoted to him, and lavished all my love on him. I made sure the other chicks were looked after too, though.

Now the chicks were transferred to the chicken run and becoming proper chickens, but they were still quite small and fluffy. I would go in and talk to them, and when I sat down Lucky would jump on my shoulder or lap and I would tell him about my day. I would take him out on the lawn and play with him until it was time for bed, then I would put him back in his pen and say goodnight.

～✽～

Barbara and Ian were still tense with each other. It was something about her underwear, but I didn't understand. It had become a cold war now; they were hardly speaking. Kevin was being his usual annoying self, swiping at me, teasing me about Lucky, but I didn't care. Something was brewing, however, and I could feel it in my guts.

One day, after school, I saw Barbara unlock one of the kitchen cupboards, take out a brown bottle and pour some of the green pills she gave me at night straight into her mouth. She scoffed the lot. Then she turned and saw I had seen her.

'If it wasn't for men, the dirty bastards, I wouldn't have to take these,' she spat at me. 'He's a filthy pig,' she said, meaning Ian. She often complained about him: how he smelt, the state of his underpants ('he doesn't wipe himself properly'), and even one time when her own underwear had gone missing and ended up in his drawer.

'He's a filthy bastard,' she said, turning and trying to take down a huge ice cream container from the top shelf. It flew out and fell on the floor, spewing bottles of pills everywhere. I was amazed by the amount of pills, and she saw me looking.

'Don't you dare tell anyone about my pills, d'you hear, you little bitch?' I nodded. 'Or you'll get what for!'

Next day I had my usual morning routine with Lucky and went to school with a furious Barbara, who was sulking all the way, still angry with Ian it seemed. After school I went out to find Lucky, as usual. I called for him and waited. I couldn't see him in the chicken run, which was strange. Barbara had gone straight out into the garden when we got back and was busy hosing around the greenhouse. I went into the hen house, and there were a few chickens on their nests, including some of the school ones. But no Lucky. I carried on whistling for him. Where was he? I ran up and down the garden, round the shed, in the bushes. No Lucky.

Barbara was at the tap, filling a metal bucket. Finally I realised I'd have to ask her. She must have seen him. I was panicking now. Lucky was my friend, my world. Had he been eaten by a fox (sometimes the foxes came in and took a few chickens) or had he got out? Barbara was swishing water around with a bamboo stick as I approached. I looked in the bucket and jumped. I could see a load of baby mice, all pink and tiny, swirling around in the water like floating marshmallows. She was drowning them, poor little things.

'If you don't get rid of them, they'll be all over the house,' she hissed venomously. She turned the tap off, threw down the stick and marched back into the house. Job done.

I bent closer over the bucket, and at the bottom, under the pink mouse corpses, was something else – a small black body, twisted, with its neck bent. I screamed and burst into tears. It was my darling Lucky.

8

Hatred and Help

After Lucky's untimely death I was sadder than I could bear. I cried and cried and cried until I could cry no more. The whole world had gone completely dark. No William. No Lucky. I felt totally abandoned and alone. I sat in the shed, my head on my knees, licking them, empty and bereft. Counting, counting, counting. Pulling my eyelashes out in little clumps. Ripping out hair, bit by bit. Wherever I was – at home or at school – I seemed to be hated. I just didn't understand why. Barbara and Ian were not talking and the atmosphere was very tense all the time.

Every so often Barbara did a lot of shouting and crashing of the pots and pans in the kitchen. Sometimes she would throw things out the back door in a raging fury. Ian would keep out of harm's way and did a lot of hiding in the garage, pottering about or watching TV. Barbara would spit that Ian 'wasn't a real man', whatever that meant. There was another upset about her underwear, which had gone missing off the washing line, and she was accusing Ian of taking it. Why, I had no idea. He had his own underwear – I ironed it. It was all very confusing.

It was a miserable house. Kevin spent his time being bossy,

picking on me or eating what he wanted in front of me and generally ruling the roost. His real dad hadn't visited for months now and he never talked about him – it was like he'd evaporated down the motorway somewhere. If I was in the kitchen, passing by, I'd get a slap, whack, kick, punch from Barbara or Kevin or both. If Ian was there he would turn away and busy himself, even if I was slapped in front of him; he pretended he didn't see it. He never intervened.

One day Barbara was in a total rage. She had bought something for the house and Ian didn't want it. He wanted her to take it back. She picked up pots and pans and started throwing them at Ian, and then out the back door and onto the grass and plants. I was standing in the garden near the chicken run, holding my breath, watching things fly out and about. When Barbara went off on a rant, it would go on and on for hours. Ian scuttled out of the house and into the garage, his safety zone. Then Barbara spied me watching. I tried to pretend I wasn't listening.

'I saw you,' she shouted across the garden really loudly. 'What do you bloody well want?'

I stared at the ground, not moving, hardly breathing. A statue.

'Oh, stop looking like that; your sort are always all right, no wonder the Germans hated you.' My blood froze. 'You filthy little Jew,' is what she spat at me then and slammed the back door.

My only place of safety in the whole world was Sean Brannon's. I went there as often as I could. The Polish people who pitched next to him were very private, although they were kind enough to me and William, and knew we appreciated the occasional piece of cake or sandwich they gave us. Yet Barbara would tell me, 'They're Polish and filthy' if she saw me looking at these caravans. She hated the travellers. 'They're Gypsies, and you need to keep away from them. Hitler tried to finish them off,' she'd say with a sniff.

I didn't know who this Hitler was, but from the way she said it he sounded like someone to be feared, but also respected as a master. She also called him a devil, so I was very confused. She was always talking about him too. I had 'the Devil's eyes', so we must be related. So I must be as bad as Hitler.

I went round to see Sean. Unusually he was talking to the Polish people. I crept through the trees, not wanting to be seen, and hovered beside Sean. When the Polish people saw me, they smiled. 'The robot' was wearing a trilby hat and a long brown mac, and was very tall. 'The witch' was wearing what she always wore: a headscarf and dark clothes with a flowery pinny in front. Her face was very thin.

'Why don't the Germans like me?' I whispered to Sean, wide-eyed. I'd never met a German person and didn't understand what the problem was. What had I done?

The Polish man looked very surprised and said, 'Vy you ask?'

I said my mother had called me a Jew. He looked pained. 'What's a Jew?' I asked. Barbara had often thrown this word at me, and I didn't really know what it all meant.

'I'm Valdek,' said the Robot. 'Vis is Sofia.' They both smiled and nodded at me. 'Vee Jews too.'

The woman leant forward and stroked my hair, nodding warmly, then squeezed my arm in a kind way. She no longer looked like a witch, and he wasn't a robot. Not at all. I felt tears prick my eyes.

Back in Sean's caravan, over milk and bread and butter, he

explained Hitler was a bad German man who had hurt a lot of people in the war. He had killed many Jews – millions of them – in a terrible way.

I couldn't take in what he was saying. Why millions? Were Jews such bad people? Did it mean people would kill me? Maybe it explained why Barbara hated me so much. Did she like Hitler? But no, she didn't, she was always saying Hitler was bad. If she didn't like Hitler and she didn't like Jews, who did she like? It didn't make sense. Sean sat and smoked and ruffled my hair.

'Never mind, girlie,' he said. 'More milk?'

Next time I wandered to the orchard and onto the common land, as I did almost every day now, I heard the Polish people making a sound like they were calling birds. I tiptoed over, looking around to make sure Barbara or Kevin wasn't spying. Sofia handed me a huge wedge of bread and jam and, on another day, a big piece of almond cake wrapped in greaseproof paper. I wolfed it down on the spot, crumbs flying. It was delicious. She smiled and squeezed my arm again. Another day they gave me sweets. Valdek and Sofia gave me a Toblerone and I hid it under an old plant pot in the orchard – a little stash for desperate times. It was near the back of the orchard, by the grass roller and the compost heap, and I didn't think anyone would look under it. It looked all old and discarded.

When my birthday came around – which I had begun to realise was sometime in June, although it was never celebrated – Sean gave me a giant bar of Dairy Milk and the Polish people gave me a little plastic wicker basket of jellied fruits. All these went under leaves in a plastic bag, under the pot and out of sight, and I hoped they'd stay safe. I also hoped Kevin and Barbara would never think to look there – I took that risk. There was nowhere else to stash them, and they kept me going, sweet by sweet, chunk by chunk, for a very long time.

Now William and Lucky were gone I felt very lonely at school. I sneaked Tony the panda into my bag and carried him about with me. One lunchtime two older girls pulled me from the playground, where I'd been standing alone by the wall, holding onto Tony for dear life, and pushed me into the smelly playground toilets. I was terrified. They pressed me back against the sinks and towered over me.

'Your mum is a witch – everyone knows that,' one of the big girls snarled in my face. 'Why does your mum beat you? Are you a dog?' sneered the other, smaller girl, making an ugly face at me. They both laughed.

'Your mum's a man,' said the first girl. 'She starves you 'cos you're a darkie.'

Tears streamed down my face and my fingers were digging into Tony, but I said nothing. I could feel the sink sticking into my back, but I bit my lip.

'Tell your mum to go and get her broomstick,' said the biggest girl – and with that they both left, laughing.

I stood shaking and realised I'd wet myself. My socks were wet and there was a puddle on the floor. I went into the toilet and cleaned myself up and told Tony we should never tell anyone. There wasn't anyone to tell. I'd been in so many meetings at the school when William was still there, with Barbara, the teachers and the Head, and we had both learnt to keep our heads down and say nothing. We knew if we said anything to a teacher in front of Barbara that when we got home it would get even worse. All hell would break loose. We actually feared an outsider's kindness as, although Barbara tried to pull the wool over the social workers', neighbours' and teachers' eyes, when we got home we would have to pay for her being shown up.

'Nobody will ever believe little bastards like you,' she would spit at us, hitting us about the head and body with her newspaper roll. 'Nobody wants you, nobody cares.' We completely believed it was true.

Now I was alone with the travellers it was even trickier. Barbara knew I went down to the orchard and onto the common land beyond as often as I could. Sean would collect his paper from a box at the end of the lane every morning and I would go down to meet him and follow him back. I would tag along to his caravan and stay there as long as possible. I even stayed the night once or twice, with Sean making me up a little bed on the sofa, with coloured crocheted blankets, where I felt safe and sound and slept without horrible green pills and medicine.

Sean went and asked Barbara for her permission and, amazingly, she said all right. He knew he had to be careful with Barbara, as she was always striding about the garden, shouting and swearing. He saw the state I was in, as he always had food and comfort at the ready. But he needed to live in his caravan as a good neighbour, as did the Polish people, and he wanted to keep the peace, so he didn't want to argue with Barbara as he knew she could make trouble and get him evicted if she wanted.

～✄～

Every so often social workers would turn up at our house. Sometimes it was because the next-door neighbours had made a complaint about the way Barbara treated me (or William, when he was still there). There had been many complaints, nearly all of them ignored. Sometimes it was after something had happened at school and we were 'investigated'. And sometimes it was just out of the blue – or so it seemed to me. Barbara always turned on some charm when they arrived and got out the tea and biscuits. (I would note the biscuits for a raid on the larder later, where I could filch one or two.)

The social workers always came with felt-tip pens in their bags. I would recognise the same packet from the previous visit, as the same pens were still dry or worn out. They would give me some paper and ask me to draw 'my family'. I would draw Barbara and Ian, and sometimes Kevin and the dog. I would also draw Sean. I always put chickens in the picture. When it came to Sean, I put a lot of effort into drawing his tweed cap, and drew a big red love heart on his chest. The social worker asked me who he was, and I said, 'He lives there,' and pointed out the kitchen window, to the land beyond the garden and orchard.

Then the social workers, two women – one older, with dark hair in a suit, one younger, who was blonde and wore jeans – talked to Barbara, who was out in the garden watering plants. I watched as they all walked down to the orchard and looked over the hedge towards the caravans. My heart started racing. Had I done something wrong? Would they hurt Sean? Would they take him away? When they came back, one of the social workers came and sat next to me. I was still drawing but I now felt scared.

'Has Sean ever touched you?' the dark-haired older one asked. I thought for a while and said he touched my hand and showed them my hand. She sat and scribbled something in her notebook. Then she asked, 'What do you do together?'

I said we played. It wasn't true, as in fact I usually just drew while he drank tea out of a big mug or read a newspaper. I felt

I shouldn't say that I slept on his sofa sometimes but, just as I began to say something about learning to plant seeds with Sean, Barbara came over and said, 'Would you like a cup of tea?' to the older woman. It was like she didn't want me to say any more. I wondered if I was doing the wrong thing talking about Sean. Maybe it would get Barbara in trouble, and then I'd get it. Or worse, I'd get Sean sent away – and then I would surely die.

When they left, Barbara was furious.

'You have to be bloody careful what you draw. That lot are bloody stupid idiots with their backsides hanging out of their jeans.'

I didn't understand what their backsides or jeans had to do with anything. Barbara ranted on about them only knowing about life from books and 'what was the use of that?' She told me they didn't understand people, not like her, anyway. However, a few days later the two women were back again. The dark one in the suit crouched down beside me by the chicken run where I'd been feeding the hens. I felt suspicious the minute she did that, as I knew something was coming that I wouldn't like. She wanted me to look at her, and to trust her. Then she said, 'Louise, you're not to see Sean any more. It's not right that a little girl spends so much time with a man.'

I burst into tears. Sean was my only friend. He was kind. He gave me food. I wanted to scream, 'Nooooooo!' at the top of my voice, but Barbara was a few feet away and I knew she was watching me like a hawk ready to swoop. Sean was my lifeline and he was being cut. What would I do?

The next days and weeks were endless. I kept going to the edge of the orchard and looking for Sean through the hedge. He would be out on his step, smoking, and would smile. I would poke my head through the hedge, wave and look at him longingly. He would wave back and give me a thumbs-up. The Polish people would also wave and I would wave back. They were kind people who saved me from starvation and boredom and I was banned from seeing them all. I was being punished yet again. All I had left now was the chickens to talk to. I cried and cried and cried talking to the chickens.

I sat in the shed, head on my knees, talking to myself. Counting. I wondered where William was now. Why had he gone like that? Why didn't he take me with him? I counted. Pulled out more hair. Ripped my eyelashes. Licked my knees. Tried to find somewhere in my head where it was peaceful. I drew pictures of the caravan and Sean, but they made me cry as I missed him so much.

It was an eternity until the social workers came again. They brought out the same old tired packet of pens, with the same dried-up ones and wonky ones. I sat at the table and they once again asked me to draw 'my family'. I had learnt my lesson, so I drew a perfect picture of Barbara and Ian, with Kevin and me and the dog. A happy family. No Sean. I didn't mention Sean, although in my heart he was all I could think about. He was the nice man who made me toast and milk and bought me Ruffles and Dairy Milk bars. The one who listened to me when things got really bad at home. He knew a little bit about how things were, although we were both very polite when we talked about Barbara. I didn't want to make a problem and I was scared of telling the truth to anybody, even to Sean. Nobody knew how bad it really was.

The dark-haired social worker looked very pleased with my drawing. With no Sean in it, I think they thought everything was all right. Also, Barbara probably didn't want to get into trouble, so she didn't tell them I'd actually slept in the caravan sometimes. It was another of our family secrets, although this time in my favour.

After this visit, I was allowed to go back to visiting Sean. It had been about a month, but it felt like a year. The next time I wanted to hear 'Hello, girlie', I went racing out the kitchen door, down the garden and through the hedge and stuck to him like glue. I couldn't get enough of him then, as I felt I had been severely punished for spending time with my one and only friend in the whole world: dear, kind Irish Sean. However, even he wouldn't be able to save me from what was to happen next.

9

Under Attack

I was now eight going on nine. Kevin was thirteen going on fourteen and was getting more boisterous and threatening. As well as punching and kicking me, he started coming up close to me and leaning over me and putting his face right up to mine. I didn't like it. I felt very scared. He smelt bad, for a start, of body odour. He was very pongy, and smelling him towering over me would make me want to be sick. I would retch. He smelt greasy, musky, like an old dog, and his breath was terrible. I avoided him as much as possible, but he took delight in cornering me in the kitchen or in the bathroom, or pushing past me on the stairs or in a corridor. He would try to lean his body against me and I wanted to scream, but I looked down and held my breath until he gave up and went away. I knew better than to make a fuss, as Barbara would always take his side and call me a rude name or two.

Then one day I was on the bed in my room – which still had the partition down the middle – when the door burst open and in came Kevin with his friend Mark behind him. They both looked funny. Their eyes were shining, and both had red cheeks. The hairs stood up on the back of my neck and I pulled my knees up to my chin, feeling frightened. I thought if I sat still and looked down, they would go away.

But they didn't. Instead, Kevin strode up to the bed and shoved me down, hurting me. I was winded for a moment. Then both of his hands were on my shoulders and suddenly I was lying down with him pressing me hard into the bed. His red stinky face was close to mine. I was so horrified that I stopped breathing for a moment. Then I realised that Mark had hold of my ankles and was pulling my legs apart.

Kevin looked back at Mark over my body and then lifted up my gingham dress. I started struggling and wriggling as much as I could. I was quite strong but these boys were much older than me, and Kevin turned back to me and pushed me hard back on the bed with his hand flat on my chest. I wanted to scream, I needed to shout, but I didn't. I certainly didn't want Barbara to come up and see what was happening – I didn't think she would rescue me; she'd be more likely to tell me off.

So I kept kicking my legs, but Mark had now caught them. Suddenly I felt my knickers being pulled down. I tried to kick and wriggle and twist my body sideways, but there was an iron grip around each ankle. I couldn't see anything except the back of Kevin's greasy head. He now had his full weight on top of my chest, and both boys were looking down at my bare private parts. I was horrified. I tried to move this way and that and attempted to sit up to bite Kevin's back, but Mark had my legs and Kevin was still leaning his whole weight on me. Then, suddenly, as if on signal, they were gone. I lay on the bed, panting. My dress was up under my armpits and my knickers were round my ankles. I sat up slowly, feeling shocked and afraid. They had looked at my bare body, my private parts. I felt sick, my heart was racing, my mind was swimming and I wanted to cry. I didn't know what had happened but I knew it was bad. But there was no one to tell – I couldn't even tell Sean. I felt too ashamed. I just pulled my knickers up, smoothed down my dress and started counting in my head. One, two, three, four. One, two, three, four. One, two, three, four.

❦

Barbara was always talking about sex. And men. 'Men will use you because they always use girls like you,' she would say to me. Or, 'Men just want what they can get.' She often called me a whore and said I was 'Like your mother, only fit for breeding.' She told me, 'You ruined people's lives by being born – look what you did to your mother, look what you did to me!' I was worthless, unloveable, ugly. I was born to be used. Plus I was a 'stupid bitch' and an 'oily Jew', so I wasn't worth anything at all. She was hardly going to help me fight against Kevin and Mark, as I was 'a wicked little girl'.

When I had been at my lovely first primary school, we had been taught some very basic things about mummies, daddies and babies, and the birds and the bees. They had begun to teach us where babies came from. Barbara had got wind of this and had gone ballistic.

'Those teachers are perverted,' she screamed. 'They've got a stupid American attitude,' she ranted. She had grabbed me by the shoulders and said, 'When you're older you'll kiss a man and you'll get feelings and then you'll get pregnant – and you'll be out on your ear, d'you hear?' I heard, but I didn't understand. What were these 'feelings' that would make me get thrown out?

Barbara often spoke about Ian in a horrible way that made me feel very uncomfortable. She would say he stank (which he did, of stale cheese and bonfires), although I never really got that close to him, as he never gave me a hug or a cuddle. She would say he stank of wee and didn't wipe his bottom properly (I hated to think of this). She would put his stained white underpants in buckets of soda to soak. But I also had to wash and scrub them for her with green Fairy soap. Barbara would also say frequently that Ian 'raped' her. I didn't know what 'rape' was or what the word meant. It sounded very bad. She spat the word 'rape' with total venom. She also called Ian a 'filthy, cruel, disgusting man' to his face and behind his back. She seemed to hate him. She seemed to hate all men.

But despite hating Ian, she liked to roll around on the carpet, wrestling with Kevin, which seemed very strange indeed. If I watched them wrestling she would look up at me and say, 'I bet you're jealous?' which was the total opposite of what I was feeling – I was thinking I was so glad it wasn't me being held down on the carpet by Kevin.

So would I get pregnant if I kissed a man? And would I be raped, as all men were rapists? However, Kevin and Mark holding me down, pulling down my knickers and looking at my bare body marked the beginning of a new, dreadful phase in my life. Kevin would touch me now whenever he could. He kept looking at my chest or touching my bottom. I was left very confused about everything to do with men and sex.

Although Kevin had his horrible friend Mark to the house when he wanted to, I wasn't allowed to have anyone round. I didn't really have friends at school, as I was usually picked on by Spencer and his gang, or by the nasty big girls. But one day I was invited to a girl's house after school, and for the first time I went.

Maisie was very sweet and also liked doing art. She had a lovely house with a warm friendly mummy who set a table with cakes, milk and biscuits. I thought this was wonderful. Barbara had drilled me in what I had to say: I had to be polite, and not behave like the little bitch I was. After tea, Maisie and I went up to her bedroom. It was a treasure trove – beautiful, all pink and white, with flowery wallpaper. She had a jewellery box, which was white with flowers and leaves painted on the outside. When Maisie lifted the lid, a little ballet dancer in blue silk slowly twirled around to a twinkling tune. I had never seen anything like it in my life – it was wonderful. I played with it over and over, mesmerised, opening and closing the lid, to Maisie's amusement. We tried on all her rings and necklaces and danced around her room. She had loads of scarves, hair clips, pretty dresses, socks and shoes. Maisie was happy for me to try things on, and we both play-acted all sorts of things. It was the happiest afternoon of my life.

All too soon Barbara arrived at the front door and Maisie's mum called up the stairs for me to go. I rushed down, afraid they would all see how strange she was. And indeed, there she was in her plain grey anorak, with her tight, wavy grey hair and pointy angry face, yanking the dog into a sitting position beside her. Seeing Maisie's mum – who was as pretty as a picture in a long blue dress, with earrings and a necklace and lovely curly dark hair – I realised how old-fashioned and funny Barbara looked.

We marched home in silence and, when we got back, I suddenly realised I still had one of Maisie's rings on my finger. It was a thin silver band with a pretend green jewel on it.

'You're a thief!' screamed Barbara. 'You're a naughty, wicked girl – go up to your room this instant.'

She pushed me in the house and up the stairs. I was crying. I hadn't meant to take the ring. It was an accident. When Barbara had arrived, I'd rushed to get everything off (I'd had a ring on every finger), and must have missed the one on my little finger. Barbara pushed me into my room so hard I fell on the floor.

'You are a wicked thief,' she repeated, 'and I'm going to call the police. You need teaching a bloody lesson.'

'Noooooo!' I screamed. 'Please don't call the police.' But Barbara was already marching down the stairs and into the hall where the telephone table and Trimphone stood. I could hear her voice booming from the hall: 'Hello, police? I want to report a thief. Her name is Louise Taylor. She is my adopted daughter and she is a nasty, spiteful, ungrateful, horrid little girl who lies and steals from people.'

I sobbed and sobbed as I heard this, and pulled the offending ring off my finger and put it on my bedside cabinet. It was like an unexploded bomb. I hated it.

'She's been to a little girl's house to play and she deliberately stole her ring. She is wicked.'

I was listening and crying, biting my lip and pulling my hair. I would go to prison. I would never see Sean again.

'Yes,' I heard Barbara continue. 'Yes, I will certainly punish her. Ten hard slaps at the top of her legs and ten hard slaps on her bottom. Thank you so much – you're right: she's no longer to go to other people's houses as she steals and she's not to be trusted.'

I was now so scared I was frozen to the spot, as I heard Barbara put the phone down and start stomping upstairs. I wanted to wee. Barbara roared in like thunder.

'Stand up,' she snapped, giving me a beady stare. 'Pull down your knickers.'

I stood up on wobbly legs; I had no choice. Barbara bent sideways and took off her Clarks K-shoe, lifted my skirt and whacked me with it across the top of my thigh. The flat leather sole smacked really hard across my skin, stinging as she bashed me as hard as she could. Her lips were thin, her eyes narrowed, as she whacked hard.

She then bent me over the bed, putting my head on it, as I faced the window. This time I had ten hard thwacks with the stinging leather sole of her shoe. When the punishment was over she said, 'You'll get no tea tonight. You will go to Maisie's house tomorrow and apologise for being a nasty little thief.'

That night I was utterly miserable. I had bruises on my thighs and my bottom really hurt. I hadn't meant to take the ring; it was a real mistake. I was so worried about being late for Barbara and being punished that I'd rushed down the stairs at Maisie's. But I'd got punished anyway. Now I was going to lose my one and only school friend. I would never be able to go to tea again. I lay in a pool of absolute misery all night.

Next day Barbara met me from school and marched me to Maisie's house. When we got there, Barbara stood at the end of the path with the dog, looking very grim. Then I was pushed up the path and told to ring the doorbell. When the door opened, there was Maisie's nice mummy, who said, sounding surprised, 'Oh, hello, Louise.'

Then she noticed Barbara who had hung back at the end of the path, looking like a grim, grey statue.

'Oh, hello, Barbara. Would you like to come in?'

Barbara sounded very stern and huffy. 'No, thank you – she

has something to say,' she said, meaning me. I stood blinking on the doorstep, looking up at Maisie's mum's kind, warm face, with her pink lipstick and sparkly eyes. I held out the ring between my thumb and index finger.

'I'm very sorry,' I said in a small voice (I actually wanted to cry, but was trying not to), 'I've done something very bad and naughty. I stole this ring because I'm a very bad girl.'

Maisie's mum looked very confused for a moment. She picked up the ring and looked at it. 'Oh,' she said, 'this is just a toy from a comic. It's okay – we didn't even notice it was missing.'

I could feel my cheeks were now burning. I could also feel Barbara's hawk-like eyes boring into my back.

'It's not a problem. I bet you just forgot you were wearing it,' she continued sweetly. I looked up at her warm face and still wanted to sob.

'Come here,' snapped Barbara. I duly turned and walked back to Barbara, who grabbed the top of my arm and dug her talons in. Without a word to Maisie's mum, she tugged me down the street. I lifted my free hand to attempt a feeble wave.

'Stupid bloody woman,' Barbara was hissing under her breath. 'Bloody hippy.'

When I got home I was sent straight to my room without tea. When Ian arrived over an hour later, I heard Barbara telling him loudly in the hall that I was a 'thief and a liar and I was going to prison'. I lay on the bed watching the evening light fade, feeling lonelier than lonely. Suddenly the door flung open and Kevin's head popped round it.

'Thief! Thief! Liar, liar, pants on fire!' he chanted childishly. 'I ate all your food – there's none left, nah nah!' Then he burst into laughter and slammed the door.

A week later I was doing my Saturday chores. One of my jobs was to take an old grey Hoover round the house and vacuum everywhere. I had to take it all the way upstairs, one step at a time, and vacuum the whole house top to bottom. This did mean that I could go into rooms I didn't usually go into – as I wasn't usually allowed anywhere other than my bedroom, the bathroom, toilet and kitchen. This meant I actually went into Barbara and Ian's bedroom. I had to hoover round the beds very carefully. I wasn't allowed to open any drawers in her tallboy or dressing table, which were all in matching dark wood. I also couldn't open the wardrobe, it was forbidden. It did mean I could hoover up any poo that had crumbled under the bed – and I always checked how things were going down there. I also had to polish the surfaces with Pledge and a yellow duster.

Barbara never wore make-up or perfume, and didn't have any jewellery like Maisie (bracelets, necklaces or beads). But she did have a little glass tree on her dressing table, which had three gold rings hanging on it. I polished the glass on the mirrors and the surface of the dressing table, and then I put down my duster and the Pledge. In my childish curiosity I slipped the rings onto my fingers and held my hand up to the mirror and put it against my face. Just like I had played with Maisie's rings. I stared at myself in the mirror and liked what I saw – three gold rings on my little fingers. I had had a taste of jewellery now at Maisie's and I loved the idea. Barbara hardly ever wore these rings, and I wondered if they were her wedding and engagement rings.

Just then the door flung open. There was Kevin. He saw me with the rings on my fingers. I jumped and put them back on the glass tree and felt very scared. Kevin disappeared as fast as he had appeared. I held my breath and listened. I could hear his footsteps going along the landing to his room. He wasn't going straight down to the kitchen to tell on me, so maybe it was all right. The threat of the police was still hanging over me. I didn't want to be whacked again with Barbara's Cuban-heeled shoes either. So I carried on dusting and Pledging and hoped everything would be all right.

Next morning, Sunday, I was waking up and Barbara shot into my bedroom, dragged me from the bed by my arm and pulled me to standing.

'You little thief,' she hissed. Ian was wandering along the landing in his pyjamas, and stood in the doorway. 'Don't hurt her,' he said meekly.

'Mind your own bloody business,' she snapped at him. 'I'll do as I see right!' Then she turned back to me, dragged me out the door, past Ian, down the stairs and into the kitchen. I was shaking. I didn't know what was wrong, or what had happened, but I knew it would be really, really bad. Barbara bent over towards me and grabbed my chin tight in her left-hand grip.

'Now look at me, you little bitch. Tell me the truth for once – where have you put my ring?'

I felt sick. The room started turning. I began to stutter, 'I haven't…' when her right hand appeared and punched me hard across the face. A tooth flew out along with a spurt of blood. My mouth was suddenly full of bitter hot liquid. She hit me again across the face, the other way.

'Where is my ring, you little lying, thieving bitch?'

I had blood and spit dribbling down my chin and my mouth was sore. I shook my head as tears bubbled over. She punched me again in the face, not holding my chin with the other hand, and this time I went flying across the kitchen and hit the larder door.

'Get up. Get up, you little bastard!' She was coming for me again. I was hurting everywhere – my mouth was full of blood, my face stung, my lips swelling. I lifted myself up off the floor and she came over and stood in front of me. She bent over to face me and I could smell her hot, musty breath as she spat out her words.

'You're playing it like that now, are you? Go to your room this instant.'

I went out the door, up the stairs, along the landing with my heart racing, my hand clamped on my mouth. I knew I had tried on the rings, but I also knew I had put all three back. I knew I had. I'd been careful this time. I felt terrified. What was she going to do with me? Were the police coming to get me? Was I going to prison?

I spent the whole of Sunday in my room. No food. No drink. No nothing. My mouth was hurting where the tooth had come out, and I had dried blood on my lips and face. I listened to life going on downstairs and in the street. I heard Ian go out the house to the garage, doors opening and closing, hosepipes spraying, lawn mowers revving. There were car doors opening and slamming, dogs barking, and voices wafting up from the garden. I even heard Sean say, 'Mornin', Ma'am,' as he did to Barbara as he passed by the house. I guessed she was out in the lane doing something.

I was very hungry and very scared. I looked out the window, over the back garden, looking for a sign of Sean. I eventually heard Kevin call to Ian, 'Dinnertime,' and, much later, 'Tea's ready.' I wanted to go to the toilet, but I was scared – too scared to go outside. Eventually I thought I would wet myself and I opened the door a crack. On the floor was a glass of water and one slice of dry bread. I peeked my head out of the door and, seeing the landing was clear, tiptoed to the toilet. I didn't flush, as I was scared of making a noise.

On the way back I picked up the bread and water and ate and drank it very quickly in my room, despite my sore mouth, then put the plate and glass back exactly where it had been. I then heard the sound of the television going on in the best room downstairs, and canned laughter wafted up as the light began to go down on the day. A whole Sunday just in my room. She didn't even come in and do the night routine – I was in total isolation. As the sun went down I watched the sky turn from blue to pink to orange to navy. I looked at the trees and saw birds gathering, swirling in bunches. I felt a bit calmer seeing colours in the evening sky.

Next morning, Monday, I was kept home from school, as I was 'bad'. I didn't care either way now, although I hated being in the house just with Barbara. When Ian left, I heard him say, 'I want her out of that room today, Barbara, or I'll call social services myself.' I was amazed. He never usually stood up to her. I heard the door slam and Barbara mumbling something.

Suddenly my door was flung open. 'Come down,' she ordered. I was still in my pyjamas, and I trotted downstairs behind her, feeling quite dizzy and lightheaded. Theatrically, Barbara put on yellow Marigold gloves and we both went outside. I was barefoot. She went to the dustbin at the side of the house and started taking all the stuff out and throwing it on the floor.

'Louise, why are you doing this to me?' she said, as she threw empty cans of dog food and paper bags on the ground. It was very pongy. I said nothing. I was made to put all the smelly stuff back with my bare hands. I was eventually given some breakfast and then sent back up to my room.

When Kevin came round after school he also pushed my door wide open and shouted, 'You're a liar! You've broken Auntie Barbara's heart, you little shit.' I sat on my bed, saying nothing, wondering what was going on. I had Tony in my hands and squeezed him to me. Kevin disappeared, after which I could hear Barbara crying, loud howls, which was strange. She never cried usually. It sounded very dramatic. I could hear Kevin saying nice things to her: 'It's all right, we'll find it.'

I was still kept home from school for the next few days, as this was a 'crisis'. I also think the bruises on my face, which now had black fingermarks and cuts, would have made people ask some difficult questions. My lip was also split, and there was a gap where my tooth had been. Barbara ignored me most of the time. Then, one evening when Ian was home, she grabbed me near the larder and gripped my chin again with her steely fingers.

'You think you can pull the wool over my eyes, you lying, thieving little bitch. You manipulate your dad against me, you have him round your little finger; you're a spoilt, nasty little cow.'

She spat all this in my face and then tossed me against the wall. I pressed my back against it, trying to shrink from view. How was I manipulating him? Was she angry that he had tried to stop her locking me in my room? I never spoke to Ian and he never really spoke to me. I was just trying to survive.

❦

Being under attack meant that I had to use my head all the time. I was constantly having to work out what was going on. I would use my head – or, rather, my imagination – to make things smaller, to shrink them down when I felt upset. I would imagine horrible things that had happened to me, or earlier to William, and then shrink them and let them float away. I used my imagination all the time: like squeezing my eyes and seeing colours, which was a great way of escaping what was going on in the room at any time. Or even during punishment. I would distract myself, and I could float out of my body and just move things around in my mind and put them away when I didn't like them.

I had to do this because it was all too much to keep in my mind all the time – the horrible things that happened were too painful. So I learnt to wrap them up and pop them in the back of my head, like wrapping a parcel or a present. I would post them right at the back of my mind, hide them away, and not come back to them until later, if at all. I didn't want to feel all the horrible crushing feelings, as they were too big and scary. I would slip and slide them around, turn them into shapes and colours, hide them and ignore them or paint an imaginary picture with them.

My main way of surviving was to rebel, very quietly and secretively, and when I was eight going on nine this became quite a complicated thing. Sometimes it looked like I was being very good, very nice, when in fact I was just *playing* being very good and very nice. Inside I felt very different, but I knew I had to keep thinking, keep working out how to survive. It would make me smile if I got away with something and she didn't notice or find out. It would make me feel better when I got something I wanted – like nice cherry brandy or the dog's Choc Drops – and she had absolutely no idea what was going on. For a moment I felt I had some power in a situation where I actually felt totally powerless. I went to the 'Louise place' in my head and nobody could see in there, not least Barbara, who was my worst enemy number one.

❧

This ring situation went on and on for two whole weeks. I heard Barbara telling our neighbours that I was 'a little thief' and 'not to be trusted'. She told my teachers and she told our local doctor. And she did actually even go and tell the police – we marched into the police station and she told the story. The policeman looked at me and said, 'You wouldn't do that, would you?'

I shook my head, speechless and completely dumbstruck. Barbara grabbed me and pulled me out of the station, huffing and puffing all the way home, shouting at the dog the whole time. An elderly couple came up and told her off for hurting the dog – and she told them to 'Mind your own sodding business!' They were very shocked and scuttled off. I felt hugely embarrassed but said nothing.

I began to wonder if I really had taken the ring, like I accidentally took the little-finger ring from Maisie's. I really thought I had put all three rings back, as I was always so careful to make sure things went back exactly the way they were. I was usually a master of covering my tracks.

It was Saturday again, and I was doing my usual household chores in total silence: the hoovering, the bed making, the polishing with Pledge (although I was not allowed to touch Barbara's dressing table now, that was out of bounds).

'You are to go and brush the rugs on the lawn,' she snapped at me after I was finished. I went outside and started bashing the rugs, which were hanging over the line. Loads of dust flew out as usual. I hated this job. I coughed and spluttered but carried on. Suddenly I heard a scream.

'Look!' I heard coming from the kitchen. I stopped. Barbara was showing something to Kevin and Ian. There was a commotion. I stopped bashing and tried to listen. All three were staring at Barbara's hand. I crept across the grass towards the door and watched. Barbara looked up.

'It was on the stairs,' she said quickly, 'under the edge of the carpet. I found it when I was brushing.'

My heart lifted. The ring! She had it back!

'I know that's where you put it,' she snipped at me, 'but at least I have it back now. It's my wedding ring. Nine-carat gold.'

I looked over at Kevin, who was smirking at me with an evil look that said, 'Gotcha!' I knew he had been behind the whole thing. What I didn't know was that worse was to come.

10

Being Dumped

School is horrible, but home is worse. Spencer and his gang are still picking on me, and now he tries to feel me up as I pass. One of his friends corners me in the playground and pokes a pink sausage through his trousers and wiggles it at me. I don't tell anyone. I keep my head down and try to muddle through. Barbara has a strange attitude to school – she tells me, 'It's really a waste of time for the likes of you,' so she often keeps me home to do chores.

Apart from looking after the chickens, I also do a lot of other housework, alongside the ironing and bed making. Sometimes the social workers drop in without any warning to find out why I'm not at school. Then Barbara shooes me upstairs and I'm told to get into bed, as I'm 'ill'. I lie rigid in my bed in my clothes, pretending I'm sick, playing along to keep the peace. I hear voices in the hall, and then they're gone. I wish I could see them alone and tell them the truth but I never get to do that, so I have to play the game otherwise she'll never let me forget it.

I'm always listening out for what's going on, as nobody tells me anything. Once the social workers have gone, I hear Barbara come upstairs with a heavy tread. She walks into the bathroom and I hear her open the mirror cabinet. In there are her bottles of pills: green ones, green and black ones, little round yellow ones. I hear her pop open a bottle and the sound of pills pouring into her hand. I hear the toothbrush glass clink against the sink and water running. I know she's taking a handful; she often does. I've seen her do it many times. She thinks I don't see her. In fact, I also do this myself when I feel very upset. I've learnt to go in and sneak a few of those shiny green ones I'm given at night, and I take them with a gulp of water, very quickly. Then I feel all woozy and calm. It's a nice feeling, a break from all the fear and pain. It's like my head fills up with cotton wool. I'm often hurting – I have so many bruises, punches, whacks – and I've learnt that I can go to the bathroom and sneak a few of these 'sweeties' and feel a bit better afterwards. I know they aren't really sweeties, they're some kind of medicine from the doctor, but I pretend they are.

Now I hear Barbara coming along the landing and I freeze. Please go past, please go past. I close my eyes, pretending I'm asleep. I'm still under the covers in my clothes and play-acting being ill. The door flies open.

'I don't know why I ever had you,' she says to me fiercely. 'You are nothing but bloody trouble.'

I'm trying to flatten myself out completely, blinking over the rough blanket. 'Those bloody idiots don't know anything about children. I'd love to see them deal with you and all the trouble you are to me.'

I know better than to say anything. I just lie, as quietly as I can. I don't even blink. I hardly breathe. She looks her at watch. 'Come on, get up. We're going to get Dad's tea.'

I have no idea what the time is, although it's probably after-noon. I should be at school, and no doubt the social workers have told her so. She has argued with them or something; that's why she's taken the sweeties. I get out of bed very obediently and follow her down the stairs. We get the dog, go outside and get in her Ford Escort.

Barbara drives like a maniac all the way to Headington, a village outside Oxford. She swears the whole way at other drivers, calling them 'bloody idiots' or 'stupid bastards', hits the kerb several times and overtakes on the bend of the road. I'm terrified, so I squeeze my eyes tight shut, trying to see the swirling colours I like. Orange, purple, blue, spots... it makes me feel much safer somehow.

When I open them we're in a car park behind a supermarket. Barbara is grumbling about having to buy food, cook tea for 'bloody men who want everything their own way'. She hates cooking, she hates buying food, she hates men. Hate, hate, hate. It's all she says, all the time. Her eyes are glazed and she's sim-mering – I know we are building up to one of her explosions. So I keep very quiet and trot along after her, trying to be pleasing and helpful.

We walk round the supermarket and she approaches one of those ticket machines with a queue system. She snatches a ticket.

'I only want some sodding meat pie. Why should I have to bloody queue for hours?' Barbara snaps at all listeners.

I feel my face go red and offer to carry the basket. We are queuing and people are looking at her, as they always do. She's building up to a volcanic eruption. I feel ashamed. I want her to stop, but she won't – she is now complaining loudly about the shop, the queue, the 'bloody idiots' behind the counter. She starts pacing up and down like a wild hen. I stand, holding the basket, wanting the ground to swallow me up.

Then I see Maisie's mum coming towards us. She smiles. I smile. Barbara sees her coming too, and her face darkens. She grabs my arm and takes the basket, half full, and throws it on the floor. She's hurting me as she pulls me by the arm, past Maisie's mum, who is looking confused. I'm crying now. I hate it when this happens. I say 'Mummy, you're hurting me,' as she drags me across the car park. People stare. I am dragged so I fall on my knees and graze them, which makes me cry louder.

'What the bloody hell are you looking at?' Barbara screams at a man standing by a nearby car. 'Mind your own ruddy business.'

I'm pulled to my feet and we get to the car. She's fumbling in her bag for the keys. I'm crying uncontrollably and my knees are bleeding. I say, 'Mummy, please stop, please stop.' She looks daggers at me and says, 'I never should have had any of you bloody unwanted children. You have ruined my life.'

Her face is bright scarlet. She opens the driver's door and I'm standing at the other side, by the passenger door, shaking, holding the car handle. She turns the ignition, revs the engine and backs out. I'm still holding the handle and I run alongside the car. Then I let go as she does a back turn, nearly squishing me against a parked car. She puts her foot down and the Escort drives through the car park at high speed and out onto the road. I helplessly watch it go. I wail. I'm standing and howling and I don't know what to do. I'm just crying and crying, my knees smarting, and suddenly there's a hand in my hand. I open my eyes and there is Maisie's mum, looking down at me, worried.

'Where's your mum gone?' she asks. I shake my head; I can't speak. I can't stop crying. Maisie's mum keeps asking what is wrong with Barbara and I can't answer. I'm scared of getting her into trouble. I'm scared what she'll do to me if the social workers and police get involved, but I'm also scared, more importantly, of what would happen to me if I gave the game away.

Maisie's mum and I walk across the car park and get into her car. She hands me some tissues. I blow my nose. She keeps asking why Barbara would leave me in a car park. Should we go to the police? I feel very scared at the idea and shake my head. Maisie's mum starts her car up, and I try and get hold of myself.

'Mum is feeling sad,' I stutter out, trying to make it into something Maisie's mum can understand. She turns and looks at me, but keeps driving. When we get home, the Escort is parked on the drive. When Barbara opens the door, I can see she is still in a rage. Maisie's mum stands with her hand on my shoulder but speaks gently to Barbara. I can see Maisie's mum doesn't know what to say. Barbara leans forward, grabs my arm and pulls me into the house, saying, 'You know what kids are like – and these ones have a chip on their shoulder.'

The door is slammed in Maisie's mum's face. I'm pulled down the corridor and whacked across the face for being 'nothing but trouble' and told to go up to my bedroom. I remember it like it was yesterday. It was confusing and humiliating, but Barbara always found a new way to torture and punish me.

❧

Barbara never said sorry, she never explained. I was to be abandoned many times by her – being dropped places and not picked up, or simply left while she was in one of her furious rages, when she would drive off. She often got in her car when in a vile mood and drove about the country lanes. At first I thought it was because she needed to get out and get a change of view from the family home. There was some truth in that. She also liked visiting farms to check out the chickens, or in answer to adverts, as she liked getting new dogs. I learnt to be wary of her when we went anywhere in case she drove off suddenly without me, or hid from me, or suddenly disappeared.

One time she drove me to a place called Shotover Woods, a park near Cowley. Barbara told only one nice story about Ian, and it was that when they were courting he took her to Shotover and picked her a bunch of bluebells. I used to think, when she said horrible things about him, that there must have been something good at the beginning, otherwise they wouldn't have got married. The bluebell wood sounded wonderfully romantic.

One afternoon I was off school, as Barbara had kept me home as usual. We got in the car and she drove very fast. I felt sick, as I often did in the car. If I felt sick she would stop the car very roughly, open the door and throw me out on the kerb to be sick. She would be furious. 'Bloody children,' she'd be muttering. There'd be no sympathy or travel sickness pills. Then we'd be back in the car and roaring at speed down country lanes.

As we drove out to Shotover this afternoon we had to pass by my school. She shouted, 'Get down,' as we did, as she didn't want anyone to see I was in the car, so I slipped onto the floor and hid as we went past; she didn't have seatbelts. Then I crawled back up once the coast was clear. At Shotover we parked in the car park, which had only a couple of cars in it. She was in one of her spiteful moods, ranting on about Ian. She hated bloody Ian, she hated the nosy parker neighbours, the stupid social workers, the ruddy school. Barbara strode off with the dog, snapping that it was everyone else's fault. She said I should never trust men, they were filthy, dirty bastards, and she ran through all the usual things she hated, including me. I guessed she had taken some of her tablets and was burning off her anger with a brisk walk involving me and the poor dog.

Eventually we reached a deeply wooded area. It was far away, so we couldn't hear the traffic from the motorway or even local roads any more. I was sad not to see any bluebells but it was beautiful, leafy and green, and I loved looking up at the trees, where their leaves were rippling in the wind against the blue and grey of the sky. I could hear birds and there were grey squirrels running along branches and hopping. I wondered if I'd see fairies or elves. I'd seen them in books at school. I started daydreaming, enjoying the peace of nature.

I walked on and Barbara was behind me, still ranting to herself, but occasionally said, 'Look at that bird,' as a magpie went past. I guessed she must be feeling better, but I didn't dare look. I loved the bird's black and white markings, and thought they were amazing. I ran on up to the trees and leant against one. It was solid, with rough bark. It felt strong. I gave it a big hug and looked up at the branches and the leaves shaking in the wind. I could see two magpies now and turned around to tell Barbara, but she was gone. I blinked. Where was she? Where'd she gone? I started running back along the little path through the trees, but it soon became several paths and I got lost very quickly. I was alone, right in the middle of a wood. I didn't know how to get out. I started crying, feeling frantic and really scared. I ran through the trees, calling 'Mummy' and 'Come back'. The tears and snot were streaming down my face. I had no coat, no hankie, nothing. I was just in a light dress.

Eventually I bumped into a man with his dog. He was old, with a cap and green jacket on. I kept thinking, *Men are filthy, dirty creatures*, so when he tried to hold my hand I ran away from him screaming. I screamed and screamed, absolutely hysterical now. Then I found three women walking together. I was unable to speak now, as I had been sobbing and running, screaming and shouting: 'Mummeeee!'

One of the women took my hand, but I hated her touching me. I felt so scared I pulled away, like a wild animal. She was kind and calm and eventually I was able to walk with her to the car park. She put me in her car and gave me a drink of water. I was still panting from sobbing and running so much. The woman said she would take me home and, again, I felt a stab of dread. I gave her my address and we drove in silence. I was so confused. Why had Barbara done this to me? Did she really want to leave me in the woods?

When we drove onto the gravel in front of the house, the Escort was parked and Barbara came out. She was holding tissues to her face.

'Oh, thank you,' she said to the woman before she could say anything. Barbara dabbed at her eyes with the tissues. 'I was about to call the police. I didn't know what to do. I turned around and she had just run off. She's very difficult to look after,' she explained to the woman. 'She's an unwanted child, and I've done my best for her. She has a chip on her shoulder – just like they all do.'

The woman handed me over and gave me a strange look. I knew I had to play the game. I went in and nothing was said – not a word. She didn't explain; she didn't say sorry. This time I was told to go and feed the chickens. I never said a word to Ian; not even to Sean. It felt so scary that she could do that to me that it sort of shut me up and made me cling onto what I had. The idea of the night in the wood alone was terrifying, but worse was to come. And these incidents triggered memories of similar things that had happened when I was even younger.

The first time I was dumped I was about six years old. She had actually abandoned me before in many places, like Debenhams, local shops or playgrounds. I usually got home with the help of a nice adult or a school friend's mother. Then, when I was eight, she drove me, again at high speed, to a place called Wytham, just outside Oxford. I had never really met people from Barbara's family, although she did have some relatives still living. This was yet another day I should have been at school, but I'd been kept home as usual because I was 'coming down with something'. I wasn't, as I had done chores all morning.

We parked up the car and she got out and started striding towards a stone cottage on a bend in a country lane. There was an elderly couple, Rene and Fred, in the cottage, and we went in. I was sent outside to the back garden but Barbara stayed and sat with them. I had no idea who they were or why we were there. I knew Barbara had worked for years for an Oxford couple as a nanny – she was proud of that time in her life – and maybe these people were old friends from back then.

She had recently begun to mention things about my birth mother, who came from the Oxford area. I didn't get any clear information but she kept talking about her, getting me quite interested. I didn't know if this couple had something to do with my birth mother. Then Rene came outside with a metal tin filled with custard creams. I took a couple and sat outside in the garden, on the cobbles in a little courtyard, while Barbara had tea and biscuits with them inside. I always amused myself by looking at things, especially flowers. The garden was full of lovely blooms – red, blue, yellow, white. Big daisies, roses, tall purple flowers, like bells. I was lost in looking at everything. I wanted to draw them but had no paper. So I set about memorizing the shapes and colours for later. When she was ready to leave, Barbara shouted, 'Louise', and I scrambled up and we said our goodbyes.

On the way back I enjoyed the view out of the window over the fields. I loved seeing the big fat cows nibbling on the grass. I said, 'Hello, cows,' to myself as we passed. I always loved animals and liked to wave to them. I felt Barbara was in a dark mood now, worse than when we arrived, and I didn't know why. She wasn't speaking at all, and she was gripping the steering wheel so hard her knuckles were white with a pink glow.

Suddenly she turned the car abruptly and we were bumping up a narrow lane through the trees. We turned right and left, and were then in the middle of woods. I was confused.

'Get out,' she ordered. So I did. We walked with the dog through the woods for a while but it was getting chilly. Then Barbara did something strange. She sat down on a big stone and started crying. She cried and cried and I stood watching her, not knowing what to do. The dog and I sat down next to her. I leant over and put my hand on her hand, which was icy cold.

'Get off me, you stupid little girl,' she snapped through her tears. I felt foolish. Stupid. I didn't know what I was supposed to do. What had I done now? What was wrong? Barbara began talking to herself and hitting herself on the head with her fists. I felt scared watching her doing this. I didn't know why she was doing it. It was usually me she was hitting, so I actually felt sorry for her. I knew how much it hurt. Still I stood watching, not knowing what to do. She looked up and saw me looking.

'Go away and leave me alone,' she shrieked. 'Get out of my sight!'

I turned around and started walking. I didn't know where I was going but I was crying now. I was scared of her. What would she do to me? Why was she hitting herself? I'd never seen Barbara like this, and I walked a little way away, hoping she would feel better. It was beginning to get dark. I looked back and she was still on the stone, pointing to a path. 'Keep walking,' she shouted. So I did, saying, 'Mummy, stop' to myself in a quiet scared voice.

When I turned around to look again, she was gone. I froze on the spot. What should I do? I knew she didn't want me to run back towards her, yet I didn't know where I should go. She had told me to keep walking, so I kept walking. The whole situation was very scary. I walked and walked. The sky was still blue, although the light was fading. There were lovely trees. I climbed over a wooden stile, and then slipped on a cowpat and got all dirty. I got up and ran through a field of big red cows, who turned and looked at me, chewing the cud. Then I realised I could see the cottage we were at earlier, the one with Rene and Fred. I ran through the field and eventually got to the house. When I knocked on the door, Rene and Fred were there but they were not that pleased to see me. I was ushered through the house and out into the back garden where I'd eaten the custard creams earlier.

Rene gave me a glass of squash and I drank it, as I was very thirsty. She went to the telephone and eventually came out and explained she'd had to call social services, as she couldn't find

Barbara, and they would come and get me. I was extremely upset. Where was 'Mummy'? Rene told me she was not coming. I started pulling out my eyelashes, pulling out my hair. Where was I going? What was happening? Would I see Sean again? I was really frightened as I sat and looked at the flowers in the garden. I willed them to help me.

When the social worker arrived it was a man wearing a leather jacket and jeans. I usually saw women in twos. He was about the same age as Ian and had brown hair and a crinkly face, but I found him a bit scary. He had a big brown moustache.

I said, 'Thank you for the squash,' and the social worker put me in the back of his green car. As we drove off I had no idea where we were going. We were driving along with me in the back seat looking out at the fields and cows again. Where was Barbara now? Where were we going? I could see the man's brown eyes shining in the driving mirror.

'Well, Louise,' he said, smiling. 'You're a pretty little girl, aren't you?'

I didn't say anything and just looked out the window, hoping to see more cows. I liked cows.

'We're going to a farmhouse for the night,' he said. 'Mrs Knight will look after you.'

I had no idea who 'Mrs Knight' was, and just kept looking out the window. In my head I was counting and pressing my thumb and fingers together on both hands, at high speed. One, two, three, four. One, two, three, four. I had no idea why this was happening to me.

Suddenly the car was slowing. We were on a very small country lane. There was a lay-by in the road – I'd been in one before when I was travelsick and had thrown up on the verge. The social worker put the brake on and opened his door. What was he doing? I looked about me – there were no houses around. I wondered if I should get out too.

Then he opened the back door and got in next to me. I was quite dirty, having trudged across the field of cows. I had a little dress on and white socks, now splattered with mud and poo. I said nothing and looked at the man, who made me feel uncomfortable. He closed the door and said, 'Want a sweet?'

I said, 'No, thank you,' although I was dying to have one. I felt very peculiar with this man. He put his hand on my knee, and then moved it up my thigh. I stopped breathing. What was he doing?

'You're very pretty, Louise,' he said. Then he moved his hand up further towards my knickers, and further up, just as an ambulance came hurtling around the corner a few feet away from the car. He took his hand away very quickly and looked out the window. The ambulance rattled by. We sat on the back-seat together in awkward silence for a few seconds. Then he suddenly opened the door, got out and slammed it shut. He got back in the driver's seat and started up the car.

I sat, shocked, on the back seat. What was going on? I looked at his eyes in the mirror and pulled my dress back down. I felt truly terrified.

'Louise, you don't need to tell anyone about this,' the man said, as we drove off. Who was I going to tell? Who would believe me? Then, without a word, I was driven to a place I didn't know and handed over to Mrs Knight, a large lady who lived in a big farmhouse.

I sat in her rambling living room. There were three big boys sitting on the floor playing with Lego and bricks. Then I heard the male social worker say to Mrs Knight in the hall outside, 'Be careful of Louise, she is known for telling lies.'

I was amazed. I heard Mrs Knight say, 'Oh, thanks, Malcolm. Good to know. You can't be too careful.' Then she came into the living room and handed me a sheet of paper.

'Read this and we'll get along fine,' she said. I couldn't read very well, and the words sort of swam before my eyes. Then Mrs Knight took me upstairs to a room with bunk beds: I was on the bottom. There were more children up there, two girls and two boys. Some were her own children, some were fostered. I didn't speak to anyone. I had no idea what was going on or why I was there. Why had Barbara left me again? Why had the old people not wanted me? Why had the social worker tried to touch me? Why was I here now, and for how long? Was I ever going home again?

When teatime came there was food but I didn't really want to eat it. I felt too upset. I had no clothes, no toothbrush, nothing. Mrs Knight found me some pyjamas. That night the children took it in turns after lights out to hold me down, pull down my pyjama bottoms and look at my private parts. They took it in turns to touch my body, like it was a scary animal, and each time they whispered 'yuck'. Both the boys and the girls did this, mostly in total silence. I just held my breath, waiting for it to stop.

I felt like I'd stepped into a nightmare that wasn't going to end anytime soon. I was at the farmhouse for two days. I didn't speak to anyone or play with the children. There was a big sheepdog outside, though, and I went and sat with him and stroked him all day. I loved being with a big calm animal with bright eyes, soft fur and a wet nose. I loved the feel of his coat and his warmth. Eventually Mrs Knight came out to find me.

'Come with me,' she said, and I got up from the dog and followed her reluctantly. On the doorstep was Barbara in her grey anorak, looking sour. I felt my heart sink. I didn't like where I was but I didn't want to leave either.

'You've worried me to death,' she said, 'running off like that.' And with that I was swept off the doorstep and into the car without any explanation. We sat in silence all the way home. Nothing was mentioned about this incident ever again.

11

Going Up and Down

When I was nine, I went up to middle school. It meant that I finally got away from the horrible school and the dreaded Spencer and his gang. The middle school was also near my first primary school, Vernon Lane, in a nicer part of town, and I wondered if I might see Miss Nickerson, my lovely first art teacher, by going back near there.

I still thought about William from time to time, although his memory was now fading. Barbara had told me during one spiteful moment that he was so stupid and bad he was now in a 'special school', whatever that was. He was also in 'care'. I didn't really understand what this meant. I had tried to call the phone number I memorised once, but couldn't get through – so gave up. It was now three years since I'd seen him and I still looked right occasionally when I went down our road, just in case I might glimpse him. I also looked around the shops whenever we were out, just in case I spied a red toothbrush of hair. But I never did see him again, and I had no idea where he was or how to contact him. He was the only other person who really knew what it was like in our house. I certainly couldn't ask Barbara where he was, Ian wasn't interested, and Kevin I avoided as much as possible.

Middle school was smaller and seemed much nicer all round. The teachers were friendlier and the children not so harsh. I knew I didn't look right, as I was still wearing the horrible maroon slippers or Barbara's old-lady shoes, and my uniform was second-hand and not the same colour or quality as the other children's. It was navy, and I had yet another knitted tie. Barbara still walked me to school with the dog, and we were still late. I got strange looks when she turned up and I could see people looking at her, and at me, and thinking, *Who's this strange lot?* I wasn't sure if the teachers could see I was different from Barbara, as although I called her 'Mummy' I knew we were not blood related. She never stopped telling me I wasn't hers and that I wasn't wanted.

I was beginning to feel very self-conscious, as my breasts were starting to develop. I could feel my clothes clinging to my body and I didn't like it. I didn't like boys looking at me, after all the things Barbara had said about them. The constant touching, teasing and poking I had endured from Spencer, Kevin, Mark, and even the male social worker in the car, made me feel very awkward about my body. I knew I smelt quite bad, as I didn't have enough baths, and washing was very quick in the morning and almost non-existent in the evening. I hated smelling. I had started to sweat now, and I asked Barbara if I could shower after school, especially after PE.

'I'm not wasting water on the likes of you,' she spat. I tried again and asked if I could have deodorant. 'You're too young.'

So I was stuck with trying to wash myself with carbolic or green Fairy soap with a flannel, but I knew I smelt sweaty and my clothes were awful. I would wear the same white shirt all week and it would end up grimy yellow under the arms, with a grey collar. Other girls mocked me for being dirty – they had Impulse sprays in their bags called wonderful things like 'True Love' or 'Romantic Spark'. And they all had shiny hair in beautiful ponytails, with sparkly bobbles and lovely fashionable hairbands, while I had a black pageboy, cut very short (real pudding basin style) and dandruff. My hair was greasy and it itched, so I had snow all over my blazer. It was awful.

When I was sweating I would stuff toilet paper into my armpits to try to soak up the moisture and then, when I took it out, it would smell really bad and I would flush it down the toilet in disgust. The toilet paper was that hard, greaseproof stuff, so it chafed my underarms and they got red and sore. I couldn't buy any toiletries as I didn't have any money, and now, in my new school, I began to get bullied about smelling all over again. Then the soap and flannel disappeared from the bathroom; Barbara had taken it. Children began to move away from me at school, and refused to sit next to me. I would take refuge in the toilets at lunchtime and cry. I would never make a friend if I smelt like this.

Then we were called into the headmaster's office for a meeting. The night before, Barbara spent a long time pinning up her hair to make her usual demi-wave style. She put rollers in and covered it with a net, and manicured her nails using Nulon hand cream. She wore a dress and jacket and looked unusually smart, but I was grubby as usual and was called out of class before the morning break. I could smell myself; it was awful.

When I got to the headmaster's office Barbara was already there. She was standing looking very smart – for her – and she nodded at me as I came in. I could see she was in one of her strange moods. She looked quite smug, so I didn't know what she had already been saying to the headmaster, Mr Phillips, who was very nice. We both sat down in front of him on high-backed chairs.

'I've asked you in,' Mr Phillips began politely, looking at Barbara, 'because we are concerned about Louise's hygiene.'

'Oh, yes, sir,' said Barbara, in a polite voice that I didn't recognise. 'We are also very concerned. She refuses to wash. She is such a dirty girl. I've tried my best to teach her but she just won't learn.'

I was speechless. Fat, salty tears started rolling down my cheeks. The truth was further than I could possibly explain. I had started really happily at this new school and I was again being bullied for being smelly. And I was smelly because I wasn't allowed baths or showers and even my soap and flannel had been taken away. But I was so upset I couldn't speak. That was the end of the meeting and we were ushered out.

I looked at Barbara. Why was she doing this to me? She seemed to really enjoy my humiliation. She smirked at me, turned and walked away. When I got home she gave me an old frayed towel that she used for the dogs, a white bottle of MUM roll-on deodorant and a flannel. I was told I would be allowed two showers a week from now on. I made sure I didn't look too excited, as I knew now that if I liked something it was a good reason to take it away. So I bit my lip and said a very polite 'Thank you, Mummy,' and behaved like a good little girl. Inside I was cheering; outside, I looked demure. That was how the war had to be won.

✦

Although I'd started my middle school enthusiastically, and had a bit of a difficult time over my body odour, two things did get better around this time. The first and most important thing was art. This school was much more interested in helping its pupils express themselves with both art and music, and one day the art teacher, Mr Tunning, told us there was going to be a competition. I got very excited. Art was the one thing I could do. I was drawing all the time at home, on any spare piece of computer paper that Ian left around. He had loads of it, big white and green striped sheets with holes down the side, that I asked to have – and I would draw and draw and draw. I loved making pictures, especially of people and things, like flowers and the dog. I would sit with Sean and draw his knick-knacks or plastic flowers and his chocolate Labrador, Frida. We were told we had to draw our 'Family Tree'. I realised, as we walked home, that I had no idea what my family tree was. I didn't really understand what it meant. I had no sense of where I had really come from, or who belonged to me. I actually felt that I had no one. I was constantly told I was unwanted, thrown away, discarded. I didn't have the same blood as Barbara and Ian. I didn't 'belong' to William (who was gone anyway), or to Sean or the Polish people. I did ask Barbara and Ian and they both just shrugged off the question. I never got an answer.

However, I had an idea. I begged paper from Barbara, Ian and Sean, old boxes and stuff from the shed and garage, and I built a huge five-foot tree with Sellotape and cardboard. It was based on an old apple tree in the garden, which was an interesting shape. I stared at the trees in the park, too, and saw all their wonderful colours and shapes. It was huge, with a greeny brown and purple trunk and loads of big branches with blossoms made out of collage from magazines and newspapers. I made it in the corner of Ian's garage. I laid the cardboard on the ground and Sellotaped it all together. Then I got to work. It was a fantastic experience, and I didn't notice anything around me. I even forgot I was hungry for once. I drew on birds in a nest with wonderful feathers. I coloured it all in with felt-tips.

It was a huge work of art. I carried it into school wrapped in two black bin bags (which I begged for), and placed it next to all twenty-nine other pictures, which were of 'typical' family trees, drawn on a single piece of A4. Mine looked really big, colourful and different.

When Mr Tunning came in he looked at all the work and said, 'Wow, everyone has done an amazing job.' We all beamed. Then he looked at mine – which was literally standing out above the rest – and he said, 'Who did this?' I put my hand up very slowly.

'This is the best in the class,' he said. 'Louise, this is truly fantastic – you've won.'

To my utter amazement, the whole class clapped. Me. They clapped *me* – the smelly odd girl in weird clothes who no one usually wanted to sit next to. The girl who couldn't really read or write properly. The one thing I could do, though, was draw and paint. I felt my heart swell with pride and tears prick my eyes. My tree was best! It was a fantastic moment. And all because I had no idea who my family actually was!

A week later it was announced that the prize was a trip to the Tate Gallery in London. I had been chosen to go with six of the children who had done the best pictures. I couldn't believe it. We were going in a minibus with our art teacher. I had never been on a proper day trip to something like a museum or gallery, and it was a really fantastic prize. Of course, Barbara didn't say 'well done' or anything like that but the night before the trip I was incredibly excited. When I got home from school I asked if

I could make a packed lunch for myself – but Barbara refused to let me touch the kitchen. I also asked if I could have a clean shirt and skirt, as I really wanted to look good for the trip.

Suddenly she turned and bore down on me with a nasty look on her face. 'That bloody school is filling your head with ideas.' I felt my enjoyment freeze completely. 'You're nothing special, my lady, you're just a stupid little girl who can't read or write properly.'

She looked down her pointy nose at me and sneered. 'The likes of you will never make a living from art. Don't be ridiculous. Only rich people can do art. People like you have to work.'

I felt all the excitement and happiness drain out of me. Then she said, for a final slap, 'Your mum is a slut and your dad is a drunk, and if you don't watch it you'll go the same way.'

My bubble was burst. The next day I went on the school trip in my dirty shirt and skirt. There was a grubby brown stain round the neck and I smelt fairly bad. I felt like I had a heavy stone in my stomach and I no longer wanted to go on the trip to London. The prize already felt spoiled. All the popular kids jumped on the bus past me and grabbed all the window seats. I just sat at the back of the bus feeling nothing. I didn't care any more about the trip to the Tate, or the bus journey or the packed lunch. I just felt heavy.

'Are you all right, Louise?' Mr Tunning asked kindly when no one sat next to me.

'Yes, sir,' I said in a small voice. How could I begin to tell him what was going on for me, or at home? It all seemed completely impossible to explain. Who would believe it? Where would I start?

As we got nearer to London – my first time there – I did

begin to feel my heart lift a little as I took in all the buildings, the shapes, the lights, the colours, the roads, the cars, the clothes, billboards – absolutely everything. I didn't even feel sick. Everyone on the bus was excited as we neared the gallery. We parked the minibus and walked to the Tate, an enormous building. I fell in love. I was amazed by the pictures, the art, the colour of the walls, the light, the little white cards with things written on. It was all completely wonderful.

At lunchtime we had our food outside on the steps. I watched as another girl took out a purple plastic Disney box, which had a little note to 'Darling Sarah' inside, 'from your mum, with love – have a wonderful, creative day'. She had gorgeous fresh food, lovingly prepared. I took out a plastic sandwich bag with a plain white cheese sandwich in it. No drink, no extras. And certainly no note. I wondered what it would be like to have a loving mum like Sarah's who wished me well and wanted me to have a nice day, and who packed food for me with love, not hate.

After lunch, we wandered round the gallery some more and I saw some amazing things made of wood, and brick, and metal. My eyes were opened. Near the end of the day I stood next to a big American man who was talking to a woman, saying, 'Art is for everyone.' He had dark shoulder-length hair and sideburns, a green shirt with a strange, lace-up collar, and was younger than our teachers. His blonde friend was beautifully dressed in a long flowing dress with lots of beads. I was as interested in these two people as I was in the gallery.

On the way home, in the bus, I could smell my shirt wafting up after a long day walking about and felt embarrassed. But I kept seeing the two beautiful people: the man and the woman, and how he said, 'Art is for everyone.' I realised I was part of 'everyone'. I loved art. It was for me, too – smelly or not; unwanted or not.

I suddenly realised, watching the light become dull and the streetlights flicker on as the roads whooshed by, that I wanted to be an artist, and that the world of the Tate was also the world for me. Those people were people I liked, too. But that also the most important thing would be to keep this idea to myself – it was too precious to be smashed by the likes of Barbara. It would be secret. All mine. I hugged it to myself. However, there were even more challenges to overcome.

Apart from art, the other thing I liked doing was singing. I had spent many afternoons and evenings with Sean, with him singing old Irish tunes and sometimes playing his tin whistle. It was magic. He also had an old radio that we could listen to together while he read the paper and I drew. He taught me some songs, and even though we didn't have music in the house, I really loved hearing his tunes. At middle school I always liked the singing we did in class, and at Christmas and the end of term. I didn't think I had a great voice but singing made me feel happy.

I think because I said so little at home – and had to watch what I said all the time in case I got into trouble – that I liked the freedom of singing, of making sound. After the art competition and day trip I made a couple of friends at school. Actually, a lot of the children asked me to draw things for them when they were doing pictures, like arms and legs and things, so I became a tiny bit more accepted. One of my new friends at middle school, Janet, was in the choir. She kept saying, 'Why don't you join?' It was after school on a Thursday. I really wanted to try but I felt very shy about singing in front of the teacher, Mrs Isaacs.

One lunchtime we were sitting in the school field and Janet got out *Jackie* magazine, which we all loved reading. At the back were the words for a Marie Osmond song called 'Paper Roses'. We both sang this song out loud to our heart's content and we even harmonised with each other. We smiled and laughed. I felt carefree for once. It was fantastic making music together and it was a whole new experience for me. I loved it. There was an audition for choir coming up the next Monday and Janet kept saying, 'Go on, Louise, you can do it. Pleeeese.' It was great that she wanted me to join. I was beginning to make a friend. I felt wanted for once.

That evening I spent time thinking how I could ask Barbara. In the end I plucked up the courage and told her about the audition and singing 'Paper Roses' with Janet in the field. She burst into nasty laughter.

'Why would anyone want you?' she sneered at me. 'Are you completely mad?'

Nonetheless, I was determined to have a go. This was a real chance for me to start joining in things despite my appearance and lack of learning. The art prize had given me a real boost and I felt I could at least try for the choir. So on Monday, despite being one of the shyest children in the whole school, I went along to the audition. Singing out loud in front of Mrs Isaacs, standing by the piano, was a pretty big deal. My knees were knocking and I felt really sick. As I started singing 'Paper Roses', my palms and armpits were sweating. I was so nervous I was shaking visibly. But Mrs Isaacs was nice and said she would count me in, and she did: 'Louise – are you ready? One, two, three...'

I had to stop and cough a couple of times but I got through

it, despite my little coughs and splutters. My friend Janet was sitting on the floor smiling at me, along with some other children who were waiting for their auditions. There were also some dinner ladies I liked (and who were nice to me) across the hall by the kitchen door that backed onto the hall. At the end of my song a couple of the dinner ladies clapped. My friend Janet also whooped. I went bright red but I felt amazing. I had actually done it.

'Well done,' said Mrs Isaacs, smiling. 'I will let you know tomorrow.'

I was desperate to go to school the next day, Tuesday, to find out if I had got in. But Barbara kept me home: 'You're not looking well,' she said. I was fine but, as always, she wanted me to help her with the garden, the chickens, the housework. I was eager to get to school, and just wanted to know if I had got into the choir.

'I doubt you'll get in with your croaky voice,' said Barbara, as we hung out the washing. 'They want proper singers. You can't hold a tune.'

I didn't think she would know if I could or not, as I'd never sung anything with her; she wasn't interested in music. But I said nothing, and just hung up Ian's discoloured underpants and her grey underwear in silence. I was then put to weeding the vegetable patch. Later I heard Barbara's voice wafting through the kitchen window out over the lawn – she must be on the phone: 'Oh dear, she will be disappointed.'

She came out and stood over me, looking grim. 'That was the school,' she said. 'They said you're totally tone deaf and you are not in the choir.'

I hadn't heard the phone ring but I was devastated. I felt so ashamed. I must have been horrendous as a singer. I felt such a failure and tears filled my eyes and fell on the hard ground as I pulled out weed after weed. I felt angry with Janet – how could she put me up for something so embarrassing? I was as useless as ever. I felt ashamed, hurt and desolate, as my world had suddenly collapsed. Yet again.

I was off school for two weeks then. Barbara kept me home to do housework and I didn't care, as I wasn't in the choir. I had imagined singing in a little group round the piano next to Janet, smiling. Or being in musicals and concerts. And now I was outcast, yet again. Not good enough. I didn't want to go to school now, as I felt so embarrassed. I had humiliated myself in front of people. Even in front of the jolly dinner ladies, who were often nice to me and gave me extra food. I went back to school with my eyes firmly down on the pavement. I didn't want to see anybody, and I didn't want to talk to Janet. I stayed very quiet and hidden in the back of the class.

That lunchtime I passed Mrs Isaacs in the corridor and she stopped right in front of me. I held my breath and wanted to disappear.

'Hello, Louise,' she said warmly. 'Are you coming on Thursday?'

I blinked up at her, confused. 'You got in, you know,' she said.

My heart leapt. I didn't know what to say. How had Barbara got it so wrong? That evening I told Barbara my news.

'Well, you can think again,' she said. 'I'm not picking you up late. Don't be stupid. You're not going to choir. They just took pity on you, that's all.'

So, on Thursday, I really wanted to go to choir but I didn't think I could. How could I explain it to Barbara? After school

I hovered outside the music room, listening to them warming up, and then I realised: if Barbara came to the school to get me she would pull me out of choir in front of everyone and make up some story. So I went outside to the playground and just waited for her. She was late, as usual. I missed choir, and also the chance to attend.

'I told you, you weren't going,' she said when she picked me up, finally. 'They said you sounded terrible. You must have got it all wrong.'

And that was the end of that. I was very unhappy after this. Although I'd had the experience of the dinner ladies cheering me, Janet whooping and Mrs Isaacs telling me I had got in, I missed choir and all the fun that went with it. I had a real complex then about my voice. I was sure I couldn't sing very well, as Barbara continued to tell me I was terrible. It was hard to hang onto the good things when I was told all the time how bad I was.

❦

As compensation for feeling terrible, or when I had been very badly beaten or punched, or left in my room all day, I would find a way to sneak down and have a swig of cherry brandy. It would help take the pain away. It reminded me of the good times with William, too, when I was not alone. Disappointment and punishment always made me want to have another drink, and another, and I got very clever at disguising the bottles and myself after drinking. It was my quiet act of rebellion, but it was also an act of survival.

Around this time there was a family wedding on Ian's side (it was a rare event to go anywhere, especially with family). I wanted to be a bridesmaid in a pretty new dress, but Barbara put paid to that: 'Why would anyone spend money on you? Have you looked at yourself? Anyway, you're not real family. You're not blood.'

So at the wedding I spent my time going round all the tables and slurping the leftover drinks. When the adults weren't looking, or were doing something else, I would sneak their leftover champagne and get under the table and drink it. I got very squiffy at that wedding. It was a lovely feeling. I felt warm, muzzy and fuzzy, loose, and it felt like nothing mattered to me now. I felt free. I loved it. But I was always careful to stop. I never went too far, as I knew I couldn't give the game away. Nobody noticed. Or if they did they didn't say anything, either to Barbara or me.

I was very careful how I did it in my usual very secretive way. I watched the adults carefully, noticing when they were chatting to or laughing with others, or turned away, and then I saw my chance. I was usually aware of when I had Barbara's gimlet eye on me, and then I was a perfect little girl, being quiet and orderly. I knew if she got wind of me supping the drinks I would have been punched not only into next week, but into next year and beyond.

After the disappointment of the choir and the bridesmaid dress and all the usual punishments, I wrote a letter to one of the social workers saying how unhappy I was at home. I found an official letter on the kitchen table and copied down the address and name. I wrote and told them, in my awful English, about how miserable I was. I drew a picture of a little house with no door and a girl trapped at the window that showed how I felt. I hoped that someone would come to the house and talk to me, see the truth and rescue me. Surely someone would visit and I could tell them how horrible everything really was at home?

I waited and waited but no one came. I carried on going to school some days, and then being kept home out of the blue by Barbara for days and weeks at a time. When the social workers did come round, I was kept away from them in another room. So I didn't know if they ever got my letter. At school I was always falling behind and trying to catch up, and feeling very stupid as a consequence. There seemed to be nobody to talk to except for dear old Sean, so I would pop round to see him and have milk and biscuits, or bread and cheese, whenever I could. He would always make me feel just that little bit better about things. Just for a while. He was really the only thing that kept me going.

12

A Dog's Life

We always had dogs and cats. Barbara was keen on particular breeds of dog, such as Poodles, Shih Tzus and Tibetan Terriers, although she often got crossbreeds as well as pedigrees. She liked driving around the countryside to find puppies, and sometimes chickens. She scoured the papers for special offers and sometimes we went to see breeders and farms, as she was very particular about what she bought. Barbara always liked babies, puppies and kittens, as well as chicks. Just like her weird doll collection, which she adored, she liked things that were small and helpless but hated them the minute they got a bit bigger and had a mind of their own.

During my early years we had many dogs, but they never seemed to live very long. There was Rover, Topsy, Spot, Milo, Misty, Scruff, Kizzy and so on. She often had high-maintenance dogs with topknots and ponytails or special coats. She would buy expensive brushes and shampoos, little coats and leads. She probably spent more on the dogs than she ever spent on me. She would take them for training, and then lose interest halfway through. Typically she was keen for a while, when they were tiny, and would carry them around like babies, put them on her lap and dote on them all the time. Then suddenly she would lose interest. Something would trigger her off. After that she would be very rough and tough with them. She would pull them this way and that on their choker leads till they bled, like poor old Topsy, or she would smack and kick them, and even starve them, just like me. They were always being punished for something. And then they were gone and the doggie cycle would start all over again.

When I was about ten, going on eleven, she had Spot – a white Jack Russell with a black spot over one eye – who came after Topsy, who had died very suddenly. He was still only a puppy and keen on biting shoes and slippers, like all puppies do. I thought he was really cute, if a bit yappy. He had nice brown eyes, sticky-up ears and white fur. I liked stroking him and he wagged his tail with a lot of energy and affection.

Barbara nearly always got into a really black mood on Sundays. Everyone kept out of the way and Ian hid in the garage, as usual. She was angry and resentful about cooking and let everyone know it. As I got older I offered to help but she wanted to keep me out. 'You'll only mess things up,' she said.

This particular Sunday she was in a blinding rage. I had no idea what was the matter with her. We were all treading round her like she was a hand grenade. She was in the middle of preparing the food when, all of a sudden, things started flying out into the garden, like they often did. I could hear her saying, 'I'm bloody well fed up with all this,' and, 'I hate my life,' as I heard chopping sounds.

Then I saw a saucepan fly out the back, followed by a cauli-flower, then a plate and some cutlery. It might have been funny if she hadn't been so scary. I was by the chickens and kept a low profile, as I didn't want to be in the firing line. The gun might come out next, as she kept it in a kitchen cupboard. I never knew what she might do: she was completely out of control. However, this morning things were flying everywhere and I could hear 'bugger this, bugger that' coming from the kitchen.

All of a sudden I saw something white fly at speed in an arc out of the kitchen and land with a loud crack on the path. Was it another cauliflower or pan? Loud yelping followed. I was hovering by the chickens, watching the drama unfold, when I realised that the last missile had been Spot the puppy. *Oh no!* I ran over as fast as I could and he was lying on his side at a funny angle, his tongue lolling out. He was still breathing but he was winded, sort of panting and whining very badly. He couldn't seem to move.

Barbara came beetling out of the kitchen. 'What's wrong with the bloody dog?' she spat. She didn't realise I'd seen her throw him. I looked at her wide-eyed and the dog was still moaning and whimpering. I scooped him up carefully, and by now Ian had appeared and was watching the scene from a safe distance.

'Stupid dog's sick,' said Barbara, storming past Ian and into the kitchen through the back door. Ian stood looking like he had no idea what to do. Barbara then appeared with her handbag and anorak and the puppy was wrapped in a towel and taken to the local vet.

Once they'd gone I went to sit with Sean to avoid being in the house alone with Kevin. I poured out what had happened. Sean sat smoking calmly and shook his head sadly, stroking Frida all the while. I cried and cried, thinking, *She could throw me out the door just like poor Spot. How could she do that? The poor little pup.*

A while later I heard the kitchen door open – Barbara and Ian were back. I ran through the orchard and went to the house, looking for Spot. He was gone. Ian whispered he'd had to be put down. I ran upstairs and got into bed, grabbed Tony, my broken panda, and sobbed my heart out for the defenceless little pup. I heard later that the story Barbara told the vet was the puppy had had 'an accident'. I overheard Ian telling Kevin on the landing that she'd told the vet Spot had run into the road, in front of a passing car. How could she do that? What a lie! It was all wrong. It was sick. Not only was she lying but I had seen her throw poor Spot like a doggie rugby ball. I had actually heard something snap. It was awful.

Afterwards I kept replaying it in my head. Then I remembered that years before I'd seen her swilling water around in her famous metal bucket by the outdoor tap, and when I looked in there was a whole load of drowned tabby kittens. Their dead bodies ended up in the dustbin like vegetable peelings.

I was inconsolable about Spot. He wasn't my dog but the way he'd died had upset me deeply. I felt I should have been able to save him. The following week I was sitting in uncomfortable silence in the car with Barbara as we were going to pick up Kevin from his Saturday job. He was now sixteen, whereas I was eleven going on twelve, and he had a job in a builder's yard. I didn't want to go on this trip, but Barbara never liked leaving me in the house alone. She told me to my face that she didn't trust me not to steal something. She still referred to the ring episode, as if I had actually stolen it. She never forgave and she never forgot, whether it was a true incident or not. Whatever happened I was always in the wrong.

This day I just looked out the window and counted: sheep, cows, hedges, trees, clouds — anything to pass the time on the journey. I loved looking at nature; I found it soothing. And being with Barbara in the car was such a hell-ride, as she always drove too fast along the country lanes, swearing at everybody, that I would spend the time pressing my thumbs and fingers together, counting nice things out of the window and hoping we would get there alive.

When we got to the builder's yard, we went into a white Portakabin to fetch Kevin. He was still finishing up, so Barbara spoke to the friendly woman behind the desk. The company was run by a friend of Ian's from work, which was how Kevin had got the Saturday job. Kevin was still at school and becoming bigger and more difficult for me to deal with by the day. I avoided him at all cost. He was still kicking and punching me, trying to touch my breasts or look at my private parts, teasing and bullying me, so I wasn't keen to be picking him up after work. I hated being anywhere near him; he was such a brute.

By now his lorry driver father, Sid, had moved in with another woman in a neighbouring village. Kevin had been furious and refused to see his dad or accept the situation. She had children of her own and he refused to visit. Kevin seemed to take out all his anger on me, with Barbara's permission. I hated being with them when they were together.

Luckily, in the corner of the Portakabin, there was a big wicker dog basket, and in it a lovely black Labrador spread out on old blankets, suckling a litter of six pups. I went and sat next to the dog and stroked her fine head. She was like Sean's lovely Frida. The warm, friendly woman in the office, Joan, came over and talked to me.

'They're eight weeks old,' she said to me. I loved looking at their furry bodies, all round and cute, with their tiny paws and soft eyes, as they piled up on each other, fighting for a nipple. Just then one little one came bowling over and sniffed my hand.

'Looks like you've found a friend,' Joan said kindly.

I picked up the little ball of warm fluff and she sat in my hand, sniffling and snuffling. Barbara came over to see what was going on.

'Your girl looks like she's found a new friend,' Joan said to Barbara, who said nothing. 'She can have her if she wants,' she added, with a big smile. My heart leapt but I said nothing. I didn't dare.

However, somehow, by the time we left, a deal was done and I was to take the puppy home. Maybe Barbara saw it as a cheap replacement for Spot. I had been so upset all week, and she had shouted at me to 'get over it' the whole time. Perhaps she was trying to shut me up. Anyway, the little ball of black fluff was to be my own puppy. Not Barbara's – mine. I couldn't believe it. It was true we had no dog at the moment, after Spot's terrible end. And it was also true that I usually did a lot of dog care. I was used to feeding them or taking them for walks, grooming them or giving them their Choc Drops. I decided to call the pup 'Blue', as her lovely black hair had a bluish sheen, rather like my own.

'Stupid bloody name,' snarled Barbara, but I stuck to my decision. Blue it would be. Blue very quickly became my new best friend, my companion, the centre of my life. I looked after her with love and devotion. Barbara told me that as I was so useless I would have to do more housework to cover the cost of Blue's injections and food. I had to clip hedges in the garden, cut the lawn, clean out the dustbins, strip and make the beds with crisp hospital corners, do even more dusting and vacuuming than usual. This was to 'pay' for Blue's upkeep. I didn't care. Blue was my own little puppy, and I was going to treat her right.

One day I was stripping Kevin's bed and I noticed a big dark stain the middle of the sheet. I opened the window to let in fresh air and then I went back to the stain and looked at it. Was he wetting his bed? At sixteen? Barbara came in and found me staring at the patch. She leant over the bed, touched the stain with two fingers, brought them to her nose and sniffed.

'Wet dream,' she said, and laughed oddly. I had no idea what she meant. 'He was probably thinking about you,' she laughed again – a real menacing laugh. I still didn't get what she meant. Why would thinking about me make the bed wet? But an icy feeling shot through my veins. I felt very unsafe and scared as Barbara was looking at me with a strange eagle-eyed look. I just pulled the disgusting sheet off the bed, pretended to not hear and carried on working.

I had seen Barbara sniff things very strangely before. She'd had some female neighbours round one time, and when they left she did the most peculiar thing. There were little sponge seats on the kitchen chairs that were covered with material and tied to the back of the chair. Barbara bent over and sniffed the seats and then stood up and said, 'Wee. These seats smell of pee.' She pulled the sponge seats off the chairs and stripped off the material covers and threw them in the washing machine.

'Dirty bitches,' she snapped. 'Smelling of wee. They don't wipe themselves properly.'

She often had all sorts of strange things to say about bodily functions, and was constantly commenting on the state of people's underpants and ability to wipe themselves. I felt embarrassed that she was saying such a thing about the neighbours. I was glad they came, as it meant there was a fresh supply of biscuits I could try and filch when the coast was clear. It was also ironic that she restricted my washing myself, which, as I was growing, was becoming more and more urgent. Did she want me to smell?

Kevin was allowed to wash as much as he liked but he still stank disgustingly, despite using oceans of Right Guard on his stinking armpits. Barbara was often hinting to me that Kevin would find me attractive and this was becoming a pressing problem, as he stole into my room or followed me round the garden and tried to touch my body as often as he could. I had to fight him off on more than one occasion. It was a constant battle to keep myself away from his nasty grabbing hands.

Once Blue was big enough, I started taking her for walks every day. I loved doing it: it meant some freedom from the house and I could walk along the lanes, look at the sky and trees, see some cows, sheep or other dogs and smile at people as they passed. I had a game at the time of packing a small red child's suitcase that I'd had in my room since babyhood. I'd walk around my room and the landing, pretending I was leaving home. When I took beautiful Blue for a walk I began to get a sense that there was a whole world out there beyond the confines of our horrible house, my prison.

I would glimpse into people's living rooms or peek inside doorways to see what real family life was like. I would see TVs on and a family sitting on a sofa, smiling. Or people just talking to each other, laughing and eating. There were people out in gardens together, cutting hedges or snipping the roses and co-operating nicely with each other.

People strolled past holding hands or even kissing each other in public. There were young girls whizzing past on roller-skates and small boys on bicycles with training wheels. There were older boys with jeans on, being cool on skateboards. I began to see that people went out and did nice things together, and I began to smell some kind of possible freedom in the future. I wanted what they all seemed to have: a normal life.

I just had to be careful what I did right now. I somehow knew that getting to school was important. So far my education had been patchy at best. I'd had so much time off that I was always way behind and unable to catch up. Art was the only subject I shone in and, deep inside, the idea had already formed after the Tate trip that this was going to be my future. Somehow. I just had no idea what the stepping stones towards it would be. But I knew I would find them one day. I also know I'd have a fight on my hands every inch of the way.

Meanwhile I appeased Barbara and tried to be a 'good girl' as much as I could. Keeping the peace, staying quiet, taking my punishments and being as secretive as I could be about scavenging things was my way of life. Dutifully I got up at six every day to take Blue down the back lane by the school. I loved these early-morning walks. She did too. I would get to University Parks, a big area, and let her off the lead. She would gallop off happily and I would throw sticks for her to catch. She'd bring them back, panting, pleased with herself, all drooly, wagging her tail and I'd say, 'There's a good girl,' and pat her and give her loads of hugs and cuddles. We were both good girls. After school, if I managed to get there, I would take her out again. If I didn't get to school because Barbara kept me home, I would be told to go for the walk before school was out.

I knew she didn't want me to be seen by anybody from school. We never spoke about it, she never spelled it out, but I knew this was the case. Blue wasn't allowed up in my bedroom, although I would have loved her to sleep with me at night. But

I often crept down during the night (I could undo the bed strap now, and also Barbara often left it off, as I was bigger), and I would stroke Blue, lift up her silky ear and talk to her. I'd tell her I loved her. I would give her a kiss on the head and squeeze her lovely soft paw. She was a beauty; she was my world. I knew she loved me and I loved her with all my heart.

One afternoon I was walking Blue along my usual route, down the back lane to the University Parks. I often daydreamed on my walks to the park. The dreams were an extension of my walking around my room with my little case packed. I was still only twelve, but I was beginning to imagine a future life when I would be free. I fantasised as often as possible. I would have a nice place to live, with Blue, of course. I would be painting and drawing all day, with a fridge full of lovely food and drink that I could have whenever I wanted.

Suddenly a man was upon me. I was in a back lane, and there was a tall man with glasses, in jeans and jacket, with wild greasy hair and staring eyes, who had me by the shoulders. He dug his fingers in and pushed me hard and I fell back on the brambles. He was grabbing at my chest and my trousers, trying to lift my T-shirt. I was speechless and terrified. The man had one hand on my chest, pressing me down, and was pulling at my clothes with the other. After the initial shock I started wriggling and kicking. I'd had plenty of experience with Kevin and his horrible friend Mark, who had pulled my clothes off several times now.

I started making a loud noise and suddenly Blue jumped into action. She grabbed the man's wrist with her mouth and bit hard. He yelped, 'Ow, ow, you fucking whore, you bitch,' and tried to swipe at Blue. When he let go of me, I wriggled out from under him. Blue was growling and tugging at his wrist now and the man was clearly in pain. He tugged and pulled his arm out, and I could see it was bleeding, and he turned and ran away as fast as he could.

My wonderful Blue! She was barking after him, but stayed with me. I sat on the floor for a few minutes, my heart racing, totally dishevelled. Blue licked my face and wagged her tail. My trousers were halfway down, my top round my armpits. I straightened myself out, as Blue nuzzled me and leant her body against me. I then hugged her and we sat together by the side of the path for some time, as I tried to make myself calm. Counting, counting, counting. I hoped no one had seen this happen to me as it was so embarrassing. Eventually we walked home very quietly, with me shaking like a leaf. Blue stuck to my side the whole way. I felt like I was in a dream.

When I got back Barbara was taking the washing in. By now the tears had started, and shock had given way to me feeling really shaky. I walked slowly into the garden with Blue and didn't know what to say to Barbara.

'What's wrong with you?' she asked snippily. 'You look a fright.'

I wanted to tell her, wanted her to put her arm around me, and to listen for once. I wanted her to reassure me, to phone the police, to make a fuss. I began to tell her what had happened. I felt really shy and confused but, bit by bit, I managed to get the words out. It was horrible to say what he had done to me. Barbara stared at me with her beady, hawk-like eyes.

'What do you expect when you go out looking like a slut?' she said. 'It's your own bloody fault.' Then she picked up the blue laundry basket and walked away, back into the kitchen.

I went into the orchard with Blue, sat behind a tree and cried my heart out. I felt dirty, hideous, ugly. I couldn't tell Sean either; it was far too shaming. It was clearly all my fault. Maybe I was a slut. Maybe that's why everyone kept grabbing at me. Blue leant against me and I hugged her warm body and stroked her fur; she was all I had at that moment. She understood, as she'd been there. She'd saved my life. However, next morning, same as always, I had to do the early-morning walk with the dog. I took Blue out on the very same route. Even so, I was scared to death. When I got to the place where the wild man had pushed me in the bushes, I burst into tears and felt sick. But I got through it somehow and shook all the way home. I thought the worst was over, but I was wrong.

When I got back and had my little bit of breakfast, Barbara said, 'You'd better go to school today, it'll do you good.'

My heart lifted. I thought, *Wow, she's actually thinking about me.* Barbara didn't say anything about the incident with the man, and I did wonder why she didn't call the police. She was ready to call the police if I did something wrong, so why not now, when someone did something really bad to me? I'd been taken to the police station to 'teach me a lesson' more than once, so why not report a man who actually attacked me in a public place?

The thing is, with Barbara there was never any logic or reason. She would do exactly what she wanted when she wanted and it was often one thing one day, and another the next. However, it was actually good to go to school even though I'd missed about another two weeks. I was way behind in everything and felt despair that I would never catch up. I didn't tell anyone about the University Parks man. I tried to push it to the back of my mind where I put all the other horrible things that had happened.

I still felt sick and shaky but, as the day wore on, I realised that being at school had been a good idea. Maybe Barbara actually cared about me after all. When I got home I rushed in to find Blue. I wanted to tell her about my day. Oddly, she wasn't to be seen. I ran around the garden, looked in the orchard; maybe she was locked in the shed. I couldn't find her. Eventually I ran into the kitchen where Barbara was at the sink, rinsing soap off some mugs.

'Where's Blue?' I asked breathlessly. Panic was rising. 'I can't find Blue,' I said, tears starting. 'Where is she?'

'She's gone,' Barbara said coldly, 'and that's the end of it.'

'What do you mean, gone?' I nearly screamed. 'Where is she?' I was losing control.

'I took her to the vet,' said Barbara, still rinsing. 'She's dead.'

My knees gave way and I fell on the floor in a heap and howled.

'Stop that,' shouted Barbara. 'Shut up, you little bitch. Go to your room.'

I was beside myself. I couldn't compute what was going on. Or why. Why would she do this to my wonderful dog? Blue was fine, she was healthy and young. I trudged up the stairs and threw myself on the bed. I sobbed and sobbed and couldn't stop. Whatever happened, there was always something worse just around the corner. I cried for days and spent time in bed, not getting up, staring at the ceiling, sobbing into my pillow. I didn't want to get up or go to school and that suited Barbara fine. I was forced to do chores, which I did through clenched teeth. I wouldn't look at her. I didn't speak. There was a giant dog-shaped hole where Blue should have been.

꙾

A few days later Barbara had a couple of women from the village round for coffee. Numb and exhausted, I crept out of my room and sat at the top of the stairs listening to them. If Barbara caught me there'd be hell to pay, but today I didn't care. I was totally heartbroken. I listened to the women talking, as the living room door was half-open, and I heard Barbara explaining I was home as I was getting over the shock of being attacked in the park. I heard her say, 'Yes, we've all known about that man in the Parks for weeks now, and sadly he struck my poor Louise.'

I stopped breathing. So Barbara had known there was a man in the Parks who was a problem – and yet she let me wander about on my own with poor Blue. She never warned me, or came with me. I heard the other women say it had been in the paper for weeks that women shouldn't go out in the area alone. Yet I'd been blamed for being a 'slut' and told it was my fault. Worse, my darling Blue had been destroyed in the process. Why? What had she done wrong? She had paid the ultimate price – but for what? Saving me? Maybe saving me is why she'd lost her life.

I knew then that I really wasn't safe; my life was one long punishment. I didn't know what it was I'd done that was so bad to make my life such a living hell. But I knew then that I would have to leave this house, to find a way out, to find some safety and care as soon as I was big enough to go, or I would end up being destroyed like Blue. One of Barbara's favourite phrases was 'I will kill you one day', and I feared she would actually do this. What I didn't know was that for years she had been working on a plan to get rid of me.

13

Nobody's Child

As long as I could remember Barbara would say really rude things about my birth mother. She didn't have a name for her, as such. I had no real information about her, or who my family actually was. It was all shrouded in mystery. All I knew for definite, because Barbara had told me so many times, was that she was a 'whore' and a 'stupid bitch'. I would be swiped by her hand, or kicked by her foot, spat at and told I was a 'stupid bitch, just like your mother.' So the picture I had in my head was of a terrible person, like a witch, who I was just like. Or some awful floozy woman in terrible clothes – was I like that too? I simply had no proper, hard information about where on earth I came from or how I ended up living with Barbara and Ian (and the really horrible Kevin – who was a permanent fixture in our house now because he hated his dad).

As I grew older, Barbara began to change her tune about my mother, a bit. I didn't believe this because I knew she had thrown me away. But when I was about nine years old, Barbara had begun to tell me that my mother missed me, or wanted me back. How did she know? Was it true? I had no letter from her telling me that it had broken her heart to give me away and that she was sorry. I had no picture of her, and no idea what colour her hair was or where she came from. I had no picture of her family, her town, her house. Did she have other children? Was she married? I couldn't ask Barbara any of these questions. And then there was the confusing issue of me being painted with the 'tar brush' and being an 'oily Jew', as Barbara threw at me, over and over. How was that? If that was so, where were they? And where was my father? Why wasn't he with my mother? Were they married? Had he died? Why didn't he want me either? I had an endless list of questions and nobody to answer them for me.

When I was alone at night, or wandering round the garden, I wondered if Barbara had ever met my mother. What I did know was that Barbara was always late picking me up from school wherever I was, and I heard one day that she'd been off driving quite a distance. What I didn't know then, and only found out later, was that from when I was really very small Barbara was on a personal mission to give me back to my birth family. She did a lot of hunting down of my real family members without talking to the social workers or going through the proper channels. She wanted to be rid of me. She had also done the same with William, I found out much later. She had actually gone and located his grandparents and tried to give him back. It didn't work, and he ended up in care, as nobody wanted him.

During this time I wondered about Rene and Fred, the two old people she'd driven to when the male social worker tried to touch me and took me away to strange foster parents for a few days. I found out much later that these were actually my mother's parents. So I'd met my grandparents without knowing it was them. But they didn't want to know me either, so they sent me away. Yet another rejection. I didn't know at the time what was going on, but Barbara had developed a plan to find my birth mother so she could give me back.

It was Barbara who wanted to throw me away. Just as she had William. And our dogs. She often threatened me with: 'I'll send you back where you came from' and I eventually realised she actually meant it. Naturally she had no idea whether my birth mother – when and if she found her – would have any real interest in taking me on. I had no idea about this until one Saturday morning when I was twelve, Barbara barked at me: 'Go and get a dress on and get in the car. Your mother wants to meet you.'

I was feeding the chickens, pulling old straw out of the hen's boxes, and what she said set my heart racing. I stopped and looked up at her, stunned.

'Finish that now. Get ready and be quick about it.'

I threw clean straw around all my clucky hens, feeling sick. Was she coming here? Obviously not, as we were going somewhere. Why was she coming? Was she going to be alone or with my father? Chickens done, I raced upstairs and threw on my one and only 'best' dress, which was a horrible brown flowery affair, a Barbara cut-down. I put on my only Clarks bar shoes, brown ones with grubby white socks with my big toe poking out of a hole. I pulled a comb through my pageboy haircut. Looking in the mirror I could see that my eyebrows had been plucked to non-existence on the right side of my face and that my eyelashes were almost gone. I had blue eyes and a button nose and a very serious expression.

I had recently started my periods, and I had little bumps growing tightly under my dress, which I felt very self-conscious about.

I hadn't got a bra although all the girls at school were sporting cute little Berlei ones with pink roses and white bows. My little breasts were hovering under a frayed white vest. In fact the coming of my periods had brought with it even more humiliation from Barbara, who would openly discuss me being 'on', or would say, 'It's Louise's time of the month,' in front of Ian and Kevin.

There was no privacy or sensitivity coming my way. She also gave me a hideous contraption, a big piece of elastic that went around my waist, which had a huge sanitary towel clipped onto it, back and front. This was bulky, awkward and smelly. As washing and soap was still rationed as far as I was concerned, I often had spills of blood on my underpants and clothes, which then required soaking in soda and scrubbing with a brush (which I did, of course). Barbara would sniff at my garments and mumble 'filthy little bitch' when I produced them for the wash. It wasn't my fault. The other girls at school had nice pads or even Tampax, but I wasn't allowed any of that – 'waste of money' – so I had these huge old lady pads and had to deal with the embarrassing fallout (literally).

Luckily, on this day I was to meet my mother, I didn't have my period. But I did have a migraine. I had started having killer headaches about a year earlier and now they came at regular intervals. It felt as if half my head had been chopped at with an axe. I was nauseous with black and white vision and swirling lights in my eyes. I often got the headaches around the time of my period, but also when Barbara was in a particularly shouty mood. I clenched my teeth, tensed up and would curl up in a ball and wait for the sickness and headache to go away. Now, today, I was going to meet my mother with my temples pounding and my stomach swirling with nausea. I knew better than to ask

Barbara for anything, so I snuck to the bathroom cupboard and swallowed a couple of green pills, knowing they might make my head feel a bit more like cotton wool.

We drove for hours. Barbara had a new dog now, Mimi, a white poodle who was thrown in the back. I sat in the front feeling sick most of the way, and in fact I had to jump out the car and throw up outside of Oxford, before we got on the motorway.

'Hurry up about it,' snapped Barbara. 'She won't wait all day for you.' And then she added, as a sweetener, 'She really wants to meet you.'

How did she know that? Had my mother said anything? Did Barbara know her? All the way I stared fixedly out of the window. All my life I had wondered who my birth mother might be: was she a famous ballerina? Or had she been a glamorous pop singer and not allowed to keep her baby? I imagined someone like my old friend Maisie's mum, who was warm and kind and wore long, floaty clothes.

There were many 'hippy' mums at my school, wearing gypsy print blouses and long swishing skirts. They always wore beads, bracelets and earrings and put henna on their hair. The thing I noticed was how much they loved colour. They were 'rainbow' mums, so different from the steely grey Barbara, who wore clothes like a prison warder: black or grey polyester skirt, grey jumper, grey anorak, sensible grey, black or brown shoes. She looked old, grizzled, plain.

I imagined my real mum to have flowing black hair, like mine, especially if she was Jewish, like me. Maybe she was like Mary in Peter, Paul and Mary, the singers, with nice long hair and a sweet face. Maybe she was like Joni Mitchell, singing 'Both Sides Now' with blonde locks and high cheekbones.

As the houses gave way to fields, then to endless roads, then to more houses, now mostly built in grey stone, I realised we had driven for nearly two hours. We were in a place called Swindon, which looked somewhat nondescript. I had heard the name, but had never been there. We drove through the town and out the other side.

The whole journey Barbara and I were silent. I just needed to keep myself quiet, with my thumping headache, looking out at the trees, the passing houses, the clouds, the other cars. Occasionally I would feel sick or nervous and I would put my dipper finger along my eyelid, find a little bit of stubble and pull. It hurt, but it was somehow satisfying. Then I would do it again, and again. And then I'd tell myself to stop – I didn't want my real mother to think I had no eyelashes.

We eventually drew up to a house that had fields all around it. It was quite a flashy big house with a gravel drive in front, and two shiny new cars. Barbara got out and pulled poor Mimi roughly off the back seat.

'Get out,' she snapped at me.

I opened the door and unfolded myself on the gravel. I stood there feeling completely dazed. Barbara was already crunching up the drive, so I followed. She rang the doorbell and we stood for ages, my heart thumping. I was about to meet my real mother for the first time! Would she sweep me into her arms and give me the biggest hug ever? Would she kneel down and weep and say how sorry she was for abandoning me? What would she look like? Would she show me to my new bedroom and ask me to live with her for ever?

Then the door opened to reveal a small, round woman with platinum blonde hair.

'Oh,' she said in a high-pitched voice like a cartoon character, looking extremely uncomfortable. 'Oh, it's you!'

'Hello,' said Barbara, trying to be charming. 'Yes, we got here in the end.'

'Oh… oh, yes,' the woman said awkwardly. Barbara turned to me and pushed me forward.

'This is Louise,' she said, as if handing over a parcel on the doorstep.

I saw a plump woman with a slightly blurred face and shocking pink lipstick. She went red and became flustered.

'Oh dear, oh yes, well, oh, um, er, you'd better come in.'

We followed the woman round the side of the house and into a back garden. There was a long lawn surrounded by plants with big trees at the end. In front of the lawn, just at the back of the house, was a stone patio and on it a table around which sat many people eating, drinking and chatting loudly. When we came in they all stopped and looked up. I wanted to disappear.

My 'real mother' was very panicky. She clearly didn't know what to say or how to introduce us and was flapping her arms in the air.

'This is… er… this is… er… Louise,' she said to the gathering, pointing to me. No mention of 'daughter'. 'And this is Barbara, her, her… mother.'

Barbara stood there looking grim, keeping a firm grip on Mimi. The people round the table looked confused, then nodded. Some said 'Hello', and then they all went back to eating and talking. I stood between the two women, looking up, feeling completely overwhelmed.

'I'll be back later then,' Barbara was saying to this strange woman, and I suddenly panicked. Was she going to dump me?

Do one of her driving off and leaving me tricks that she had done so many times?

I felt panic rising. As much as I hated living with Barbara, it was all I knew. It was 'home' after all, even if it was horrible. Was I going to be dropped here and left with these complete strangers who clearly didn't want me? And whom I didn't know?

Barbara said nothing to me and just whisked Mimi up the steps and through the house and out. I stood on the patio and wanted to cry. I bit my lip. The strange, over-made-up woman stood next to me in her pink trousers and flouncy top with ruffles and loads of beads and looked very awkward. She then bent towards me.

'Call me Julie,' she whispered, trying to smile. I smelt a waft of sweet flowery perfume and looked at her, wide-eyed. It was a high-pitched giggle, like a little girl. I felt very uncomfortable, and still said nothing. Then she said, 'Your mother told me you've been asking to meet me for months – but I didn't know you were coming today.'

I tried to take this in. I hadn't said a word to Barbara. I never said anything to her about my real mother – I was just told all the time she was a 'slut' and a 'whore'. I looked at her hair: it was dyed so platinum it looked like dolls' hair. No sign of the dark locks or shiny bluish black hair that I had. Julie looked at the people around the table and decided to do something – she took me by the hand and introduced me as 'Louise' and 'a friend'. She told me all their names. They said 'Hi' one by one, and then went back to eating. So I was a 'friend', not her daughter?

She found me a chair, sat me down and put some things on a plate, like a sausage roll and some crisps, and left me to it. I wasn't hungry – for once. I just sat tight-lipped and watched all these people chattering away to each other. I wanted to die. I felt totally out of place. I knew I looked grubby while all of them had nice trendy clothes on. They were laughing, smiling, happy. There were two younger people there, in cool clothes, and Julie moved over and chatted to them, putting her hands on their shoulders and touching their hair. I worked out after a while that they were connected to her – were they her children? Then I realised the big man at the party – tall with silver hair – must be her husband, as he kept touching her on the shoulder and asking her things.

As I watched, a whole scene unfolded of a family life I knew nothing about. I felt like an alien who had landed on the lawn and been taken in and given a sausage roll. I couldn't eat it. I just sat and wanted to cry. Eventually the man who was with Julie came and sat next to me.

'Hi, Louise,' he said. 'How are you doing? I'm Brian.'

I couldn't say anything. I just burst into tears. After a bit he went away and I just sat by myself in silence, digging my nails into my palms, willing myself to disappear. I waited all afternoon for her to take me aside and say, 'Hi, I'm your real mum' or 'Tell me all about yourself', but instead she just kept saying, 'Call me Julie,' and doing her high-pitched giggle. I watched her shaking her bracelets, tossing her hair, flirting with all the men. Nobody knew who I was or why I was there. Nobody cared, and definitely nobody wanted me.

Barbara arrived in the early evening and we made our awkward goodbyes. We drove in silence most of the way back. I realised that Barbara had somehow found out there was to be a party at Julie's house and had taken it upon herself to get there – she had crashed the party on a whim. I shut my eyes and a vision of Julie in pink floated up. Was she a 'slut' and a 'whore' as I had been told my whole life? Barbara made no attempt to explain anything, and I was too crushed and distressed to ask. I just looked out at the sky and watched the clouds change shape and disappear behind trees, houses and hoardings.

Why had Barbara told Julie I wanted to see her? There was I thinking that Julie wanted to see me when she so obviously didn't. I longed to see Sean so I could tell him what had happened and try and make sense of it all. If this was my real mother, did she want me? It didn't feel like it. She hadn't told anyone who I was, so no one welcomed me into the family. Was that going to happen later? Who were all those people? Was Brian my father? Were they Jewish? I was none the wiser, and much more confused than I'd ever been before we went. It seemed I really was nobody's child. So nobody would help me with what was to come.

14

From Bad to Worse

Things got worse after this trip to Julie's house. I didn't dare ask Barbara anything about her or what would happen next. I really wanted to know – would I see her again? Would I become part of her family? Would we visit or would she come and see us? In my memory the colourful party assumed the status of a dream, and Julie's world was one of laughter and smiling people, nice clothes and plentiful food. I decided that she had been so surprised to see me that she wasn't quite ready to welcome me into her life, but that would surely happen sometime soon.

In the meantime, Barbara was in a fury, stomping about, banging doors, snapping at everyone. She picked up her air gun once or twice and aimed at pigeons in the garden – I hid in the shed until it was over. Then her new game became darts and she bought a dartboard, which she hung on the end of the airing cupboard on the landing outside my room. If the mood took her she would come up to the landing and throw the darts from one end to the other, and they would land with a thud on the board. If I was in my room I had to hang back until she had finished. I didn't dare go out and get caught in the crossfire. Barbara wouldn't stop for me to come out and go down the stairs; she'd made that clear. She would make an animal-like grunting sound as she threw the dart, and she had a lot of strength for a small wiry woman.

One day I really wanted the toilet and I started coming upstairs from the hall. Barbara was on the landing playing darts and I waited for her to throw them all. I asked politely, as always, if I could come up and go to the toilet.

'Have you finished the washing up?' is all she said in reply, as she pulled the darts off the board. I answered yes, and then started walking past her, to the toilet. I didn't make eye contact with her, as I knew it was safer to keep my head down and look at the floor. Making eye contact could lead to accusations of 'rude bitch' or 'what are you looking at me like that for?' So I kept my head down and scuttled past. However, just as I got to the door to turn the handle, I felt a sharp pain in my back. I shrieked and turned around. Barbara was standing at the top of the stairs, two darts still in her hand. Suddenly a dart dropped out of my back and fell at my heels.

'Pick it up,' she snapped at me. 'Give it to me.'

My back was throbbing. I gave her the dart, shaking, and then scurried to the toilet. Afterwards, in the bathroom, I took off my top and I could see blood oozing out of a hole beneath my right shoulder blade. It was painful and sore, but what hurt more was the cold, calculating way she threw the dart to hit me in the back. When I left the bathroom she was gone. I hung around for a while, not knowing what to do. Then, when I went downstairs, she was in the kitchen crashing about and nothing was mentioned about the dart. She didn't even look at me, pretending that nothing had actually happened. I knew better than to say anything. Inside I was quivering with fear and worried what she might do to me next. The next day, Kevin and Mark were playing darts on the landing and I heard her say, 'Be careful, or you will hurt someone – I don't want to be driving up the hospital.' I, on the other hand, was fair game for target practice.

❧

I was soon going to move up from middle school to secondary school, which I felt very nervous about. I had enjoyed quite a lot about middle school, although I was still way behind in my education. Barbara had kept me home for so many days and weeks that I was forever trying to catch up. I had huge holes in my knowledge, especially of maths, geography, history, science and English, as I was always dipping in and out of class, and not able to follow what was going on.

Art was still my favourite lesson, and I longed for the hours in the week where I was free to make lovely pictures on clean white paper with charcoal or pencils, ink or paint. I was good with my hands and loved making collages or cutting out shapes, or sewing or using clay or even plasticine – anything where I had to use all sorts of materials and let my imagination roam free. I loved colour, and the paint and materials brought a huge amount of joy and happiness into my life – which seemed to be mainly grey and beige the rest of the time.

The only really nice times outside of school were when I was sitting in Sean's caravan eating some lovely crunchy bread or a Ruffle bar, with him telling me colourful stories about his life working as a navvy on the railways around Oxford or on building sites. He always had stories to tell, and he might put on some Irish music on his little radio or get out his tin whistle and play. I would sit with him and imagine things as he unravelled his memories. I would look at his cloth caps hanging in a row on the caravan wall, or his crotched cushions in rainbow colours. He loved to laugh and he would tell stories and roar with laughter, and I would laugh too. I didn't always understand the whole story, but it felt warm and safe in the caravan and I loved just to sit with him as he opened a bottle of Guinness and supped.

He would give me a little sip, saying, 'This'll do yer good, girlie, loads of iron in this.' I would take a gulp of the dark brown liquid that tasted like earth, but I liked the fact he shared it with me. He would sing, 'I'll take you home again, Kathleen' in his deep, fruity voice and a tear would come to his eye. But he would smile again after and say, ''T'is lovely,' or ''T'is life,' and I felt calm with him.

I never once felt unsafe with Sean. He would hug me or pat my head and feed me and make me laugh. But I felt a new strange experience with him: respect, care and love. I just dreaded tiptoeing back to the house afterwards and creeping upstairs to my bleak, lonely bedroom.

One day I had a brainwave. If Julie knew I had won the art competition, would she love me then? Would she come and get me? So I wrote to her using the address in Barbara's kitchen notebook.

'Mum does not no abut [sic] this letter – it is secret. I'm not happy… you never come to see me… I can't get on with Mum, can you help me?'

I stole stamps from Barbara's purse, posted the letter and waited. I then wrote to my social worker, also telling her I was unhappy at home. I waited and waited, but in vain. What I found out much later was that Brian, Julie's husband, had already written to the social workers to say that they didn't want anything further to do with me. I didn't know this; all I knew was that my pleas for help were falling on deaf ears.

After this I would spend hours throwing a ball up on the garage roof and waiting for it to roll down so I could catch it – over and over and over. I would be shouted at in the end by Barbara, who would tell me to get on and do something useful. I would go upstairs to my room and watch other people going about their lives, observing my neighbours in the garden with their children, and listening to the sound of children playing or singing, or lawnmowers in action. I would see a mother walking down the road holding hands with her child, chatting. I loved to see this. I wondered what it was like. I tried to push the idea of Julie out of my mind. But I would go back to the summer's day, the garden, the chatting, the people, and wonder what they were doing. What did they think of me? Would I ever call her 'Mum'? Meanwhile, I had to work out how to live with the one I had – who was forever shouting, kicking, hitting, being grumpy and treating me harshly.

The problem for me was I longed to be loved by Barbara, for her to want me and to care for me. But all I got was punishment and hate. I was dependent on her and I needed her, yet all I got from her was violence and put-downs. Now I had met Julie, it was a huge disappointment. I'd been led to believe by Barbara that Julie wanted me. It was very clear she didn't. While Barbara was harsh and strict, Julie seemed silly and uninterested. I found myself imagining being whisked off to a beautiful house to live happily ever after with her, while I knew, deep down, that the longer I waited for a response to my letter, the less likely this was to ever happen. There I was, with two mothers, and neither of them wanted me or cared about me.

I hoped that when I went up to secondary school the bullying would finally stop. It was as if the other kids saw 'kick me' written all over me when I walked into a new school. I still thought about William and wondered where he was. Did he remember me? Was he okay? Was he alive? I was still hungry all the time, still pulling out my eyelashes and still counting to get through the difficult times of the day – and night.

I was desperate to go to a school with people I already knew. There was a comprehensive nearby, which was friendly and near my middle school. I knew it did a lot of arts, drama and music, and the pupils didn't have to wear stiff uniforms. It was famous for having a great mix of boys and girls and nice liberal teachers and parents. I wanted to go there.

However, there had been an incident with a boy that had turned Barbara dead against me being at school with boys. She was always talking rudely about men anyway, and at school I had become friends with a black boy from Africa called Ayo. He was very sweet and gentle, and he taught me African games and dances. He wasn't mean to me and didn't judge or bully me like the others. He smelt differently, too, which I liked. The white boys were often pongy, but he smelt nice when he was sweaty. I was curious about him: he had big brown eyes and lovely skin and he treated me like a friend. We didn't have many black children at our school, and I made a beeline for him. He was also bullied, and we helped each other stay safe.

One day Barbara arrived to pick me up and I was still talking to Ayo. As he said, 'Goodbye, see you tomorrow,' he touched me on the arm. He often did that; it was friendly. Barbara saw him do it and, when I walked home with her that day, with Mimi choking on the lead, she spat out, 'You'll have a black baby, you dirty girl.'

Next day, Barbara went to the headteacher and Ayo was moved out of my class. 'You will not speak to him again,' she shouted at me that evening. 'You are not to sit next to him in class.'

I felt terrible: he was a sweet, kind person, my only proper friend, and I had got him in trouble. I had got close to someone and Barbara had worked her usual magic and got him removed. I was back to being isolated, back to being shunned and laughed at. I would see Ayo across the playground after this and he would look at me with a sad, blank face. I couldn't go and speak to him in case it was reported or Barbara saw. After all, he and his family had been embarrassed by Barbara and me, so I guessed he wouldn't talk to me either. I wondered if he thought I had told on him to get him into trouble. It broke my heart.

At home, I had to be careful not to mention Ayo's name again. Of course, Barbara never mentioned it, as she pretended that nothing had happened. However, the upshot was that I was now to be sent to a girls-only senior school. My heart sank. I wasn't asked; I had no choice. I didn't want to go there. Barbara filled in the forms and said, 'Like it or lump it.'

It was a longer journey, there was a horrible grey uniform and it was strict. Strict was what Barbara liked. And the lack of boys was what she also loved. I dreaded what the future would hold.

Yet, despite not wanting me to go to a mixed school, or to

talk to boys, Barbara kept dropping hints about me marrying Kevin. He was still refusing to visit his father and Barbara seemed fine with that – she wanted him for herself. I hated him. As I developed my breasts, he got more and more bold with me. He would still punch and kick me whenever he could, and we often wrestled and tussled. I got good at pushing him off, even though he was much bigger and taller than me. He was now seventeen, while I was nearly thirteen. He had a moped, and Barbara kept trying to get me to go on it with him. I didn't want to, but I was forced to get on the back and put my arms around him while he roared off down the road. I hated every minute of it, and didn't want to touch him. I loathed him. When we got back I ran up to my room and hid. I hated being near him. But Barbara had other plans on her mind. One day she came into my room and put a black 'babydoll' nightie on my pillow.

'Put it on, Louise. Kevin would like to see you in it.'

I was horrified. I waited until she left, then I hid the outfit and hoped she would forget about it. Barbara would say things like, 'You could do worse than Kevin. Then you could marry and look after me!'

Clearly she was already brewing a terrible idea for my future: marriage to Kevin. Kevin! The bully who had made my life hell. The boy who had held me down and tried to rip my clothes off. Barbara was aware he hadn't had a proper girlfriend yet, and she saw me as a good training ground. He was constantly looking at me, brushing past me, touching me, leering at me, making comments. Barbara would laugh or turn her back. Ian was nowhere to be seen, as always.

One evening, before going up to the new school, I was in my

room, lying on my tiny bed. I could hear the family having their tea downstairs. Kevin had his horrible friend Mark with him, as he sometimes came to tea. I avoided them both this evening and got out of the kitchen after my usual 'baby' tea, which had never changed. A smell of gravy, meat, potatoes and cabbage wafted up to me. I was thinking about how much I didn't want to go to the high school. I was frightened. I was also still hungry and wondered if, later, I could sneak to the larder and get something. There might be some cold potatoes, or even just some Complan. Something, as my tummy was still rumbling.

❧

I'm drifting off, daydreaming, when the door opens a crack. A head looks round. It's Kevin. I sit up smartish. Before I can get up, he's in the room, with Mark close behind him. Kevin puts his fat finger up to his lips and says, 'Sshhh!' forcefully. I go to get up off the bed, but Kevin is standing over me, pushing me down with his hand on my chest. I start kicking but Mark has my legs. Kevin sits down next to me on the bed, his back to me, his body lying across me, pinning me down, and Mark is at the end of the bed. Panicked, I start wriggling and kicking with all my might. I can feel Kevin's iron grip across my chest, holding down my arms so I can't move. He plays rugby, and it's a tackle. Mark is pulling down my trousers, pulling down my pants, with one hand holding one ankle. I try and kick like a goat with the other ankle but they are two hulking boys. They're not looking at me or talking to me. All this is done in whispers and silence. I can't see Mark's face or what they're doing, but I can feel my body from the waist down is now naked.

I am stripped bare, and they're looking at my private parts.

They've done this before a couple of times, the same kind of attack. They must dream these things up between them. I've seen Kevin with some magazines with naked women on the front. *Ow!* Then I feel it. I feel something hard and cold and sharp right up against where I wee. It's hard and cold and pushing. *Ow! Ow! Ouch!* It's sharp. Real pain. I really start trying to wriggle out from under them now. I'm panicking. What are they doing? Something is really hurting; it's agony. 'Ow!' I shout.

Kevin turns around, red-faced, and spits at me, furious, 'Shut the fuck up.' Then turns back.

'No! Stop! Don't,' I scream. I'm wrenching my head off the bed, straining to sit up, twisting my body, trying to see what they're doing to me. Mark is bent over my legs and I can see his arm moving while the other still holds my ankles. I see a flash of what looks like an empty Coke bottle in Mark's hand. A Coke bottle! What's that for? I scream very loudly now. At that, they both jump up and run out the door, and I'm left on the bed, dishevelled, panting. I know Barbara won't come, as she never does when I scream or shout when I'm with Kevin. Ian doesn't ever come either.

My trousers are round my ankles, my T-shirt is under my armpits, my private parts are exposed completely. I put my hand down, touch, and bring it up to my eyes: bright red. Blood. I sit up and look down at the mess. There is blood dribbling down my legs on the inside and onto the bed cover. I feel again, more blood on my hands. I touch below where the wee comes out, and there is torn flesh. Whatever they were doing with the bottle, it has cut me – down there. The room starts swirling, and I feel sick.

I lie back and start counting wildly. One, two, three, four;

one, two, three, four. I spend ages doing that, staring blankly at the ceiling, holding myself tight where it hurts. Following cracks, going along lines. Eventually I feel steady enough to pull my clothes off and put on my old pale-blue nylon dressing gown. I hobble down the landing to the toilet, feeling very vulnerable. I sit on the toilet and wee red water. It is not my time of the month. How will I explain the blood on the bed? How will I get it off? Barbara will not hear anything against Kevin. Or Mark for that matter. I hate Kevin – and Mark – more than I can possibly explain right now. I am bleeding, torn, in pain and feel scared. But I also know, sitting there, that there is absolutely no one I can turn to for help for something like this. So obviously it must be my fault. I desperately need a friend to confide in – someone who might help me get away from this place. I can't tell Sean, as it's too embarrassing. I pin all my hopes on finding a friend in my new school.

15

Fighting Back

I knew the minute I got to the high school that it was the wrong place for me. It was strict, gloomy and rigid. I was put into the bottom stream right from the start as I was thought of as 'thick'. My grades were terrible, obviously, as I had missed so much school over the years. All I could do was draw and paint. My 'remedial' history was like a neon sign around my neck spelling 'Dummy'. So I ended up in the cookery and needlework classes with the dead-end girls who were going nowhere. The school only paid attention to the clever girls in the top classes who were going to go to university. I was shoved in with the girls who were going to get pregnant as soon as blink. I couldn't spell, my maths was terrible and my general knowledge was poor. I hadn't been allowed to watch TV or the news, so I didn't know what was going on in the world. I was a dunce, according to the school.

Right from the start we were at odds and it wasn't going to get any better. It was a rigid, cold institution and I didn't feel at home there. The headmistress ran everything with an iron rod – which was something I was used to, and sick of. She had a traffic light outside her office, and when you were summoned you had to sit and wait until it went green. It felt very humiliating somehow. I didn't know how to learn. I couldn't sit and pay attention in class because my mind was whirling with everything that was happening at home. I just couldn't focus. When the teacher started talking I would drift off. Or I would panic, not understanding what I was supposed to be doing, as I'd been daydreaming too much. Everyone else would have their heads down, scribbling notes or writing an essay, and I'd be looking out the window at the trees. School hurt my head. I just couldn't do it and I wasn't interested any more. I couldn't get engaged with it; I felt it was all too late.

I realised I'd been stupid to think I might find a friend among these girls in their neat little uniforms, who could have no idea about my sordid real life outside school. They all seemed to have nice mummies and daddies who took them on holiday or to the cinema, or bought them nice clothes and LPs, and took them out for meals. I was in a different world from all of them, or so it felt. I even seemed to be in a different world to the poorer girls from the council estates, all of whom seemed to have more than me. I had all these nasty secrets, this hideous way of life, this shameful background, and nobody knew about it. Or perhaps they might guess, as I was still wearing shapeless clothes and the wrong kind of shoes. I'm sure I still smelt fairly bad. Somehow I had the mark of the 'loser' on my forehead and everyone could see it. I'd been told all my life that I would amount to nothing, and I was now amounting to absolutely nothing. And I hated every minute of it.

However, despite everything, I gradually began to create a new Louise. Maybe the contrast between me and everyone else became too hard to bear and I had to do something to shape

myself. It started with little things and then began to grow and
grow. One Sunday morning, around this time, I went into Ian's
garage when he had unusually taken the van out to collect something. Increasingly I snuck into his garage. I didn't hide my poo
there any more, but I felt it was a bit of a hidey-hole from the
house. I did sneak a bottle of cherry brandy in there (they never
drank the bottles that Ian got from customers at Christmas; they
sat there from one year end to the other). So I hid this bottle and
slugged some brandy from time to time when things got tough,
such as after the Cola bottle attack.

Kevin and I were now at war. If he came near me I blanked
him or spat and fought like a rabid cat. I hated him and fought
him at every turn. I wanted his father to come and take him
away so he'd leave me alone. So sneaking into the garage was
a wonderful break from it all. This morning, for some reason,
Barbara was also out – probably walking the dog. Ian had a
Roberts radio, and I went and turned the dial – something I
would never usually have the nerve to do. I found Radio 1, and
a fantastic, wild, loud music started. I suddenly burst into life
and was jumping up and down on the spot, dancing crazily to
the music. It was fantastic. It was angry – there was a male voice
shouting stuff I didn't really understand – and it was loud and
gritty, and I jumped around, spun about, and felt absolutely
marvellous. I felt free in those five fantastic minutes. Freer than
I'd felt in all my life. Wild. Happy. Mad. Powerful. When the
music stopped, the voice said it was the Clash singing 'White
Riot'. I didn't really understand what or who that was. I'd heard
about punk, which was all the rage at the time, and had seen
people in town with weird and wonderful hairstyles in bright
neon colours, wearing black clothes with safety pins and slashes.

My pulse was racing, my heart was beating hard, but in a good way. I felt alive. I felt good. I turned the radio off and snuck out of the garage, making sure I left no trace. I had found punk – would I now find me?

Around this time I began to see more of the wider world outside of our horrible house. We had always been surrounded by neighbours but Barbara would frown on any contact, particularly because they had so often written to the council and reported her for cruelty (albeit nothing was ever done). We still had social workers dropping in but Barbara handled them like a fine art. She knew just how to play her cards right and deny everything.

Now I was bigger I was able to walk out of the house myself, and sometimes I met a couple of lads from down the road and we'd go to the park. They were at the local comprehensive, or 'comp' as we called it – the one I wanted to go to – while I was at the high school, which was supposed to be a cut above. However, what they didn't know was I was in the thick stream and hated every minute of it. So I learnt to smoke with these lads. At first they taught me to smoke cigarettes, like Players No. 6 or Benson & Hedges, like breathing in a bonfire, which made me cough and retch. But I did get that nice light-headed feeling that I also got with Barbara's green pills or with the cherry brandy. Then we would mooch down the 'Rec', the local park, which had swings and slides. I always liked being out of doors, as I loved nature, and one day they handed me a strange kind of cigarette that had tobacco but also a strong-smelling herb in it.

'Wanna try it?' said one of the boys. So I did. I had nothing to lose. I felt a nice warm glow. Then I began to feel nicely light-headed, and started giggling. I loved laughing. I had almost never laughed at home, as it had always been like a funeral parlour, and I was terrified most of the time. We stood by the benches, or by the trees and the swings, and smoked the joint and everything got swirly and pretty and light and funny. I felt good. I felt happy. I didn't care any more. I felt free.

I had to keep my new friends and smoking a secret, however, as there would be hell to pay at home if Barbara got a whiff (literally). I was good at disguising myself, though, and was a master at keeping control after my years of being pleasant and polite to her, hiding everything and trying not to show her how I really felt inside.

The one subject I still loved with a passion was art. Somehow with art it didn't matter whether you were academic or not. Everyone was all mixed up together. I began to copy the album covers of people I was beginning to hear about. I got hold of David Bowie's 'Diamond Dogs' from someone at school and sat in the art room copying the cover. When I brought home my pictures, Barbara was horrified. 'That's weird nasty stuff,' she said. I thought it was wonderful, so I hid my drawings to save them from being torn up and put in the rubbish bin.

As most of the girls in my class were heading for early motherhood or the Cowley Road – where there were gangs of nasty, gropey men wanting to drool all over them – I started trying to hang out with the girls in the 'top' classes at school. I was drawn to the cleverer girls, and wanted to be part of their gangs, but at first it was impossible. So I watched them. I began to copy them, and then began to create a new image for myself.

I did go round for tea one day to one of the posh girl's houses and it was a complete revelation to me. Miranda's family lived in a big red-brick house with lovely front and back gardens. They had huge white lampshades from a shop called Habitat, which were all the rage. They had lovely Moroccan carpets, wooden floors (no swirling orange carpet, like at ours), and big beautiful Indian cushions made of velvet and little mirrors. I was in awe of this house. I also watched the parents let the children speak. Miranda was allowed to join in the adult conversation – something I had never been allowed to do (I was always told to 'Shut up, you little bitch'). Even though Miranda was in the middle stream (not the top), her parents let her talk about things on equal terms with them. I was shocked. I was always told that only the adults had any say in a matter. All decisions had been made for me, and I'd never been asked about anything.

After this, I wanted to voice my opinions more. For years I had been silent. Whatever happened, I bit my lip and put up with the punishment or the slagging off. I was amazed that Miranda's parents were interested in what she had to say, and never missed a parents' evening. Barbara and Ian had never shown up at any parents' evenings at any of my schools. It was only the difficult meetings with social workers that Barbara actually turned up for – because she had to.

I began to steal make-up from local shops and use it. I wanted to try fashion, to create my clothes, to change my appearance. I began using colour on my eyes, lips and hair. Of course Barbara forbade it and shouted at me, or slapped my face, calling me a 'slut' or a 'whore'. But I'd heard it all before. I was getting tired of her violence and her attitude. I was beginning to think for myself, just a little bit. I didn't know why she thought she could slap me about and starve me all the time like she did. I began to create a whole personality for myself, a new persona. I started to play her like she played me. I would tell her what she wanted to know, so she wouldn't 'kill' me, as she constantly threatened to. I began to tell lies, to create stories. Some were complicated lies. Some were sad. Some were just to survive. Sometimes I told them to Barbara to get out of being punished. Sometimes I told them to new friends, to make them like me, or to reduce Barbara's oddness.

One girl at school said to me, 'Your Mum is really scary,' and I just said, 'Oh, she used to be a nanny and believes in discipline.'

Of course, this was the truth, Barbara had been a nanny, but it wasn't just discipline she believed in; she was out to destroy me. She hated me. I never confessed what was happening at home – I was too ashamed. Sometimes I turned my mother into a wonderful 'happy hippy' mother, or a 'Waltons' type of 'mom', and I described how wonderful she was to the other girls. I made out she was a fabulous mother, and home was great.

I was so desperate to fit in, to stop being the odd one out, that I almost starting believing in these fantasies myself. I gave the impression that my parents loved me, that I mattered, that they would do anything for me. It was a complete pack of lies, but I began to need to believe it. I told some new girls that I was from a large, happy family, a bit like the Osmonds, and I had a lovely bedroom with white furniture and a white phone. I told wonderful stories of the travels we'd had to faraway places. The other girls lapped it up. I was rich, a princess, and nothing was too much for me. They believed it, or so I thought.

One day I was embellishing on this, out on the hockey field at the back of the school. Somehow it got back to the headmistress, who called Barbara and me in to see her. We sat in her office (once the traffic light went green) and I was told to stop telling lies. Barbara sat there saying, 'I have no idea what to do with her, she is such a liar.'

I said nothing, but I remembered all the years when she had told everybody how wonderful she was to me, and then beat me up at home. Inevitably, once we got home from school, Barbara ripped off my clothes and whipped me with a wet, smelly floor cloth. She kicked me in the belly, spat on me and I was utterly humiliated. After this punishment I didn't speak to her for days. She starved me completely too, but I didn't care, as I now refused to eat.

From then on, every time I said anything at school I was accused of being a liar by the other girls, and it was an embarrassing situation to be in. Whatever I now said, it was a lie, so no one believed me about anything. I had cried wolf once too often. The upshot of all this was that I was furious. I was livid and boiling with rage underneath, but I didn't realise how much. I wanted to change myself, my image, my life, but it was all too slow. By inventing things I had tried to create a better me, but it had all backfired. Everything I tried always came back to Barbara feeling she had the right to kick and slap everything out of me, to torture and blame me. I hated the way she twisted everything all the time. I was always under suspicion. She never took responsibility or owned up or said sorry. Never. It was always my fault, all the time. Thus, I was coming up to the boil.

One weekend morning I put on jeans and a T-shirt (I had now managed to get some younger-looking clothes from a second-hand shop), and I asked Barbara if I could go out for a ride on my bike. I had a second-hand (of course), dark-green ladies' bike. It was very old-fashioned.

She said, 'Okay, fine,' and I went to the shed to get the bike. Just as I was getting on it, on the gravel drive, Ian came back from being out in his van. In front of him Barbara said to me, 'Where do you think you're going, young lady?'

I was straddled across the bike, foot on the pedal, ready to go, and said, 'Out to see Miranda – you just said I could.' Barbara looked at Ian and shook her head, dramatically.

'You bloody little liar,' she said. 'You open your sodding mouth and out comes another lie.'

I was amazed. Usually I would say nothing, but I suddenly felt really upset. 'But you said—'

'I said nothing of the sort. One day you'll end up dead in a ditch with all these lies.'

I was flabbergasted. But suddenly I'd had enough, and got off the bike and started to walk past her. I heard Ian say, 'Barbara, stop now,' but she was on her mission. As I walked down the gravel to the gate, pushing the bike, she was behind me saying, 'Little bitch, little liar…'

I just kept on walking, wheeling the bike, but she wouldn't leave me alone. I was determined to open that gate. I could hear her saying, 'You always make trouble between Ian and me; you're a nasty piece of work.'

By now she had got to the gate and nipped in front of me, blocking my way. Usually I would turn around and go back obediently, waiting to be beaten, kicked or slapped. I was used to being punished; I expected it. But in this moment, out on the gravel, about to get on my bike and leave to see a friend, something snapped. I saw Barbara in front of the gate and I threw my bike aside and ran at her. I grabbed her shoulders and shook her, and started shouting: 'You fucking cow, you evil cunt,'

(I'd seen 'kunt' written on the school toilet doors, so I knew it was rude) and every bad name I could think of. I pushed her against the gate as hard as I could, and then ran to the dustbins at the side of the house, pulling them over, spilling the rubbish everywhere. I suddenly felt I had superhuman strength and I went over to a climbing rose on the side of the house (Barbara's pride and joy), and wrenched it violently off the wall. I cut my hands on the thorns but didn't care.

I was raging. I was beside myself. I was powered by such fury as I had never experienced before. I was shouting and swearing at Barbara all this time, and she was now cowering behind the front garden gate. I was showing my strength, my depth of feeling. I was wild with shouting. I had had ENOUGH! I went on and on and on; I was a volcano. I was exploding – it was my turn! All I wanted was a bike ride and I was sick of being stopped, sick of being called a liar, sick of all the mad twists and turns in Barbara's head, sick of all the nasty evil. Sick of being blamed. I was experiencing the endless fury that I had seen Barbara display so many times over the years, which she threw straight at me for the slightest thing.

I didn't know it then, but while I was on the rampage Barbara had slipped inside and called the police. I was still running about, ranting, when two policemen eventually turned up on foot. They were both quite old and both very polite. When I saw them, I began to calm down. All this time Ian was hovering in the background, looking very pale and awkward. The two policemen just talked to Barbara. She played the whole thing as a sob story in her favour: 'You don't know how hard it is to look after these sorts of difficult children,' she said, dabbing her eyes. 'They have chips on their shoulders. They are such hard work.'

Ian listened and said nothing. I looked at him and saw finally how weak he really was. He didn't explain anything to the policemen about what had really happened. Ian had seen everything, and yet he said nothing at all. He knew what she was like and he never, ever, protected me. I hated him in that moment, even more than I hated Barbara. He was weak. He was useless and he had never done anything for me. Barbara was saying she had tried everything but someone like me was always angry and ungrateful. I was now much calmer, but I looked at the two policemen and I thought, *You are such idiots*. They didn't ask me a thing and then just went on their way.

❧

After this incident I felt like I was enveloped in an invisible cloak. I had finally seen exactly what the situation was that I was in: Ian would never help me, and Barbara would always twist everything so I was in the wrong. Even the police would do nothing to her, no matter what she did. There was nothing I could do about it. All I could do was protect myself. I had to survive. I had to create a new self. I had to create a me that could go out into the world and get on. I realised that I would have to leave as soon as I possibly, humanly could. I was living in hell and I no longer wanted to be there. I had to be clever. I needed a campaign to save my own life. I had to find some way out.

For years I had been taking my little red suitcase round the landing, pretending I was going on a journey. Today I had actually wanted to go on my bike and instead I'd been stopped maliciously for no reason. My explosion helped me to begin to find myself. I found something inside me that was ready to say, 'ENOUGH' and 'NO' and 'SHUT UP'.

I was surprised at the level of anger I'd felt, and how much destruction I'd caused, but it was also a good feeling. (Of course, I had to clear up my mess and be punished as usual.) However, I realised I would have to put all my attention on preparing myself for the real world – the world of white paper lampshades and people in offices, of putting on work clothes and earning money. I would have to be big enough to be that person. I had never wanted anything so much in my whole life and I was going to do everything in my power to make it happen. I would have to create my new self and leave as soon as I was able. And that was that. Little did I know, things would get even worse before they got better.

16

Broken Promises

The doorbell rang one afternoon. Barbara answered and I listened from the safety of the banisters, vigilant as ever. I couldn't see who it was and then I heard Barbara say, 'Well, you'd better come in.'

Straining to see, I was amazed to witness Julie, of all people, walk into the hall followed by two smallish children. They all followed Barbara out to the kitchen and the door closed. I had been confined to my room for yet another punishment but my curiosity was burning. Why on earth was she here? I tiptoed halfway downstairs to my usual listening place. Ian and Kevin were both at work. I was supposed to be at school, but was home 'sick' as usual and actually about to clean out the chicken run.

We had yet another new dog, Sissy, a small crossbreed terrier that Barbara was training up. She heard me creeping down the stairs and yapped at the kitchen door, signalling to Barbara and Julie that I was around. Barbara whipped open the door, stony-faced. I looked past her to Julie, who was sitting at the table dabbing her eyes with tissues. The two children were out in the garden, playing with a ball. Barbara controlled herself in front of Julie. I could see it was an effort and she hissed through tight lips, 'Yes?'

I just stood gawping at Julie. Why was she here? Barbara answered my unspoken question: 'Julie will be staying. You will have to sleep in our room on the spare bed and Kevin will sleep on the sofa. You can go and change the sheets.'

I dutifully trotted off to do my household chores. Julie hadn't noticed me, or even looked up or smiled; apparently she was too deep in her grief. I had no idea what had happened, but I knew better than to question Barbara and make a scene in front of Julie.

Since the day we'd gatecrashed what had been Julie's husband's birthday party, I had heard nothing from her. I had written her letters – without Barbara knowing (she would have killed me) – begging her to come and get me. Although I didn't know Julie, her husband had actually been kind to me that day (even though he had later rejected me through social services). Their house looked nice, with pretty clothes and toys, and there was food – lots of it! The children also had looked clean and happy. But I had had no answer, and as the days and weeks developed into months I assumed I would never hear from her again. Now, a year later, as I ripped off the old sheets from Kevin's horrible stained bed and put on clean ones with crisp hospital corners, I was struck how strange it was that I was in the house with my two mothers. Two mothers! One, my adopted, grizzled grey witch of a mother who didn't love me (actively hated me, rather) and punished me at every turn; the other, a pink, fluffy floozy of a mother who didn't know me, had given me away, and didn't seem that interested in me at all – yet. What a situation! How was I to deal with this while going to a school I hated and being kept home to do housework most of the time?

After a day or two, I found out that Julie had left her husband. This was her second marriage, she said. She cried and cried, dabbed at her eyes with Kleenex and drank gallons of tea.

'Why are men so mean to me?' she sobbed. 'What have I ever done to deserve this?'

The two children, Diana, who was eight, and John, six, were complete strangers to me. We were all shy and awkward with each other. Nevertheless, I showed them the chickens, telling them they were all named after the Osmonds, my favourite group from my younger childhood. They liked playing with Sissy, who was still a pup. Then I took them to the orchard and they were fascinated by the caravans. We waved to Sean and the Polish people, who waved back. They thought it was really strange to have these people living there.

Meanwhile, I had to sleep in the main bedroom with Ian and Barbara, which made me feel so scared that I hardly slept at all. The single bed in their room had all Barbara's dolls on it. The day Julie arrived I had to go and get permission from Barbara to move them so I could make up the bed. Julie was so distressed she didn't notice this.

Barbara snapped, 'Don't break anything,' so I was ultra-careful transferring them one by one to the top of a chest of drawers in their bedroom. There were two teddy bears, Edward and Duncan; a blonde doll with a china face in a lacy christening dress, and loads of others, plastic and rubber ones, with dark hair, orange curls, blonde plaits, knitted clothes and fancy out-fits. Barbara adored her dolls and I sometimes peeped through the door and saw her playing with them on the spare bed. She would talk to them and then rock one in her arms like a baby, whispering that she loved them. I saw her singing lullabies to them and calling them 'mummy's little angels'. It made me shiver to think about it, especially as she was so nasty to me. One time she caught me spying on her and shouted: 'What are you looking at, you nosy little bitch?'

Julie stayed for quite a while. At first I thought, *Yippee, I can get to know my real mum*. But I soon found this was a very difficult task. She talked about herself all the time, but it was a strange kind of talk. She constantly looked in the mirror, or put on lipstick, fluffed her hair or changed her clothes. She would go out to the shops and come back with loads of bags of new stuff, then put it on and twirl around the hall and living room, doing a fashion show, giggling in her high-pitched, breathy voice. Short mini-skirts, way too short for her; frilly blouses, very low cut. She would get her hair bleached and permed and come back with lots of new shoes and jewellery. I watched all this, amazed.

I had imagined we would sit down and talk about things. She might ask me about school or be interested in who I was. Not at all. I wanted to show her my favourite drawings, but didn't know how. I wanted to ask her questions – especially about my father – but never found the words. Barbara was being less aggressive with me, and even Kevin was behaving himself a bit more. Having Julie there, in the daytime at least, meant they were not so openly bullying towards me.

After a while, Julie started going out every night. She was supposed to be looking for somewhere to move to. She'd also have to find some kind of job (the mention of which made her cry). Apparently she and Brian had fallen out over how much money she spent and she said, 'This time it's really over,' hinting they'd fallen out before. This was her second marriage (did that include my dad? I wondered). She'd come to us, she said, as she had nowhere else to go.

When she sat and talked about this, she would sometimes look at me and say, 'Of course, you can come and stay with us when things are sorted.' My heart would leap. But then she would go back to talking about her problems and nothing more would be said about it. I wanted to ask her when but I didn't know how. She never mentioned it again, either. Her children seemed quite sweet, but they were close to each other, and only really spoke to one another. I was a stranger, although I was a half-sibling, and, I guess, I looked dirty and not very nice, so they kept their distance from me.

I snuck out whenever I could to talk to Sean about it, and he would feed me milk and biscuits and shake his head. Then he'd put on some Irish music and we'd have a little sing together, or we'd put some seeds in his tiny garden round the caravan and water them with a silver watering can. Or I'd draw something with him while he drank a mug of tea. Then I'd come back to the house with my two strange mothers, but feeling quite a bit better.

Then the rows began. Julie was going out every night now, and coming back very late. She was visiting a local pub and had hooked up with someone – a taxi driver called Vernon. I saw her dress up and go out every night in a different outfit, and then I would hear the commotion when she came back and stomped up the stairs.

Barbara would leap out of bed and shout, 'What time of night do you call this? This isn't a hotel, you know!' Barbara would slam back into the bedroom, fizzing like a firework.

I was also more and more spooked by sleeping in the same room as Ian and Barbara. She refused to have the curtains closed, as she liked the light. This meant it was hard to sleep. They slept far apart in bed, one on either side, facing away from each other. They never touched. It was such an odd atmosphere. I would lie there in the gloomy room, hearing him snore, and watch the dolls sitting on the cupboard with their waxy faces and shiny, spooky eyes staring right back at me. I lay there at night thinking about the fact that I had two mothers in the house, but neither wanted to know me. Neither seemed to love me. I hadn't found out anything about my father, as Julie would never sit down and talk to me properly. She didn't seem interested in getting to know me, and avoided me most of the time. She was only affectionate with Diana and John. They seemed not to want to get to know me, either, which was sad. I was desperate to know more about where I had come from, why I had been sent away – especially to someone like Barbara – but there never seemed to be a time or a place to ask.

Occasionally Julie would say things about me going on holiday with them or visiting their house, but it was so vague. I would latch on to it, and then it was never mentioned again. I hoped she might mean it, but something inside me made me not really trust her.

Things finally came to a head when Barbara lost her temper in her usual volcanic way, becoming utterly furious with Julie. The row blew up one evening when she was putting on her lipstick in the hall mirror.

'You're not going out again!' spat Barbara, standing behind her. 'That's every night this week!' It sounded like she was talking to me, rather than Julie.

Julie stopped, mid-pout, and looked back at Barbara in the mirror. 'What do you mean?'

'Where the bloody hell are you going every night?' snapped Barbara. 'You're using me like a babysitting service! This isn't a sodding hotel!' I watched this from a safe distance, behind the upstairs banisters.

'You're not my bloody mother,' said Julie, affronted. 'I can go out if I want.'

At this, Barbara went red and exploded. 'Right, that's it! You're out, all of you.'

Julie nearly dropped her pink lipstick. Her mouth opened like a goldfish (I could see it in the mirror). 'What, now?'

'Yes, now. Out!'

I could see the blind fury on Barbara's scarlet face and I scuttled back into the toilet and peeked out. Barbara was suddenly stomping up the stairs to my room, where Julie had been sleeping, and started throwing things into her bags. Julie hobbled up the stairs behind her in her stilettos and I could hear the two women shouting, and then fighting, in my old bedroom.

'Leave that alone!' I could hear Julie shrieking.

'Get out!' shouted Barbara. 'Now!'

Diana and John appeared in their pyjamas and came and stood with me in the toilet. We could hear the two women squabbling like children, and I put my right hand up to my eyebrow and started pulling.

A few minutes later, a white-faced faced Julie appeared, grabbed the two children, and they all went downstairs. I crept and looked through the gap in the door. She was dabbing her eyes and mumbling to herself. Barbara was in the kitchen, crashing pots and pans. Julie had called a taxi on the hall phone.

When it came, she said to me, dramatically, on the doorstep, 'I'll be in touch,' and then she was gone. Half of me wanted to believe her, but the other half felt it might be a promise that would be broken as soon as she said it. Julie seemed the kind of person who couldn't mean what she said, or say what she meant. I wasn't sure if I could believe or trust her. In my heart, I really hoped against hope that I was wrong.

❧

After this episode, things got worse again. Barbara and Kevin went back to their reign of terror. There were slaps, kicks and punches for every little thing. Ian was becoming an even shadowy figure and spent a lot of time slumped in front of the TV of an evening. I wasn't allowed to watch much, if any.

Ian and Barbara were arguing a lot and not getting on. She had developed a new habit: buying things and then wanting to take them back. Ian was not happy about this, and there were many arguments about money. I was now twelve going on thirteen. Some days there were deliveries in our best living room of big brown boxes: a fridge, a washing machine, a new cooker (which was mustard and brown in colour). Barbara had gone on a spending spree in Debenhams. When Ian came home there was a big argument. Usually he didn't stand up to her, but when it came to her spending he stood his ground a bit more. They argued and argued, and finally Ian said they would have to be sent back; he was not paying for them. Barbara was livid, so the next day I was kept home from school, as my job was to wait for the men to come and take them away. Barbara was so furious at this that she got a carving knife and hit the old cooker and fridge with it, making long, dark lines on the white surface.

She literally cut the paintwork in her anger at Ian. The battle may have been lost, but the war was not over.

A few weeks later, a new mustard-coloured cooker was installed and Ian was painting the kitchen a cornflower blue. She had won in the end due to the state of the paintwork of the old appliances.

'I deserve better, after all I've put up with,' claimed Barbara, and the thing she particularly thought she deserved was a fur-lined leather jerkin from a famous furriers in town. I was taken into the shop and made to hold her bag while she tried it on. It was extremely expensive, and something unlike anything she had worn or had before. Barbara usually wore her old lady uniform of grey and black, with a bit of beige, and now she wanted this glamorous jerkin, made of expensive dark-brown suede. Barbara kept saying, 'It's very practical' and 'It's warm and it looks great,' as she described it to Ian later. He said no. He didn't think it was worth the money. Plus, they couldn't afford it. Barbara's face tightened into a white point, her mouth thin with annoyance.

'You're just a man, what do you know?' she taunted him. 'You're a bloody rapist, just like the rest of them.'

Whenever Barbara was furious with Ian, he was called a 'rapist' – it was the worst thing she could say. I didn't really understand what it meant, but he would go very pale and walk out the room, so it was obviously bad.

The next day, however, I was hauled into town (instead of going to school) and we bought the jerkin. Barbara was pleased. I'd never seen her so happy about something. She brought it home, put it on, and admired herself in the mirror. I wondered, fleetingly, if having Julie around had made her think a bit more about her appearance. Julie had bags and bags of new clothes all the time (no wonder her husband thought she spent too much, as she obviously did). But Barbara had never really spent on herself. She spent on the poor dogs – at least when they were puppies – and vet bills when they were put down (which was a frequent occurrence). She certainly didn't spend on me, as all my clothes were second-hand. And Ian just wore the same old clothes and overalls all the time.

The next day I did go to school, which was largely a waste of time, as I spent all day looking out of the window at the trees, sky and birds, not following anything much. When I got home there was a real commotion going on. Barbara said Ian had changed his mind. He had put his foot down about the jerkin, so it had to be taken back. She was in a total fury. The next day I was kept home and sent into town with the jerkin in a bag and told to take it back and get a refund – on pain of death.

I went into the really posh fur shop, feeling completely out of my depth. The manager looked down his nose at me – I must have looked a sight in my grubby second-hand clothes. I made up a story that my mother was too fat and the jerkin didn't really fit her now. This must have seemed crazy to him, as Barbara had bought it herself just a day earlier. After pondering for a while, he said he would return the money, but looked pretty annoyed and said he hoped this would be the end of it. I felt embarrassed, but thought: mission accomplished.

When I got home, with the refund in my hand, I handed it over to Barbara. I thought she would be really pleased, as it was a lot of money. I thought she would smile and say thank you for a change. Instead, she slapped me hard across the face and told me to go to bed without any tea. I had walked miles into Oxford (as I had no bus fare), and I had done her dirty work for her. I had missed breakfast, lunch and school to do this, and had dealt with the annoyed manager in the shop for her. Yet I had a slap and punishment for it.

I later heard Ian and Barbara arguing yet again, because while I was out on the errand of returning the jerkin, Barbara had gone into town in her car and bought loads of brand new bedding. There were piles of new sheets, a big duvet and cover and pillows in big bags in the hall. As they rowed I could hear plates, cups and saucers being flung out the back door and smashing on the concrete. This was followed by the old blankets that Ian loved, and pillowcases and sheets. He was trying to protest, saying he liked blankets, as they could be tucked in. Barbara was ignoring him, saying duvets were far superior. She wanted the best for a change.

The garden looked like a jumble sale, as I looked down from my bedroom window and watched the domestic drama unfold. Barbara was livid that Ian did not like the idea of a duvet – which people were turning to instead of traditional bedding – as he wanted to keep his old blankets. Barbara was not going to allow this to happen – what did he know? – so everything was chucked in the garden so she could have her own way. I climbed on my narrow bed and started counting the cracks on the ceiling, the blue flowers on the wall, while fantasising about ways I could leave this hell-hole madhouse as soon as I was big enough. It simply couldn't be too soon. But how on earth was I going to escape?

17

Saved by Art

I was miserable at home and miserable at school. I was now thirteen and getting more and more interested in experimenting with my appearance as a teenager. I would put on eyeliner and mascara (stolen from local shops and secreted in my room) and foundation. I started using gel on my hair, trying to make it look a bit punky. When I did go to school I had a method for dealing with it. I was totally bored there – it really had nothing to offer me. I was in the lowest stream for cookery and needlework, as my writing and maths and most other subjects, except art, were awful, and it was utterly boring. I felt I'd done (and still did) enough domestic work at home to last me a lifetime, so I didn't need to learn any of that. Anyway, I was interested in learning other stuff.

I would get into school and want to leave immediately. I began to bunk off, daily. I had missed so much school that I knew I would never, ever catch up. I couldn't concentrate, and had no idea where we were in most of the subjects; it was just a way of killing time. I felt I could spend my days in a much better way by myself, on my own.

I would arrive at school, chant flatly, 'Here, miss,' when my name was called out from the register, then I would get up, go out the door and leave for the day. I would just disappear. It was me, gone, totally, just like that. It would feel wonderful to escape. I could breathe at last. I would walk into town. I liked looking at things and wandering about; it calmed me down. I was also smoking regularly now, and I had got some cigarette papers and tobacco from the boys in the park, so I would roll up a ciggie (they'd also taught me how to do it) and smoke. It was a relief and felt wonderful to walk along, blowing out smoke, feeling free.

I had no money, or just enough for a cup of tea (I might have pinched some from Barbara's purse, as I never had pocket money), and I would go and sit for hours, watching people go by. I loved looking at their faces, hair, clothes, everything. I began to develop a circuit. I loved gardens. Sean had taught me a bit about plants and seeds. He grew vegetables round his caravan and I had learnt from him how to put them in the earth, cover them carefully, water them, thin them out, and watch them grow. I loved the magic of growing things.

I also loved the beauty of plants. There was something utterly wonderful about beautiful green leaves, big flowers and petals. I loved dahlias, roses, lilies and daisies especially. I loved huge plants with lots of leaves and colour. They seemed a wonder to me – the magic of life. I had to walk through the University Parks to get from our house to the city, and I found myself wandering round and round in wonder. I would always take a little sketchbook and sit on a bench and look at things and draw. The beauty of nature filled my soul; fed me where I felt empty, sad and dirty.

I felt cleansed as I took in the silence from the green,

from the colours and textures, the sound of water and birds. I walked and walked, past the lily pond and the ornamental bridge, looking at buds, branches, flowers, ducks. I loved watching people with their dogs, and couples holding hands, and single people on benches, feeding the birds or eating sandwiches. There were mums with buggies and babies, elderly people with walking sticks, young people smoking and kissing. It was all a revelation to me. I was in a world of my own, and felt calm and peaceful, removed from all that was ugly and nasty. It felt so different from my everyday life, either at home or at school, where I was shouted at, demanded of, ridiculed or hit and slapped, put down and spat on. I felt in a safe bubble out in the greenery of the Parks.

Then I began to branch out. I formed a ritual walk. Out of school, through the Parks, into town, a cup of tea, and then a museum in the morning, another in the afternoon. As I wandered, I loved looking in windows and at buildings. I loved seeing other people's interiors: the colourful walls and furniture in their fashionable living rooms. The redbrick houses, the variety of shops and cafés. I had heard of a museum called the Ashmolean, which sounded mystical. It turned out to be an amazing white-stone building with big columns and statues over the huge triangular front entrance with loads of steps. It was like a palace.

I wandered up the steps and tagged along shyly on the end of a line of Americans or Germans going on a tour round the museum. I smiled and sort of blended in. I was wearing my school uniform, so I guess they thought I was doing some sort of study trip. I would wander around with information washing over me, but just loving looking at pictures, statues, furniture and art in all its shapes and forms. I loved old crockery or pots or anything that was beautifully crafted, reeking of history. I was fascinated by the Victorian collections and the huge butterflies with luminous wings – I wondered how they had got there and where they all came from. I could breathe looking at these things.

In the afternoon, I would wander to the Pitt Rivers Museum, which specialised in archaeological things. I didn't know anything about archaeology or anthropology, but I loved sitting and drawing the pots, the spears and, of course, their famous shrunken heads. I found these fascinating. Were they real? Real people? How could you do that? I imagined shrinking Barbara's head down, boiling it in a big iron pot, and that made me smile.

By now my hair was growing, and I was styling it in a punky, spiky way, with gel, and I felt I had something in common with the long, pointed locks of the shrunken heads. It made me laugh. The Pitt Rivers only ever opened in the afternoons, so I felt it was my place for the p.m. shift. I would sit and draw quietly, totally absorbed. I became such a regular fixture in this museum that one of the guards would even find a seat for me to sit and draw on. I would have a little fold-out chair, and be left to draw to my heart's content. It was wonderful. This place was mine.

It was cool and dark, with wonderful huge wooden cabinets with glass fronts, stuffed with amazing things. There was so much to see, so much to look at, that I would get lost in it all. I would be absorbed for hours. No one shouted at me, no bells rang, there was no homework. Most importantly, there were no bullies making my life hell. No blaming. No taunting. No shouting. No smacks. There was just the quiet of the museum, safe and cool, where I could run my pencils over paper and create images of what I saw, and try out new techniques, for hours on end.

Back home, I would confide in Sean that I was looking at art, drawing and slipping out from school. He would listen and nod, and not say anything bad to me. One day he met me in town and we went to the Museum of Modern Art together. We wandered around looking at rooms full of pictures and artefacts. Afterwards he bought me cake and tea, and we sat talking about what we'd seen. I found out he'd never been into an art gallery before, but he was taking me because he knew it would thrill me. He promised not to tell Barbara where we'd been, and when we got back to the house, we parted ways like old friends as I turned into the garden and he strolled onto his site.

She was always suspicious when I had been to see him, or came in from school with him (as he picked me up a few times and walked back with me, bringing me Curly Wurlies or Ruffle bars, and talking about this and that). I always got a sense she was almost jealous that I liked him, although she wouldn't say so directly. She would just be snappy as I came in, and I would pretend I'd been at school all day. Why was she jealous when she didn't like me at all? Or was she frightened I'd give something away and she'd be found out? It was all very confusing.

When I got braver about slipping out from school, and I could lay my hands on a bit of money for a bus fare, I would hop on a bus and go all the way to Blenheim Palace and back. This was wonderful. I would wander in and attach myself to a tourist group. Or I would sneak into the shop, then slip into the toilets and into the building from there. It was absolutely fantastic inside. I couldn't believe real people lived like that. There were enormous gold mirrors, huge paintings, beautiful sofas, Persian carpets, elaborate tables and chairs. It was fabulous, and I made a vow to myself that one day I would have things like this myself. I wanted to live better, to live well, to have a lovely environment, to live with beauty rather than grotty, horrible, ugly things. If rich people could live like this, why couldn't I? I didn't think I'd ever have the money, but I thought I could create things that looked like the things in Blenheim. I just had to look at them very carefully and draw them, copying their curves and shapes, colours and textures.

As I drifted from room to room in Blenheim, I felt like I could easily live with this kind of furniture. Why not? How fantastic would it be to wake up in a four-poster bed, with heavy damask curtains; to have portraits hanging on the wall of your family because you were so important? I didn't have any family or a name I could show off, but the idea that you could be so important that all your relatives hung on the wall for all to see really tickled me.

I decided I would learn to paint portraits and began to draw people as well as plants. As the days went by and my freedom grew, and I filled myself with art and beauty, I also looked at everything more closely. I was watching people in the street, looking at fashion, seeing what people wore, how they spoke, what they did. There was a whole world out there I didn't really know anything about. It was like I was surfacing from an underground dungeon. I began to experiment with my hair more as a consequence, and wanted to colour it. I knew Barbara would go berserk, but I nonetheless decided I would have a proper colourful

Mohican sometime soon. I knew school wouldn't like it either. I didn't care; I was past caring.

When I sat in cafés like the Nosebag, which was a popular vegetarian café in Oxford, I would listen to music, watch other young people being free and easy in their clothes and style, and think, I want some of that. I began to plan how I would do my hair, change my clothes and break free from my granny straightjacket of cast-off clothes once I was alone. I'd definitely wear something more freaky, funky and fun. I was beginning to feel no one could stop me – a bit of a mistake, as it turned out.

Of course, my jaunts around town on regular schooldays did not go unnoticed. Because I was living more and more in a fantasy world in my head, I sort of believed I could get away with walking out of school. I felt so caged, so exhausted with the whole rigmarole of pleasing Barbara, which never worked, and so fed up with trying to fit in at school, that I now felt beyond it all. I wanted out as soon as possible. I just didn't know how to get out.

But, of course, school wasn't happy with my behaviour. I was turning into a rebel overnight. When I walked round Oxford or sat in the Nosebag, I saw other young people dressed in punk clothes, which I drew afterwards. I also listened to punk and post-punk music flowing out of shops, and it was exciting, angry, and spoke for me somehow.

I was also in the class with all the rough girls, many of whom were now hanging out regularly with the horrible men on the Cowley Road and getting into big trouble. Some of the girls whispered about what was going on, and it was really scary. I heard they were being given drink and drugs in exchange for sexual favours. I was now smoking dope as often as I could, and smoking cigarettes whenever I could get my hands on them. The boys in the park kept me supplied, as long as I was amusing. I didn't have any close friends but I was beginning to form my alliances.

Barbara was contacted by the school and there were meetings with teachers and the headmistress. I had warnings and was asked where I went. I sat in the Head's office, looking at the floor. I just shrugged. I was told I was getting 'an attitude'. The headmistress was 'disappointed'. It wasn't going to get me anywhere.

Barbara sat dabbing her eyes, saying, 'I don't know how to handle her. I don't know what I've done wrong. I've tried so hard with her, but she's such a difficult child to deal with.'

I would glower at her. She knew full well what she did wrong. I didn't say, because the minute we got home, she would grab me by the hair, slap my face as hard as she could, and punch me to the floor. Kevin would join in with a kick to the ribs and buttocks. They were a class double act. But there, in the headmistress's office, Barbara played the 'martyr mother' and it made me sick.

I would agree to go to school, and go straight to the art room. I loved it there; it was the only place I wanted to be. The art teacher, Miss Willetts, was understanding and kind. She just handed me paints, pencils, charcoal, and I would dive into the paper, disappear into colour, and be calm. Everyone knew I was good at art and, despite being a naughty girl now, the other pupils still got me to draw their pictures for them. I was the Queen of arms and legs, the Majesty of perspective and form.

Once home, I would sneak out over the road to the house of one of the park boys, Dave. He was older than me, working as an apprentice in town. His friends would come round and we'd hang out together. They treated me like one of the lads; it was great. They weren't university boys; they were working-class guys. They didn't try to abuse me like Kevin and Mark, either, which was a real relief. At least some boys were okay.

Dave's friends would come round, and they would play the latest albums: UB40, Black Uhuru, Bob Marley. We would smoke dope together ('mar-ju-wah-nah' or 'Mary Jane', as they called it), and I would feel lovely and light-headed, like I could face anything. I loved being with them; I felt free. We laughed a lot and they were nice to be with. I was building a new life with these boys; I smelt a whiff of freedom.

They even taught me to grow a marijuana plant, which I snuck into the greenhouse at home. I knew when I went back, smiling, with stoned eyes to Barbara, she would be sniffing round me, firing questions at me, slapping me across the face or whacking me with the rolled-up newspaper. But I didn't care any more. It was as if I had a new, thicker skin.

Another strange thing was, even though Julie's visit had ended in disaster, Barbara was still hinting all the time that I should go and visit her, or go on holiday with her. I had heard nothing from Julie since her stay, despite her saying she would 'be in touch'. I was beginning to see that she really was full of empty promises. I then heard from Barbara that she had snared Vernon, the taxi driver who she'd picked up in the local pub. She hadn't had to get a job after all, as she and Vernon were now living together somewhere not too far away, between Swindon and Oxford, with the children. Julie seemed very good at getting another man to look after her – or rather someone to buy her stuff.

I was still trying to work out who my real mother was, and who I could rely on, and finding little made sense. Then, one Saturday, Barbara got a letter and came and found me out in the garden. It was from Julie. Barbara was looking at me with her usual stony expression.

'Your brother needs a kidney,' she said, out of the blue. I was feeding the chickens, looking at the flowers and mooching around, wondering how soon I could escape to the park to see the boys.

'He's to have an operation. He's got to have yours.'

I stared at her, not understanding at all what she was saying.

'Well,' snapped Barbara, 'are you going to let your brother live or die?'

I suddenly felt terrified. What? I didn't want to have an operation. Or lose a kidney. Anyway, Julie didn't want me! John had hardly spoken to me. Why should I do that?

'If you don't give it to him, he'll die,' she stated dramatically. 'You're a selfish bitch if you let your own brother die for the sake of keeping your kidney. How can you be so selfish?'

She went on like this for days and days, trying to wear me down. For some strange reason I didn't really understand at the time, I would not say yes. I was sick of saying yes when I meant no. I felt enough was enough, and I didn't want to do it. I refused to agree. Barbara was beside herself.

'You are the most selfish bitch I have ever met,' and on and on she went. 'You would let him die, destroy his family... He's a lovely little boy, how could you do that? He's worth ten of you.'

Barbara went round our neighbours and people in the village shop and spread the news of my selfishness. She went on and on to Ian about it. Kevin ridiculed me for being a baby and a scaredy-cat. Barbara even told school about it. There was no escape. I had a lovely dying brother and I wouldn't save him. All I had to do was give my kidney to him, but I wouldn't, as I was a spoiled, selfish little nothing. I stood my ground; I wouldn't do it, but Barbara wouldn't let it go. But nor would I. I felt terrible deep inside, though. What if he really did die if I didn't give him my kidney? How would I live with that? What would the consequences be? Would Julie understand?

Then I would remember her looking in the mirror, putting on her lipstick, trying on clothes and not talking to me. Or the children, including John, whispering to his sister, giggling and running away when I came in the room. They didn't want to know me, either. No. I was not going to do it. No. I'd had enough. If the situation was reversed, they wouldn't do it for me. Nobody would.

'You will rue the day,' Barbara said nastily. 'This evil act will come back and get you.'

I was scared that it would but, for once, I just didn't care. I had to start looking after myself. Enough was enough. So I just refused, and let the violence of Barbara and Kevin rain down upon me, just as it always did. And, of course, things were only going to get worse before they got better.

18

Collision Course

I was on a collision course with school, a collision course with home and a collision course with life. At school I hung out with the thick girls in the lower classes, at least when I got to school and stayed for the first half an hour. There would be Pakistani men hanging around the gates of our school who came from the Cowley Road, and one friend, Sandy, would chat to one or two and then disappear. I would look at the men, drooling all over my friend, and watch her as she turned and waved briefly at me, and then went off with them. There were many girls doing this, lured by free drinks, drugs and unlimited male attention. I didn't like the look of it. I kept clear and worried what might happen to Sandy.

They tried to chat me up, and Sandy said, 'C'mon, Louise,' but I got away as fast as I could – my hairs standing up on my skin, sensing danger. Sandy would tell me later what she got up to. She was having unprotected sex with several of the men – who were really old and married – but she said she was enjoying herself. At least at first. I didn't really believe it, as I didn't like the feelings I got when I saw them. They were bad news. For me, freedom was what I was after. I was wary of anything that would tie me down or pin me to any obligation.

Home was getting harder and harder and I was desperate to get out. As I got taller, Kevin was taking over the regular discipline, as well as Barbara. If I was late back, he would violently grab my hair, push me against the wall, shouting, then punch me, pulling me down to the floor to give me a good kicking. She gave him total permission to damage me as much as he liked. She would be standing, smirking, enjoying my pain. Barbara behaved more and more like a helpless lady that Kevin had to protect from me, the marauding punk girl.

One day when our paths crossed in the Rec, he grabbed me, shoved me into a nettle bed and held me down. He was still sleazing at my body, trying to touch me all the time. One time he pushed me up against the back of the shed and shoved his tongue in my mouth. I managed to escape. Just. It was utterly disgusting. I hated him. With all my might I pushed him off and sent him flying. But it was a daily battle zone.

Meanwhile, Ian was floating around ignoring everything. I'm sure he could hear the screams, the shouts, the fights, but he ducked into his garage and put Radio 3 on loudly to block it all out. He was a total coward.

❧

I was still wandering around the city as much as I could, despite being given detention after detention. I became a regular on the benches in the various locations and in the University Parks, and was on nodding terms with many academics and mature students. I now took clothes to school to change into, so I didn't look like a schoolgirl any more. I was turning fourteen but felt ancient. I got hold of some money somehow and, with one of my friends, bought some dye and began to experiment with my hair. I made it very black to start with, like my music heroes. I was listening to as much punk and rock music as I could – usually in my favourite cafés, sometimes in the garage on Ian's old radio when people were out. I was loving Toyah, Debbie Harry, the Stranglers, Patti Smith, Chrissie Hynde and the Pretenders. These voices, these songs, spoke to me: raw, passionate, angry, energetic.

I would 'pogo' wildly for five or ten minutes, jumping up and down like a maniac and getting my fury out in the garage. It was wonderful. I loved their look: dark hair, pale faces, big molten eyes, serious gothic looks. I began to make that my own style. I loved make-up and creating a face, a mask. It was my body art. I experimented, scouring the second-hand shops (familiar territory for me) and found black satin Chinese slippers, lime socks, pink socks, black clothes. Dirt cheap. I got some old Doc Martens boots. I'd use my needle and thread to customise things. I wanted a 'don't mess with me' look, like Chrissie, Blondie or Patti. I wanted to look beautiful; I wanted to be a new me.

I would get studs and push them through my ears in several places with a needle and cork. I was used to pain, so I didn't flinch. I was used to not feeling things happening to my body, so there were no tears. I loved the Human League, so I began to train my hair over one eye like the lead singer. Earlier I had found a way of putting on barely-there mascara, foundation and lipstick, as make-up was banned at school. But now I was coming out as me, I began to sculpt my own image. I was attracted to all that was theatrical, dramatic and wild. I loved burnished gold, shiny silver, multi-coloured glitter, bright colours like shocking neon pink and purple. I craved colour, colour, colour – just like the colours adorning beautiful flowers.

I loved the look of Cleopatra in the film with Richard Burton and Elizabeth Taylor: I copied her fabulous eye make-up. I wanted lashings of black eye-liner and mascara. I wanted to do everything that both school and home disliked. I found cheap, multi-coloured scarves and wound them round my head, African style, and I had ponytails and thick frizzy backcombs. I loved old prints and weird styles, which I changed into strange garments. I wore pale lips and blood-red lips, according to my mood. I became my own focus.

Because I was so sensitive to smell (and always smelling bad), I got some patchouli, chocolate and coconut oils from the Body Shop, which was a revelation to me (best part being you could fill up and re-use bottles cheaply). I was my own art project. Bowie was in my soul: I was creating myself, creating my image, feeding myself. I had been starved for so long of any self-expression that it was beginning to burst out of every pore as 'ME'. I was becoming a Rebel with a capital R; a Dropout with a capital D. Nothing was going to stop me now.

When I did hang out at school, under threat of this or that, I signed up for Religious Studies CSE. It wasn't a popular subject, but I ended up having one-to-one lessons with a great teacher. He was a nice Greek man, Mr Papadopolous, much younger than the other stuffy teachers, and we would sit on the windowsill next to each other and talk about politics and ideas. He explained about Nelson Mandela and his fight against oppression in South Africa that was raging at the time – he was still in prison, still fighting.

I understood, instinctively, how bad apartheid was, coming from my own oppressive, unfair regime at home. We talked about Mahatma Ghandi in India, Hinduism and Buddhism, and the problem of British Colonialism. I hadn't really understood any of this before. He also explained what was happening with women's rights in the UK and America, and I began to get very excited about these ideas. Women were demanding equal pay, they wanted sexual equality, they didn't want to be wives and chattels. He explained how the contraceptive pill had changed women's lives for ever in the 1960s; now they had choice when and if to have babies. He told me to read Germaine Greer's *The Female Eunuch*. Mr Papadopoulous told the story of what had happened to Martin Luther King in America and I was appalled: shot for fighting against the oppression of his people. I hated slavery. I could understand the anger of people who had been put down, imprisoned, oppressed, violated, used and abused, and it was like he was opening up my mind to a whole new world.

Being with Mr Papadopoulous was wonderful. He treated me like an equal. He spoke to me like I wasn't stupid. He made me think about things. I had lost the plot with the rest of school (except art), but he didn't speak down to me. We talked about social problems, about identity and class, and the bad things going on in the world. I asked him, 'Why do people do such bad things in the world?' and he said, 'They do it because they can – until they are stopped.'

That stayed with me: people could hurt others *unless they were stopped*. And it seemed – in America and in South Africa and even in the UK – people were trying to stop people hurting black and minority ethnic people. Women were trying to stop being hurt across the world. I thought about Sandy going off with the creepy men, and wondered if she knew about women's rights.

I started questioning my own identity (as Jewish, for instance). I started writing poems and drawing all sorts of new things. I felt, when talking to Mr Papadopolous, that there were some beginnings of hope after all. While I spent the mornings hanging out with the rough and tough girls, or dropping into art or religious studies, I would often go round to the 'popular' and 'nice' girls' houses in the afternoons and some evenings. I liked hanging out with their families and their mothers, in particular. I began to find other girls' mothers to talk to. I had learnt for a very long time with Barbara to be polite and to present myself well. I was never really part of the family at home, always the stranger, and I had to ask permission for everything as an out-sider. So, when I met new people I knew what to do. I could make myself very presentable, could be polite and charming, despite looking increasingly punk.

I guess I was now looking more 'artistic' too, and the more middle-class friends and families actually respected it (unlike at home, where I got criticised all the time for everything, especially anything creative). One of my 'posh' friends, Petula, had parents who were both working: her dad was an architect and her mum was a teacher. Their house was a huge ramshackle pile with Heals furniture, giant beanbags and lampshades that hung low over the dinner table. They ate brown rice and interesting vegetarian food with spices and colourful salads. I'd never before had anything spicy, and I loved it straight away.

Her mum was kind and took to me. Their cat had just had kittens and she was gentle and sweet with them. I was used to crude violence towards animals, including drowning them in buckets, once Barbara felt they got in the way. Petula's mum reminded me of the hippy mums I'd found so welcoming when I was younger. Even though she'd long stopped wearing flowing dresses, beads and bracelets, she still came across as 'alternative'. I would sit at the dinner table, next to Petula, and discuss with them things I'd learnt from Mr Papadopoulous.

Petula's mum ('Call me Susie') would put her head on one side and listen. Listen! I was being listened to. This was a whole new experience. As we forked rice and peas and vegetables into our mouths and drank red wine (she poured me a glass), we actually conversed about things. I was included. It was a wonderful experience. We talked politics most of the time: Germaine Greer's *Female Eunuch*, or about the Common Market. We listened to the Stones and the Beatles quite openly, all together. Everyone laughed as Petula's dad ('Call me Jimmy') danced round the kitchen, washing up. It was fun. Life could be fun. Families could have fun. They could actually be nice to each other, and co-operative. This was a total revelation to me.

However, the one topic of conversation I never entered into was what was really going on at home. This was a dark, shameful secret that I kept totally to myself. I did not want people to know. I didn't want to be pitied, or to be different, so I tried hard to fit in. My lying continued, and sometimes I made up huge fibs about what we were doing for our holidays or what my parents were up to: 'Oh, we're trying France this year.'

The only holidays we actually had were day trips to the asylum to visit Barbara's long-lost youngest brother – he was a permanent inpatient in a local mental hospital, and we brought sandwiches with us and ate them on the dry, brown grass. Apart from that, there were no holidays. But I was too ashamed, too humiliated, to really let on what life was like in the house of horrors. I wanted to fit in with the nice posh people. I didn't want to be different, the oddball. I was so tired of all that now.

One of the nice things about the 'New Age' mums was that they respected and appreciated me as an artist. They could see, in the way I was dressing, that I was artistic and it didn't put them off. If anything it gained me respect. This was amazing for me. I wasn't put down, slagged off or criticised. I was accepted. Everyone knew I was good at art. I was now determined to go to art school, and that was something I talked about to the groovy parents.

The one thing I did reveal about home was that my parents were not keen for me to go. One day, unbeknownst to me, Petula's mum dropped in on Barbara without warning to talk to her about me going to art school. This was after a particularly heated row at home, when I'd been slapped about by Barbara and told, 'Don't be so stupid, you're not going to any bloody art school. Over my dead body.'

I wish, was my thought.

Apparently Susie had just turned up at the house unannounced and knocked on the door. When Barbara opened it she was already red in the face, as she was in a fury about something else altogether, and she snapped, 'Who the hell are you?'

I was out at the time, probably with the boys down the Rec, and had no knowledge of this encounter. I was told afterwards by Susie that when they went through to the kitchen, Barbara had already thrown a lot of crockery out on the lawn and smashed it. The lawnmower had been turned on its side and there were other things, like saucepans, lurking in the flower-beds. Susie had thought this all very strange. So when she reported this back to me, over macrobiotic vegetable curry later in the week, I wanted to disappear under the white throw rugs.

She asked me about Barbara's behaviour. She looked at me with sincere warmth and kindness, and I just said, 'Oh, she's had some bad news about her family, so I guess she was feeling upset.'

I didn't explain anything about the terror regime, or that Barbara would pick up a dog and throw it and break its back if she was so inclined. I had no idea how I could explain such crazy behaviour to people who were so friendly and normal and kind. I also feared it becoming known by my other friends, and then the bullying at school would get worse. I was trying to escape all that, and finally recreate myself, so I withheld the mess from nice, innocent people for as long as I could. I didn't want to be a victim or someone people felt sorry for. I didn't want to be a charity case.

No one usually went round to our house – for good reason. I did feel hugely embarrassed about Barbara's behaviour towards Petula's mum, though. She had gone out of her way to plead for me to be allowed to go to art school and was met with typical short shrift: 'No, that's not for the likes of Louise. I know best, I'm her mother.'

However, things were about to come to a head in an unexpectedly dramatic way.

~❧~

Now fourteen, I had finally been to the hairdresser and got a punky Toyah hairstyle. It was a shocking-pink Mohican, standing right up on top, with sea-green shaved tramlines at the sides. I was proud of my confection; it was wonderful. I put on fairly heavy make-up and black punk clothes. Around this time at school I had a careers chat, which was useless. I said I wanted to go to art school – it was my only desire. I was told I had not a chance; my grades were too bad overall.

I was livid. No one spoke to me about what my options were; I was just left hanging with the idea that I would just have to go and work in a shop or factory. Or worse, just get married (like Barbara's fantasy of me marrying Kevin, and looking after her in her old age – no thank you!). The careers teacher just shrugged and moved onto the next girl; I wasn't worth bothering about. I was furious, but kept it all inside, as usual.

I was beginning to get a bit of a hard, rock 'n' roll reputation at school. The other girls could clearly see I didn't fit in and had had enough. I was on a collision course. It all came to a head in one of the poxy home economics lessons. I felt genuinely insulted by these lessons and I couldn't stand them. I had spent my entire life being cheap domestic labour at home, so it seemed crazy to me to teach us to be housewives at school.

Mrs Deacon was a plump woman in a brown Crimplene suit, with glasses and ratty hair. We all had to stand behind our tables while she taught us how to bathe a baby in a plastic tub. Mrs Deacon reminded me of Barbara. She had a sharp nose and beady eyes and I didn't like her. She always spoke in a crisp, condescending way, especially to me.

'Girls, first you have to make the casserole for your husband when he is coming home after a hard day's work. You put it in the oven, and then you have time to bathe the baby.'

I couldn't believe my ears and eyes. I thought about the words of Mr Papadopoulous, and the fact that there were loads of women questioning these traditional roles now. Is this all I was good for? I thought about my so-called home, where the evening meal was doll food, and the rest of the family ate proper meals, minus me. My blood was boiling. What was this rubbish for teaching? So I spoke up.

'I don't want a husband, miss,' I said, with as much attitude as I could muster. 'I don't want to do this.'

Mrs Deacon focused her beady eye on me. 'Louise, you will do this task along with everyone else.'

We stared each other out. For ages.

Eventually Mrs Deacon moved on round the class. For protest, while her back was turned, I put the baby in the bath, put in some water, and splashed about, making a huge mess. Then I drowned it. The other girls round me tittered. I was mucking about and they loved it. I was now playing a rebellious clown. What a stupid exercise. How ludicrous. I could feel my blood simmering away, ready to explode.

In my house, babies were drooled over for five minutes and then battered. Hubbies hid in the garage while children were tied up and beaten or raped. Was this the happy family life Mrs Deacon had in mind for us all – or just me? Mrs Deacon turned her back, and we were supposed to put our babies in a cot with neat nappies on, while putting the perfectly prepared casserole in the oven for the master's tea. Yeah, right!

Something came over me, something snapped, and I put the baby in a baking tray and shoved it in the hot oven. I then put the casserole in the baby bath and it sploshed, smelly, steaming and brown, all over the place. Then I put my hand up provocatively and said, 'dunnit, miss,' to loads of giggles and titters from the girls around me. I was killing myself laughing. All the girls were falling apart. The class was in chaos, as smoke started billowing out of my oven. Thick, black, acrid smoke.

Mrs Deacon's eyes popped out of her head. 'Louise!' Then the sprinkler system started and girls began shrieking at the tops of their voices. It was raining in home economics, all over everyone. The girls were beside themselves – all their neat plaits and ponytails were getting wet. We were drowning in class. It was hilarious. At the same time, sprinklers were also going off all round the school, which I didn't realise then, and girls doing mock exams had ink running down the page.

It was utter mayhem. The school bell was ringing at the wrong time of day, girls were being ushered out of classrooms, giggling and delighted to be let out early. Mrs Deacon pulled open my oven and out gushed black smoke and everyone started coughing. My 'baby' was a molten mass of plastic. Mrs Deacon switched off my oven, grabbed me by the arm and pulled me past all the girls, who were looking at me with shining eyes full of admiration, trying to stop laughing. Everyone was spluttering, gasping, giggling. I didn't care, as she shouted at me, 'You are going to the Head. Right now!'

This was the best fun I'd had at school for a very long time. Did I care? No! I smiled. Bring it on.

19

The Worm Turns

The next day the traffic light outside the headmistress's office turned green. Barbara and I went in and sat on our usual chairs facing Mrs Drayton with her tight grey perm and crisp navy suit. I crossed my arms and stared at her.

'Well, Louise,' she began stiffly. 'What have you got to say for yourself?'

I said nothing, and just stared back. Mrs Drayton pushed a big box of men's Kleenex across the desk towards me, and I leant forward and pushed it back. She looked totally outraged. Playing Mrs Drayton for all she was worth, Barbara chipped in: 'I don't know what to do with her. I've done all I can. You can see what she's like…' Barbara dabbed at her eyes with a hanky. Mrs Drayton looked pointedly at Barbara and then at me.

'Louise, you know full well that you are not allowed to wear that hair and make-up at school.' I glared at her, not giving an inch. 'And you know that you have done a terrible thing in home economics – not only did you disrupt the exams, but the entire school.' I continued to stare at her. 'Do you realise how serious this is?'

I wanted to smile, but barely repressed it. Of course I did. In a way. But I didn't care. I knew how serious everything was all the time. I'd simply had enough. I didn't say anything; I just continued to stare at her, eyeball to eyeball.

'Very well,' she said, looking down and shuffling papers on her very tidy, wooden desk. 'You will be suspended for the next two weeks. You need to think very hard about what you have done.' She was scribbling notes. 'Oh, and I want that hairstyle gone when you come back.'

Yeah, right. I was thinking very hard. I was thinking about what a bad girl I had become and I was amazed by myself. I was bored, bored, bored. I was fed up with everything. I knew what would happen the minute we got out of that office: I would be sworn at, berated, put down, and then, at home, I would be punched, slapped and kicked. I was absolutely sick and tired of it. I was bad here, and bad there. But I didn't care if I was suspended: good riddance. In terms of my life, it just meant more of the same: more of being kept home to do the housework, as always. And more wandering around looking at lovely things, escaping into the healing calm of beauty when I could, drawing all the time and preparing myself for the great day when I would finally be free.

At this time I tended to go to a couple of local cafes: I loved the Nosebag, and there was also the Omni. Both were vegetarian and attracted young people in hordes. I hung out most the time with the pupils who were at the 'comp', the school I had wanted to go to in the first place. They didn't wear uniforms; they were creative and artistic, musical and fun, real individuals, and a lot of them came from the 'nice' families who had professional parents. But they were interested – like I was now – in talking about things going on in the world: politics, art, music and animal rights. We played music all the time in the cafes: Sex Pistols, Eurythmics, Blondie and Siouxsie Sioux. I felt at home there, and although I was poor I was able to disguise myself with my art and be punky and funky. I could hang out over one herbal tea bag for hours on end. It was great.

However, on the school front, there were now endless meetings with social workers, the local authority, and even educational psychologists. Things were hotting up. When I went back to school, after the two-week suspension, I still had my Toyah Wilcox-inspired shocking-pink and sea-green, crazy-colour hairstyle. I was also sporting dramatic black eyeliner. So I was called in again to the headmistress and told in no uncertain terms to get rid of it. I crossed my arms and said no, defiantly. We were on a collision course all right. Mrs Drayton was clearly beside herself (which I secretly enjoyed watching), and then I was sent to talk to an educational psychologist in another room.

No one spoke to me directly about what was going on or why I was rebelling like I was. They all swallowed the Barbara line of me being a girl with a giant chip on my shoulder. They all believed Barbara and, because of that, I was untouchable. They could all believe that garbage if they wanted to – I knew the truth – but I wasn't going to tell it to anyone either. It was mine. My secret. My life. My power. All the conversations that were going on about me went on behind closed doors. No one sat down with me and asked me anything. I had never told anyone about the madness at home as I simply thought I wouldn't be believed. I also felt too ashamed to admit to it. All through this, despite me looking like a punk, I was extremely polite. The one thing I had learnt from my imprisonment in the house of horrors was to be polite and gracious – even to (or maybe especially to) my enemies. I wasn't rude even if I wasn't going to comply with everything they wanted me to do.

So I went to the room with the educational psychologist and I sat down next to him at a big wooden table. He got out some big black files, and started turning pages. I had never met this man before in my life. I was sitting in this room with him, on my own, feeling a bit spooked. ('All men are filthy rapists' had been drummed into me by Barbara, although she'd deny it if I ever mentioned she'd said it to me over and over.) He was a little man in his forties, in a brown leather jacket. He had a ginger moustache and longish hair with dandruff. I didn't understand why I was there with him or what he wanted, so I braced myself.

'Hi, I'm Robert,' he started, trying to be jolly, and then put in front of me some white sheets of paper with huge black ink splodges on them.

'OK, Louise,' he said, talking down to me a bit. 'Let's look at these pictures together.'

As he was talking, I took my pen (which was always in my pocket) and I started drawing on the pictures, embellishing them, making lines come out of all the curvy shapes.

'No, no, no!' Robert was outraged. 'No, no, Louise, you can't do that!'

I looked at him, innocently, as he was now wide-eyed, sweating and looking very agitated. 'I thought you wanted me to do something with these?' I asked calmly.

Robert was looking very distressed, and shuffling his papers.

'These are very expensive. They are special tests,' he tried to explain. He was clearly rattled.

'But they look like pictures I could draw on and play with,' I explained, sweetly.

'No, no, no,' he was shaking his head. 'Oh, dear me, I don't know... Look, you are supposed to say what they remind you of.'

'Oh,' I said, blinking. He was now really cross with me, and I realised that I had even broken the rules in this 'assessment'. I didn't actually mean to, but it had just seemed obvious to me to draw on the pictures. I drew all the time, on everything, everywhere. I also felt deep down that I had met so many social worker types in my time that I was used to giving them what they wanted. I was like a performing seal. I assumed he wanted me to 'express myself'. They always thought they were making me 'open up', but I had learnt to play them. I was playing Robert, to some extent, and now he was rattled.

I knew he would give a bad report of me to the headmistress and tell her I wasn't playing the game. I was just thinking, *Okay, so I've messed this up, so I can get out of here. Yippee! Bring it on.* I could see that Robert was totally frustrated by me, like Mrs Drayton, as I was not playing his nice little ink-blot game. I was playing my fuck-it-up game, instead. At the end of the meeting he seemed actually hurt that I'd ruined his expensive set of pictures. I felt elated. I had won something at last.

Of course, this meeting led to yet another meeting with even more do-goody officials. A few days later I was ushered into a big room in the centre of Oxford. There were about six people sitting round the table with notes in front of them, all with lanyards on. It was just me on one side of an enormous table against six of them. Barbara was outside the room in the corridor, waiting for me, getting even more wound up. I had been slapped, kicked, punched, shouted at and starved a lot over the past few days for the shame I was bringing on her and her family. I just laughed. I didn't care any more. I was sick of her and her bloody family. I wanted to be rid of them – and everyone else who told me what to do all the time.

Now I was sitting opposite a middle-aged woman in a coral-pink cardigan and lanyard in the middle of the table, with people either side of her. She had big glasses on, like TV screens, and a plump, moist face and body. She leant forwards over the table towards me.

'Sooooo, Louise,' she hissed sweetly, 'how do you feel?'

I looked at her in her ridiculous lobster-pink cardi and huge breasts that were leaning on the table, and I wanted to laugh. How do I feel? I wasn't going to tell her and a room full of complete strangers how I felt. Was she mad? I sat there thinking, *You want me to play the game – to do that thing you like, to tell you I'm sad and angry or whatever, so you can write down your stupid notes in your poxy little notebooks. Well, I'm not gonna do it.*

I felt like I was on fire. I crossed my arms and gritted my teeth. I was not going to help. I was not going to be useful. I was not going to say anything she wanted me to. The worm had turned. And this worm had big fiery teeth, and it was going to bite. I felt like I was going to bite the lot of them, in a place that hurt. And the way to do that best was through silence and not giving them what they wanted.

Mrs Lobster-pink Cardi started again, trying to smile at me. She had big rabbity teeth. 'Sooooo, I see you seem to have trouble staying at school.'

I smiled at this. 'Yes, I do,' I said simply. Wasn't that obvious?

See how easy this was. She was getting the hang of my game. I felt I was in charge. I could see exactly what she was doing. She had these silly questions and she was going to ask them, and then I had to answer and she would tick her boxes. And then they would go 'Um' and 'Ah' and 'Er', and then there would be a lot of talking to each other, ignoring me completely, and with Barbara, and with Mrs Drayton – but not with me!

Nobody had bothered to ask me all these years what it was like, so I wasn't going to tell them now. I would play their game and play them at it better than any of them would ever realise.

'Well,' said Mrs Cardi. 'Um, er… the school has a problem with children like you.'

Like me? Like me? What did she mean, 'like me'? Then I launched at her when she didn't see it coming. I told her how boring the school was, and how there was nothing to do if you were put in the lower stream. I was sick and tired of doing cookery and needlework – was that all they had to offer? I could see the cogs whirring in their tiny heads, as they had me down as thick, thick, thick. Yet there I was being articulate. I was telling them that they were not giving me enough to do, to think about, to work on; that I was bored with their stupid school and system. I watched as they all looked at each other significantly, and Mrs Lobster-pink scribbled something else down in her notes.

'Sooo,' she began again, showing me her rabbity teeth, 'where do you go in the daytime?' She leant forward and gave me one of those 'you can tell me all about it' looks. She had to be joking.

My daily circuit was precious to me. It was my refuge, my

hope. I didn't want to spoil my wonderful times at Blenheim, or in the Pitt Rivers or the Ashmolean. Telling these idiots would just ruin it all for me. Why should I tell them? Why should they know?

'Well,' she began again, in strained social worker tones (I could tell she was beginning to get fed up with me now), 'we are concerned you are in danger.'

In danger? In the daytime? This was when I was *not* in danger. The danger I was really in was at home. But who had ever done anything about that? I couldn't begin to explain all this to this ridiculous do-gooder of a woman in a stupid pink cardigan.

'The only danger I'm in,' I said, 'is dying of boredom. At this school!'

I could see Mrs Cardi was shocked and exasperated. Looks shot round the table and they all sat back for a moment in their chairs. There was quite a pause, and then she started again.

'Okay, Louise, do you want to come to school?'

I sat up in my chair and looked her straight in the eye, arms crossed. 'Look, I never wanted to come to this school in the first place. I wanted to go to the comp, as it was a better school.'

Ripples of shock round the table.

'I don't want to come to a school like this. I never wanted to come to it.'

'Okay, okay,' she said. 'So how do we keep you here?'

'You don't,' I said with a huge grin. 'Not unless you lock me up. I'm beyond this. I'm too far beyond this.' I looked round the table. Six adults. Me opposite. Mr Ink-blot Test was there. No one told me their names. They all looked at me like a specimen in a jar.

'Oh dear,' said the woman in pink, sitting back finally, shaking her head. 'Louise, you will end up on heroin and be pregnant by the time you are sixteen.'

❧

The next day I was thrown out of school: expelled. The letter came and Barbara was absolutely beside herself.

'I wash my hands of you!' she screamed. 'After all I've done for you, you ungrateful bitch! You're going into care!'

She smacked me around the head and face, and I didn't flinch. I had heard it all before. I just walked out and went into town, and wandered and wandered. I found myself at the Museum of Modern Art and crept in, and there was an exhibition on of Robert Mapplethorpe's photographs. I looked at the amazing black-and-white images, feeling sick to my stomach. I wasn't going to show Barbara or the school anything but inside I was definitely terrified. I also felt as if a surge of volcanic-lava-like rage was building in me: I'm not doing this, I'm not having these people control my life any more, I'm not doing what they want. I didn't want to stay with Barbara, but I didn't want to go to another, unknown foster family either. I didn't want to stay at home all day, but I didn't want to go to school either. I was churning, fuming, shaking as I went around the exhibition.

As the images hit my retina, I was wowed by them: they were edgy, graphic, angry, violent, beautiful. They spoke to me. I thought, I don't get any of 'normal' life, but I do get this. I understood the photographs and the feelings in them. I wanted to be part of that world – the world that made those sorts of things, so people like me, in the state I was in, could go and look at them and feel healed and understood by them.

The pain in some of the pictures reflected exactly the pain I was feeling inside. A brutal, scary, empty, awful, terrified, exhilarated feeling.

Robert Mapplethorpe's pictures saved my life that day, as did Patti Smith's *Horses* album, which expressed exactly how I was feeling. I felt the pictures and music were honest; they expressed raw feelings as I understood them. I didn't feel anyone else in my life was honest. Nothing was true. I didn't trust anyone. I thought of Julie and her weird high-pitched giggle and barmaid clothes, and her odd comings and goings. She had never spoken to me directly, or explained anything about how I came about, or why she had given me over to the likes of Barbara. I thought of Barbara and Ian, and the awful spoilt Kevin, who was their 'favourite', and how they had made my life hell, in every way, every day. I thought of my friend Sandy and other girls at school who were being hunted daily by the seedy men down the Cowley Road; being used for sex because they were so lonely and desperate for affection, drugs and drink.

I felt like getting expelled was a defining moment, when I had rolled up my sleeves and said, 'Right, you lot, bring it on.' I felt it with clarity, with every pore of my body. I was in danger anyway, every day. Threatening me with being put into care was the last straw. I wouldn't stay there. I wouldn't go anywhere anyone wanted me to go. I would refuse. They couldn't make me. I was done with being made to do things I didn't want to. I felt like I suddenly owned my life. I was really on my own now. But I was fighting back!

I left the exhibition and wandered down to the Omni café. I got a herbal tea and sat in a corner, letting the atmosphere seep in. The coloured walls and chairs, the posters of punk and rock bands, the hiss of the coffee machine, the music from the jukebox, the murmur of students and young people chatting and laughing. By now it was 'home coming out time' from school. I sat and nursed my cold tea, and watched as a gang of pupils came in from the comp. There were a couple of girls I knew, Jan and Alex, and they saw me and said, 'Hi'. I nodded and smiled back. They were 'cool' alternative girls, with crazy-colour hair, safety pins on their black clothes, ripped jeans, dramatic eye make-up. I liked how they looked; they felt like my kind of people.

I noticed there was a guy with them, good-looking with dark hair and fine features. He was wearing a black T-shirt and had slicked his hair all spiky with gel. He had a lovely, intelligent expression and a gorgeous smile when he laughed at a joke one of the girls made. I continued sitting at my table, and then the group mooched over from the counter and Jan indicated the seats round me.

'Sure,' I said. The guy sat down and my heart started pounding faster.

'Hi, I'm Tim,' he said to me.

'Louise,' I said back and smiled. I watched them all talking, and they were discussing their exams. I thought I should go, but continued to hang out at the table, watching Tim talk to the two girls. I thought the conversation sounded very intelligent and knowledgeable. I was aware that my education was limited and I felt awkward about it. But I also felt I was done with hanging out with the 'townie' boys from down the Rec. I didn't want to be identified with the Cowley Road girls either, as the idea that I was going to end up on heroin and pregnant had outraged me. Was that all they thought of me? Was I not good for anything else?

I knew in my heart I wanted to go to art school. It was all I had ever wanted to do, and I knew I would have to find a way to get there. I had been expelled and had no qualifications and, by tonight, I might not have anywhere to live either. Maybe I would be moved to another city? Or go to live with Julie? The very thought filled me with horror – the idea of starting again in another town, with new people. What if they were worse than Barbara? And, anyway, I still had Sean. I couldn't leave him, as he was my real family. I knew I could always creep in and see Sean. I even slept over at his when I felt I'd had enough of everything, no questions asked. He was still my safe haven in the midst of it all. Eventually the group made moves to go. Tim turned to me, shyly.

'We're all going to the Lamb and Flag later, for a drink. See you there?'

I had a curfew of 10 p.m. if I went out, and I had no money to spend, but my heart leapt. I had no idea what I was going to do from this day forward, either. However, I looked into Tim's handsome face and twinkly auburn eyes and I said, as casually as I could, 'Yeah, sure. See you later.'

And with that, they were gone.

20

Finding My Hero

When I saw Tim in the pub early that evening with his friends, including Jan and Alex, I felt shy and excited. I hadn't gone home yet, as I didn't dare, and I'd no money, but I'd hung out, trying to look like I went there every day. When Tim saw me, he made a beeline.

'Hi, want a drink?' I nodded, and we elbowed our way to the bar. Tim was about to go to university to do psychology. He already had his place organised and was finishing up his A Levels. Summer was here and he was getting ready to go.

We stood sipping our beers outside in the balmy evening air, as starlings circled overhead, and we talked about music, art, politics. I was now just fifteen and he was coming up to eighteen. Every time I looked at him my stomach flipped over with a tense excitement. I loved his eyes, his look, and he was warm and easy to talk to.

When Tim went to the loo, Jan leant towards me and said, 'I think he fancies you.' I felt my face turn ruby red and I tingled all over. He was very attractive and, in fact, all the girls in our group seemed to find him fanciable. Surely he didn't fancy me? He was so out of my league. What were the signs?

I didn't know what to look for. However, I was the one he was talking to.

I was dreading going home after getting expelled that day, but I couldn't tell Tim. I didn't want to make him think I was a 'loser' right from the start. I was trying to make a new me, away from the horror of my home. I really liked him, but couldn't really tell if he liked me, despite what Jan had said. I really didn't care either. I seemed to be beyond caring at the moment, beyond everything. I drank my warm bitter and watched the swallows diving over the rooftops, and just enjoyed the moment. I didn't know what would happen next, but somewhere, deep down inside, I felt a sort of faint hope brewing.

When Tim returned he made straight for me again and said 'Hi' warmly. At least he was speaking to me – just to me. I asked him the time, as I had no watch, and realised I was getting dangerously near my curfew of 10 p.m. I had no door key – I'd never had one of my own – and I knew the chain went across the door and it was bolted at ten exactly.

'I have to go,' I said to Tim. I didn't want to explain, as I would seem too young and uncool. He looked a bit disappointed.

'Oh, okay. Oh, er… see you around then?'

We held each other's eyes for a moment and both smiled. I felt my heart leap in my chest as something electric passed between us.

'Yeah, bye then,' I said, grinning at him, and left.

I started walking as fast as I could. I had no money, so couldn't get a bus. It was dark now, and I walked fast, head down, hands in my pockets, thinking about Tim's gorgeous smile. I was walking down Longwall Street when I became aware of footsteps behind me – lots of them. I speeded up and didn't look round. However, the footsteps sounded closer and closer, so I crossed the road. The footsteps crossed the road. My heart really started pounding, as I was in a dark narrow street now and there were no residential houses around.

I was half-running when I suddenly heard, 'Filth', and 'We're gonna fuckin' kill you, bitch.' I glanced over my shoulder and there were four huge white skinhead-type boys. They didn't like punks. They had obviously come out of a pub and seen me looking very 'alternative' and decided to have a go. I was terrified.

Luckily, at the end of the street there was a red phone box with a payphone in it. I darted in and closed the door and held it. The boys surrounded the phone box and started shouting through the glass at me, like rabid dogs: 'Bitch!' 'Whore!' and 'Slut!' I should have been used to these names by now but I was feeling very tired and vulnerable. I felt in my pockets and found one ten pence piece. I dialled the house. When it picked up Ian answered. I was desperate and said, 'I'm in St Clements and some boys are trying to get me.'

Ian just said, 'I'll pass you over to your mother.' They were clearly already in bed. A second later I could hear Barbara sniping down the phone: 'Well, serves you right. You should be home, you shouldn't be out.' And she slammed down the phone. Just like that.

I held onto the phone, trying to think.

'We're gonna fucking rape you, cunt,' came at me from a huge, spotty bloke with a beer gut, tattoos and bald head. Then they started trying to rock the phone box, and one tried to climb up the front of it. I had no idea how I was going to get out of this situation. I didn't think of calling 999, as my experience of the police had not been a good one. They'd probably take one look at me in my punk gear and join in with the thugs.

'Oi, leave her alone,' I then heard, in a dramatically loud male voice. One of the four thugs turned shouted at him, 'Make us.'

The one on top jumped down. Then there was a huddle on the pavement outside the phone box and I suddenly saw, to my amazement, Tim, on his bicycle.

'I'm getting the police,' he shouted loudly. In a flash the thugs just loped off drunkenly, shouting, 'Fuck you,' as they went. Then Tim came and opened the door, and I was shaking.

'Wow, thanks,' I said, feeling I'd met my knight in shining armour at last.

'What on earth were you doing?' Tim asked.

I explained what happened. Apparently Tim left the pub just after me, and was coincidentally whizzing home on his bike through his usual short cut, when he found me pinioned by the thugs. He then insisted he walk me home and we strolled, with him wheeling his bike, all the way back across town to my home. I didn't want him to come in, or even see the house, so I hovered on the pavement outside. Tim seemed concerned about me, checking I was okay and not too scared the whole time we walked. I wasn't used to someone being concerned about me at all, so I didn't know what to say. We hung around on the pavement for ages, and it was way past eleven now. I had no idea how I would get in the house. I didn't think I would. But I didn't tell Tim, as it was too complicated to explain.

Tim didn't want to go, and I didn't want him to go. We just kept talking and talking. He said he'd never met anyone quite like me before. There was still a force field between us and I felt like I wanted to hold him close. There was a kind of magic in the air.

'Can I take your number?' he asked in the end, and I gave

it to him. No one had ever called me before, so I was worried about what would happen if he did. Would Barbara even let me speak to him?

'I'll call you tomorrow, to see how you are, if that's all right?'

'If that's all right?' All right? Here was my hero, my life-saver, walking me home, showing he cared, taking my number. I was in seventh heaven. We stood closely and said bye and I felt we might kiss, but we didn't. I felt entirely smitten by the time he left, like my life had changed completely – for the better.

Once he was gone I tiptoed carefully over the gravel to get in but the door was bolted, predictably. I went around to the back of the house, where the gate was still open. My only option was to sleep in the shed – the horrible shed where William used to be imprisoned and where we would eat the birdseed. I bedded down on some sacking, and although it was damp and musty it was fine for the night. Neither Barbara nor Ian came to check I was home safely – I guessed they thought I'd creep in like a feral cat, at some time, and I should be ignored completely, to teach me a lesson. I could have been in hospital, or even dead, but they clearly didn't care. Unlike Tim.

~❧~

The next few weeks and months went by predictably badly at home. There were constant threats and rows. Barbara was threatening to put me in care, send me to strange foster parents, or hand me over to the hopeless Julie. I had spent a weekend in her house, with her new man, and it had been disastrous. She showed no interest in me and her children resented me. She was just as awful as Barbara as a mother, but in a completely different way. Julie was like a child, constantly preening herself in front of the mirror and having hysterics about everything. She spent money like water and didn't look after the children properly, either. The two children just spent time together and left me out of things.

By then it had become clear, too, that John's kidney was fine. He'd actually had a problem with his foreskin and had to have an embarrassing operation, which caused referred pain in his waterworks. No one ever said sorry to me for making me feel as if I was killing him. Barbara had either misunderstood the situation or was using his illness as another stick to beat me with. Whatever, I was never really accepted by them and we didn't get on. So it wasn't really an alternative and certainly not the cosy home I was so craving at this time.

Back home, Barbara went on and on at me endlessly. I was ungrateful; I had shamed her; I was a waste of space. I cried a lot, but also felt defiant and angry. I was still doing all my usual household chores, and more, and I was ignoring the family as much as I could and just trying to keep out of harm's way. I would retreat to Sean's caravan as often as possible to get a breather; to help him with his garden or sit and talk with him. He was still my kind ally. He even tried to calm Barbara down when she was ranting at me.

Sean always trod carefully with her, as he didn't want anyone complaining to the council about his caravan or the traveller site, but he was also polite to her at the same time as trying to protect me. He was clever doing that. Despite all the drama at home, Tim had phoned the next day, to my delight, and we became pretty inseparable. Every waking moment I wanted to be with him; we would talk and talk, and we kissed soon after we met, and I knew I was falling in love with him. I also knew that he was going away in the autumn, so I wanted to be with him as much as possible. He was teaching me I meant more than all that but I missed him terribly all the time when we were apart.

Luckily I spent most of that summer, post-school, hanging around the posh houses of Tim's family and his other friends. I had wonderful meals around big pine tables smelling of bees-wax, with white scatter rugs on the floor and lots of lovely William Morris-designed furniture and vintage crockery. Tim's mum, Lucy, had things like an ice cream maker and a yoghurt maker, which I'd never heard of. She ground coffee beans and we had wonderful hot steaming mugs of fresh coffee with frothy milk. They made their own bread. I drank wine and talked politics with nice parents around the table loaded with gorgeous food – and I could eat as much as I wanted.

Once Tim and I became a couple, his mother invited me to stay over at the weekend. I never told his family anything about my home, but I guess there was something about me that spelled out that I was very unhappy without my saying so. I think they picked up how restrictive things were. Lucy would phone Barbara and explain politely that I would be staying 'in the spare room'. In fact, although Tim and I did cuddle up together in his bedroom, we didn't have full sex. I had almost a phobia about it, not least because of all the horrible things that had been done to me by Kevin and Mark (which I never told Tim about), but also because of Julie getting pregnant with me at fifteen (which I also didn't mention) – the very age I was. I was terrified of history repeating itself; I didn't want to be like her.

Barbara had drummed it into me endlessly that I was a whore like my mother, so I felt very wary of getting into trouble. I didn't want to rush anything, and Tim was a loving, gentle, sweet young man. He was content for us to cuddle and kiss and explore but not to rush me into anything. I was happy with him, and happy spending time with these lovely, educated, kind people who showed me there was a different way of living without violence, cruelty, rudeness and threats. It made it even more difficult for me to go back to Barbara and Ian's house, where I was attacked, threatened, hit and called rude names before I even got across the threshold.

❧

Over that summer I had to get some work to earn money, as I never had any pocket money. I found a job in a greengrocer, and loved handling all the colourful fruit and veg. I wasn't great at the adding up, which I had to do in my head, and even on my fingers, but I gradually got better at it with practice. I enjoyed working with people, and discovered I could chat to them quite well and make them laugh. I was good at the job. This made me feel better about myself. I also picked up some cleaning work. I heard, on one of our pub visits, someone saying they needed help around the home.

'I can help you,' I piped up. I had no money, and I began to pick up cleaning jobs for posh Oxford people who lived in gorgeous houses with stripped wooden floors and lovely interiors. I had cleaned all my life, so it was easy to get the work done. And I got paid cash in hand.

During this summer, a friend of Tim's family, an American author, was going away for a month and asked for someone to house-sit. Barbara protested and shouted, slapped me and threatened care, but I ignored her. Tim offered, and we both moved in with several of our friends. We looked after the place and had a little commune for a few weeks. The freedom at last was wonderful, and they were all amazed that I could clean up so well. They didn't realise I'd spent my life scrubbing and making hospital corners. I could also cook to some extent, and I could look after the garden, do pet care, and they were actually in awe.

We played David Bowie at full blast, drank wine and had a lovely time in this house. When the author returned he said he was amazed that the house was in such good condition. He'd been away before and left it with students and it'd been wrecked. With us, he'd had a great deal. All this time Tim and I were sleeping in the same bed, but I still knew I wasn't ready to 'do the deed' and he was still kind and patient. I really loved him for being such a genuinely kind and thoughtful person. He was writing me sonnets every morning, and telling me he loved me every day. He taught me to make posh food, like ratatouille, and to know my Chianti from my Pinot Grigio.

All this time Barbara said she had 'washed her hands of me'. There had been some correspondence with the school, who said they wanted me to think about coming back for my last year, until I was sixteen. They would only consider me coming back, of course, without the punk hair and make-up. In fact, some girls at school had got up a petition to get me back – they all thought it was unfair I'd been expelled for my looks and setting off the sprinklers. The school was dealing with the issue of the men on the Cowley Road preying on its girls, so my problems seemed small in comparison, at least to the girls (who also wanted to wear crazy-colour hair). They wanted me back!

I couldn't see the point, and this was the cause of a lot of rows with Barbara, which quickly descended into violence. I would then go back to the commune and spend a lovely evening laughing and drinking wine with my good friends and Tim.

On Barbara's birthday, which was in August, I baked her a vegan Victoria sponge cake in the author's house, borrowed Tim's bicycle, dressed up nicely and went over to see her. All I wanted to do was say 'Happy Birthday' and give her a card I'd made, with some flowers and the cake. I'm not sure exactly why I wanted to do this but, oddly, now I had some space away from Barbara, I felt some shards of affection for her. It's difficult to explain why. She was always horrible and cruel to me but still, I suppose, she had been a mum of sorts over the whole of my lifetime and I felt I wanted to show her I was all right and I appreciated her for something, at least. I was happy, I suppose, and felt I could spread a bit of the love. I think I knew, intuitively, that Barbara had never experienced love in her life.

When I got there, she didn't smile when she opened the door. She grabbed the flowers out of my hand, saying sulkily, 'You'd better come in.' It was a summer's day and I was hot from cycling.

'Why are you so red?' she asked me, snappily. I explained I'd been cycling. She moved towards me with a venomous look in her eye, like an eagle attacking a small rodent, and sniffed at me: 'You've done it, haven't you? You've been having sex.'

She was spitting as she said this. I looked at her pointy, grey face, her grey clothes and mean features, and thought, *Is that it?* I didn't answer. I just got back on my bike and left. That is all she was obsessed about: sex. I had no idea why. That night I said to Tim: 'Okay, it's time.'

We carefully set the scene and had the most romantic, loving, wonderful time together, as I thought I was ready, finally. We were very careful, as I didn't want to get pregnant, like Julie. If Barbara never believed me for a moment, what was the point of continuing not to do it? I might as well do it and enjoy it. I was probably reacting, but I also thought, what the hell. Enjoy! And enjoy it, thankfully, I did, with the right person at the right time and in the right way.

However, summer was coming to an end, and Tim was finally going to leave. I couldn't face it. I felt heartbroken, but I didn't want to hold him back at all. In September he set off for uni, and my heart went through the floor. We said we'd see each other as often as possible, but he was going miles away and I was stuck in Oxford and in Colditz.

He was always encouraging me with my art, as the whole summer long I had been drawing, painting and creating to my heart's content. He told me over and over that I was good enough and that I could make it. Once he had gone, and I was back in the house all the time, it was terrible. The school wanted me to go back in what they called a 'phased return', and Barbara was pressing me to do that, despite having kept me home for so much of my schooling. I was way behind because she had held me back for her own selfish, mad reasons, yet now she was making out I was the one responsible.

My life was shrinking back again, having been colourful, bold, sunny and wonderful for a few months. I felt I was growing out of the house, out of my life, out of the whole town. I didn't fit. I didn't know what to do with myself, but I was still working in the greengrocer's for money. I liked working, I liked people and, more than that, I liked having some cash of my own. I'd had a taste of independence.

At home Barbara made a big play of the fact that Kevin had had a girlfriend round. They went up to his room and came down flushed. Barbara smiled. She didn't give him a hard time about being red in the face. One evening she came into my room – I was still in the same tiny box room, with the blue flowery wallpaper – and she gave me more sexy clothes (I'd never worn the babydoll outfit), saying, 'Why don't you entertain Kevin like his girlfriend does?'

Sickened, I refused to play her perverted game and I hid the clothes. I knew now what real love felt like, and proper loving sex, and it was nothing like the horrible ugly experiences I'd had at the hands of nasty Kevin and his gropey friend.

At this time Kevin was aspiring to be some kind of alpha male. One night he came strolling into the kitchen and came right up to me, putting his face in mine. He could smell alcohol on me, as I'd been out with friends. I was quite challenging now to the likes of Kevin, as I had learnt to argue back. Kevin sniffed at my breath, grimaced and started poking at me. I pushed him off and this developed into an all-out wrestling match and fight. Ian was in the best living room watching TV and Barbara was in the garden, with the dog, Mohra (a new one, of course, as Sissy had been 'put down', like all the rest).

'You think you're so fucking smart and cool,' Kevin was saying, grabbing at my hair and breasts in equal measure, 'with all your posh fucking friends and *boyfriend*.'

He sneered 'boyfriend' at me, and punched me in the guts. I fought back as hard as I could. We fought bitterly in the kitchen, with him slamming me into the cabinets, and me pushing him back against the sink. Everything was crashing and rattling as we fought. Barbara was at the window, smirking. I caught her face, briefly, enjoying every swipe that landed on me from Kevin. He was doing her dirty work for her. And then he toppled me. He was about two feet taller than me by now, and well-filled-out, as he lifted weights.

He started kicking me in the guts, stamping on my limbs, kicking me in the face and kidneys. It went on and on, until I was retching and sick. He had boots on. He was twenty-one and I was fifteen.

'Who the fuck do you think you are?' he kept raging at me, over and over, as he kicked. 'You're nothing, you're nobody, you're scum,' he shouted. He was like the thugs at the phone box. I managed to crawl away as he was kicking, pulling myself round the kitchen. He put his boot on my head and pressed me hard into the floor. I couldn't breathe.

'I'm going to fucking kill you one day,' he spat at me. 'Mark my words.' And with that he waltzed out the kitchen, leaving the place a complete wreck.

I crawled along the floor on my belly over smashed crockery and past upturned chairs. I managed to get up the stairs, step by step, and into the bathroom, where I eventually splashed my face with water. I sat on the side of the bath for a long time, trying to breathe with bruised ribs. It was Friday night. I eventually got up and looked at myself in the bathroom cabinet mirror. My face was a mess: cuts, bruises, a swollen eye. My clothes were ripped, my arms and hands and legs had bruises appearing already. I hurt all over.

I thought, *I can't do this any more. I can't let him stop me from living my life*. I finally washed my face properly and then carefully reapplied my make-up and did my hair. I went to my room and changed my clothes. It was now or never: I knew exactly what I had to do.

21

The Great Escape

Everything hurts. I'm trembling and shaking as I stumble around my tiny room – so familiar yet so hideously ugly in every way. My heart is racing as I listen out for any sounds downstairs. I can hear canned laughter from the TV but I can't hear any voices – maybe they've fallen asleep in front of it. I slide my chest of drawers open as quietly as I can and pull out a few things: knickers, T-shirts, jeans. I pack my school rucksack carefully. I've practised this moment so many times over the years, since the days when I used to pack my little red cardboard case, imagining I was going to a faraway land, where everything was wonderful. Now I'm pulling out a little tin I hid at the back of the drawer under some old socks, where I keep my earnings. I've saved something each week from my grocery work and, counting it, I might just have enough. I stuff it in a purse and shove that in my rucksack.

I stop, hardly breathing, still listening out. Nothing. I imagine Kevin suddenly bursting through the door, as he so often does, then marauding round my room or trying to get in my knickers. He has no idea of boundaries, and I am a non-person to him. I think of Barbara coming in and bearing down over me, with her eagle eyes, narrow lips and pointy nose, always sniffing at me, being suspicious, slapping me around the head. I hold my breath. Count one, two, three, four. One, two, three, four. Heart pounding. Nothing. I don't have a watch, and there is no clock, but I know it's late. I'll have to be quick about it.

I tiptoe downstairs, holding my breath, trying to look as casual as possible. I can hear the news is on, so it's quite late now. Ian is still in the best living room, and possibly Barbara is with him. Or more likely she's in bed – I don't dare check. Kevin is nowhere to be seen, thank goodness. The chaos is still just visible through the kitchen door from our brawl earlier. Barbara will be in my room first thing to shout at me to clear it all up – as it's my fault.

My body aches as I tread carefully down the stairs; my ribs, thighs and kidneys are throbbing. I wince, but I don't care – at least I've still got both of the latter, I think wryly. I picked up some painkillers from the bathroom as I passed the cabinet – I'll need those later. I get to the front door. It's still Friday night. I can't believe it's the same evening as when I came in from the pub earlier. It seems like another era, like an age has passed. I feel like a different person, like something has changed for ever. I won't be the same again. It was a significant moment – like a slave breaking free.

I open the front door a crack. I listen. Nothing. No dog barks. Mohra is young and is probably up on the bed with Barbara. She allows the pups up with her, but once they're too big they get shunted to the kitchen. I look back down the hallway at the horrible swirling orange carpet, the pine G-Plan telephone table with the green Trimphone and phone books. There's a horrible plastic lampshade hanging round a single bulb. I loathe the ghastly cheap print of a windmill on the wall. I absolutely hate this place. I take in the magnolia wallpaper, the chipped paint, the dreariness of it all. I tread over the doorstep and pull the door closed as silently as I can behind me. Then I tiptoe carefully over the gravel to the front gate and look back. I pause. It's like the Beatles' song, 'She's Leaving Home' – one of my favourites. Then I remember Sean. Oh no! How can I leave my dear caravan saviour and the lovely Polish people?

My heart lurches, and my guts are gripped by fear. I want to cry. I want to rush back down the gravel, down the side alley past the bins, through the garden, into the orchard and tap on his window, as I always do. Three little taps, which means me. I want to see his lovely white-haired head pop out over the stable door, and hear, 'Oh, come in, girlie, why doncha?' Standing there, I waver. I'm thinking back over the merciless Kevin beating, and I know I can't go back now. It's too late. I think he might actually kill me next time. No one would stop him. Barbara would actually encourage him and Ian would look the other way. Plus Julie would be nowhere to be seen, and wouldn't care, even if she were there. I am on my own entirely. I have to face this. I can't live my life here any more. And the only person I care about right now (apart from Sean) – and who really cares for me – is hundreds of miles away. Finally I pull open the wrought-iron gate and carefully slip through. I look back briefly for the last time, and then I'm gone. The great escape has begun.

❧

There were no buses, so I had to walk to the station, which hurt a great deal. I wondered if I'd broken something, as my ribs were agony and it was hard to breathe, but I managed to get

onto one of the last trains down to London. I had no real idea
what on earth I would do when I got there. I'd never been on
a long-distance journey by train before. My only experience of
travel was by foot, bike or bus, and in the car with Barbara at
breakneck speed. We had never had holidays or trips away, so
I was totally unused to whatever it is you had to do when you
travelled by train.

I bought a ticket to King's Cross and sat in the train, looking out at the black of night, as lights, stations and buildings
flashed by. There were a few drunks on the train, some odd men
and smoochy young people. I felt my heart racing the whole
time. I had been under scrutiny my whole life. I had always
been watched, criticised, judged, beaten, hurt. I was always
in the wrong. But now it was like I was watching myself. The
experience of simply being alone on this train, hurtling into the
unknown under the cover of darkness, in pain, but free at last,
wasn't yet sinking in. I felt really sad about Sean, but I had to go.

I had no real plan of what I'd do exactly when I got there. I
would find somewhere to stay in London, somehow. I'd heard
something about King's Cross being a place for the young
homeless or something. I felt determined. I didn't want to land
on Tim. I didn't want to ruin his life or be dependent on him. I
just knew I had to get away and find somewhere to go. I was sick
of being a punchbag, sick of being blamed for everything,
sick of being labelled and hounded and misjudged. Without
Tim my life had become unbearable and Kevin's final savage
attack was the last straw. I knew I would miss dearest Sean, but
I would contact him soon and explain everything. I loved him
like a daughter, and I knew he cared about me – I felt he would
understand and forgive me.

I ended up at King's Cross at one-thirty in the morning. Suddenly it felt a very scary place to be. Drunks were lurching about everywhere, on the floor, groaning in alleyways. I walked around the station several times, with every step being agony. I wasn't sure what to do next. A couple of guys leered up to me, and I managed to duck and weave my way away from them. They gave me a bad feeling, like the guys outside school from the Cowley Road. I sensed danger, and the hairs stood up on the back of my neck the minute they started careering over towards me. I saw loads of people who were clearly looking for drugs, and plenty of heroin addicts spaced out on the floor, shivering, wrapped in blankets, or with a dog on a string, lying on pieces of cardboard.

'Louise, you will end up on heroin and be pregnant by the time you are sixteen,' rang in my ears from Mrs Drayton. I looked at the heroin addicts and thought, *No way, not me, never.*

'You are a whore and a waste of space, just like your mother, and you'll have a drink problem, just like her.' The constant prediction from Barbara also went round and round in my head.

No, not that, either, I thought, as I tried to find a corner of the station to rest in. I was shaking with fear, exhaustion and hunger by the time I found a homeless shelter for young people, which was advertised as being in a white stone gateway some way down the road, as part of the old entrance to Euston station. When I finally got there on foot, I found a notice pinned on the closed door saying simply, 'Sorry full tonight'.

My heart sank. I stood there trying not to cry. I wanted to lie on the grass nearby and holler my heart out but I had to stay safe. I started walking around a little park in front of the entrance of the station. Men kept appearing out of the surrounding bushes, buildings and from behind bins, hissing, 'Need somewhere to sleep tonight?' I kept saying no and then hobbling away as fast as I could. Eventually I found a bench. I just had to lie down. I put my rucksack under my head and my jacket over it, held onto both very tightly and hoped for the best. My head was spinning with fatigue and I started drifting off into sleep almost immediately.

Suddenly I felt a tug at my trousers. Then a yank, and I realised my jeans were being pulled down. I tried to sit up and there was a dark, ghoulish presence over me, with a guttural voice saying, 'You're coming with me,' like they knew me already. He was in his thirties, in a leather jacket, with a crew cut and piercings. He smelt very bad, as his hot hideous breath wafted over me.

I started kicking, despite the pain, and managed to wriggle out from under him and off the bench, rucksack in hand. I ran into the main station, panting, hurting and horrified, and found a place by a ticket machine and sat down on the floor with my back to it. I had to be vigilant. I was not going to sleep, obviously. Looking at the station clock, it was now coming up to four-thirty. I had found out from a guard that the Underground started running at about five-thirty, so I would get a tube from Euston and find another mainline station. I was now so spooked, so terrified and felt so unsafe that the only thing I could think of was going to find Tim, despite my best intentions not to do this. I had to get to him. That was now my mission.

London was going to be very difficult, the state I was in. I didn't want to land on Tim, but I knew instinctively that if I didn't I might wind up dead or worse. Suddenly all I could think about was getting to Tim. Once I got there I would make up some story. I didn't want to affect his life or his career but I was at a total crossroads. I had to get somewhere, to get straight, and I needed to see him so I could work out what to do next.

Fare dodging, I managed to get to Waterloo and then waited for the first train to Portsmouth at five-thirty. I hadn't enough money for the ticket, but slipped by the barrier and got on. I had no food, no drink, no nothing. It had been a very long night. Luckily I still had some ten pences for a phone call. I had to save those to call Tim. I had no idea where I was going or what Portsmouth would be like or even where Tim lived exactly. All I knew was I had to make my escape from the hellhole that was my life, in the dead of night.

❧

Tim was wonderful. He came along on his bike, even though it was only seven-thirty in the morning, after I had spent my last ten pences on a phone call from a red phone box. We walked slowly back to his shared student house with him wheeling his bike. It was like the night we met all over again. He was my hero, still. However, I didn't tell him why I had come, or that I had come from London, or that someone had tried to rape me on a bench. I just made out that I was missing him and wondered if I could stay a couple of days.

He could see my bruises and cuts, as my face was now swollen, so I guess he knew something was very wrong. But Tim was kind and understanding; he didn't press me to spill my story. He accepted me as I was. I appreciated that, as I would have cried and cried and not been able to stop if I'd told him. He took me out for breakfast, and kept asking if I was okay. I nodded, ate and then slept for a whole day. His whole attitude was one of care, kindness, acceptance and love. I drank it up. I was like a dried-up sponge thrown into a tub of lovely sudsy water. I sucked it up and recovered. Tim's flatmates were fine about me being there. Tim went to uni, to his classes and lectures, and came home and studied.

After a while I began to recover and I would clean up, cook, draw and try to work out what I should do. I had no money. Tim was kind and had just enough for two for a week or so (he could always ask his parents for more), but it became clear very quickly that I would have to do something. I couldn't tell him what was going on. I was frightened I would lose him if he knew the whole grimy, horrible truth. He might not like me any more.

He knew I'd left school early, and that it was something about my hair and make-up. I made it into a good story. Tim just had me down as a cool, artistic rebel. He was middle-class but I was gritty working-class, and I think it made him feel good to be with me. He suggested I just draw and paint as much as I wanted, and so I began to make a portfolio of my work. He encouraged me to apply for art school, but I knew I didn't have a chance, as I had absolutely no qualifications to speak of, plus my reading and writing was still way behind.

We soon started to think about moving into a bedsit with a double bed. Living together was lovely and peaceful, although our single bed was tiny. So I decided I would earn some money. I chatted to people in pubs, like I had in Oxford, and picked up cleaning and ironing jobs. Thanks to my years of housework training I was well qualified in that department. I made myself pleasant and put it about I was looking for work, and I soon had several cleaning jobs on my hands. I didn't mind, as it was cash in hand and I was good at it.

Meanwhile, once we had moved into our bedsit, which happened to be next to a posh girls' secondary school, I set myself the task of learning. I was furious about the holes in my education and I really wanted to catch up. I watched the girls being dropped off in their neat little uniforms by their mummies in their huge gleaming cars every day, and felt envy. As they were hugged or kissed on the head, given a lunch box, a wave and a smile, I realised I came from a different planet. So I set about sorting myself out.

I developed a daily routine. In the morning, while Tim would be studying or at a university lecture, I would listen to BBC Radio 4 and hear Brian Redhead explain the news (current affairs still interested me). Then, when the school bell went, I would settle down to teach myself to read and write. I got the dictionary and literally worked my way through it, trying to learn words. I'd read very few books, and I began to work my way slowly through a novel, looking up words, which Tim had suggested. *The Catcher in the Rye* was a great place to start. I got work in a pub in the evenings, pulling pints. This was good for my maths, as I had to add up in my head (like in the greengrocer's). Meanwhile, Tim and I had a wonderful time together.

I soon decided that I should try to sign on to help us financially, as things were tight. I also applied for housing benefit. At first, Tim hadn't told his parents that we were together. But it became clear after a while, as he didn't like hiding things from them (unlike me, who found it easy), and they sent him some extra money. They were kind, supportive and thoughtful: like proper parents should be. They didn't judge either. However, I didn't want to be dependent on Tim or them; I wanted to make my own way. Tim was helping me plan my way to art school. He found the pubs where the art school students hung out and we went there a lot and chatted to them and found out what we needed to do. He really encouraged me, so I started to apply. My portfolio was growing daily, and I really hoped I could somehow get in.

~ᆞᆞ~

One morning, I was jumping up and down on the bed, listening to Jimmy Hendrix's 'All Along the Watchtower', which I thought was fantastic. I was just in Tim's white shirt, with nothing underneath. The doorbell rang, and I thought it was the postman, who usually called at that time of day. Although I was in the shirt I was fairly decent, as it was big – at least to open the door a crack and take a letter in. However, when I opened the door, there was a middle-aged man in a plaid jacket and matching hat, with a clipboard.

'Hello,' he said. 'I'm Mr Jones and I've come about your recent housing benefit application.'

He showed me his lapel that had a badge saying he was from the council. I was standing on the doorstep in Tim's shirt and nothing else, looking flushed from jumping on the bed. Hendrix was still blasting in the background.

'Can I come in?' I didn't know what to say. He looked at me seriously and said, 'I need to check some things before you can get any money.'

I felt put on the spot. I didn't know he was coming but he was a council official, so I let him in. I thought, well, I really need the money, so we'd better sort it out. I showed him into our bedsit and turned off the music. I gestured for him to sit on the bed, which he did. I sat on a little upright chair opposite him, with our clothes all over it.

'Well,' the man began, looking at his clipboard and flipping through papers, 'I've spoken to your mother, and she's still entitled to claim child benefit as you are still under sixteen.' He looked me up and down when he said that, and I suddenly felt very uncomfortable and aware I was just in a shirt with nothing underneath.

I pulled the shirt down to cover my knees, crossed my legs tight, and turned sideways on from him. I didn't like hearing mention of my 'mother' – I was trying to forget her now. He cleared his throat and looked down at his clipboard again.

'Ahem, well, yes, she says she doesn't want anything to do with you, and because of that you are only entitled to £2.97 a week to live off. You are not officially here, as you are supposed to be there – she is getting your allowance. You can only get yours if she gives hers up.'

Oh God, I thought. *Typical! I'm still being ruled by Barbara. She's still trying to run my life and punish me, from Oxford to Portsmouth*. I realised I'd been foolish to put down her address as mine on the housing benefit application. I hadn't thought it through properly, and had done so automatically. I said nothing.

'You can get a proportion of your rent, however', said the man, looking round the tiny bedsit, 'as housing benefit.'

I relaxed a bit then; well, at least we would get something. We sat looking at each other for a moment as I took this in.

'Okay,' I said. 'Do I have to do anything else?' The man looked at me for a moment and then rested his clipboard on the bed beside him.

'Well,' he said, looking a bit strange. 'There are other ways of making money…' And with that he patted the bed on the side with no clipboard. For a second I didn't understand. What was he saying? What did he mean? He was looking a bit flushed now.

'Come and sit next to me,' he said, patting the bed again. I froze. Oh no, not again. I eyed up the door, sneakily, under my lashes, wondering if I had a chance to run at it and escape. I didn't want to look at the door in case it gave away what I was thinking.

'Oh… yes?' I said in a vague way, playing for time.

'There are ways girls like you can earn money,' he said, as he leant over the small space between us.

I then leapt up as if electrocuted and flew at the door like a mad bat. He thought I was just standing up, but I was out the door, down the landing, out the front door and into the alleyway. I got behind the big wheelie bins, shaking, and hid in broad daylight with just Tim's shirt on.

I held my breath and hoped to hell the man didn't figure out where I was. A few minutes later I heard the front door slam and saw his back disappearing down the path and into a parked car. Once the engine started up and the car left I crept out from behind the bins. I was barefoot and freezing. I had to hover in the chilly alleyway for three hours until the woman who lived upstairs came home, and she had a spare key for our flat. I felt absolutely furious that my safe and sacred space with my beloved Tim had been defiled by this horrible man. However, to my neighbour I explained I had locked myself out, and she seemed to believe my story. She even made me a nice hot cup of tea, as I was a human icicle by then. I never told Tim about the man because, deep down, I wasn't sure if everything bad that happened to me wasn't my fault. After all, I'd been told all my life that I was a 'slut', a 'whore' and a 'tart', so maybe it was true. Tim didn't think that, thank goodness, and I didn't want him to doubt me so, as usual, I decided to keep quiet.

22

The Long and Winding Road

Tim and I lived very happily together for two years while he was at uni. We decorated our bedsit, cooked vegan meals on a small Baby Belling stove, went on demos and to gigs and parties. He was very studious and worked hard but also made good friends. He was generous, kind and encouraging of me and my art. I held down loads of cleaning jobs while teaching myself all sorts of things (with Tim's help as my mentor) and filling my portfolio. I spent lots of time with people from the art school and started going to the local library and dipping into their wonderful illustrated art books. I was fascinated by women artists, particularly Georgia O'Keeffe and Frida Kahlo, and I loved sculpture by Elisabeth Frink and Barbara Hepworth. As I worked towards getting a place at Portsmouth Art School, I broadened my knowledge by looking at Andy Warhol and German Expressionism, and I discovered Dada.

My portfolio was comprised of portraits and collages – huge charcoal faces of Tim and myself and friends – and I used Boots Extra Hold hairspray to stick things down. I managed to get an interview on the strength of my work.

At the interview the teachers thought I was two years older

than I was, and said at sixteen I was too young to apply. I was told to come back later. I wasn't too disheartened, as at least they liked my work, and Tim encouraged me not to give up. I felt it was a big step just to get that far, given my appalling school record. It made me even more determined to try, as I loved the look of the art school and the students, and I absolutely wanted to be there. I knew it was my gateway to heaven on earth.

Then something awful happened, which shattered my world. I didn't see it coming at all. One morning we woke up in our little flat and Tim said, out of the blue, 'How would you feel about an open relationship?'

I didn't really know what that meant. He explained it meant we could have sex with other people, not just each other. I knew instantly it would mean the end of our relationship. I loved and trusted Tim entirely, he was my world, and he was asking me to share him with someone else. I said I didn't know and left it at that. However, soon after we went to a nightclub in Portsmouth, in quite a rough area, and during the evening Tim turned to me and said, 'I'm going to walk Emma home.'

She was a pretty blonde girl in his class and they'd been chatting most of the evening. I wasn't invited. He was going with her and leaving me behind. He'd never done anything like that before, so I couldn't understand it. It seemed so out of character. But I could see they were flirting and that I was no longer the centre of his world. I realised the boy who had saved me, who had made me, who had given me comfort and security and love, with whom I'd built a new, safe life, was now focusing on someone else. How had that happened? Why hadn't I seen it coming? What would I do? I wanted to fold up and die on the spot, but I left quickly and walked home crying the whole way.

It couldn't be. I couldn't take sharing him. I was more distraught than I could deal with and I didn't sleep all night, waiting for him to come back.

Next morning, when he wasn't there, I just packed my bags and left. I had nowhere to go but I couldn't stay and see Tim with someone else. It would kill me. It was so sudden. I guess he sort of lost his head, felt trapped and wanted to try being with someone else. He was also at the end of his course, so maybe he felt he needed to be free.

I guess he must have fallen out of love with me, or got bored, or wanted new experiences – but he hadn't said a word before dropping the bombshell. I guess we had fallen into a young married couple routine too soon and, perhaps very naively, I thought we would just go on for ever. I was two years younger than him, and I also guess he felt the world was his oyster. He was very handsome, intelligent, charming – and maybe we'd been together too long. He was coming up to twenty when I was still only seventeen.

Maybe she was cleverer than me and he felt tired of training me up. I would never know. His parents had totally accepted us as a couple, although Barbara disapproved, and of course had never visited. We'd done everything together – gone to films, gigs, meals with friends. He was at the end of his studies and we hadn't talked about what would happen next; we hadn't dared. I was still trying to get into art school, while he was talking about doing an MA. But all of a sudden he was into someone else and I couldn't stand it. Open relationships were quite common at the time, as people experimented sexually and emotionally, but we'd been so close. I wasn't going to fight over him though; it was too humiliating and I was too proud. I was also sensitive to rejection, so all I could do was pack up and melt away into Portsmouth. But how would I survive?

On the bus into town I felt like I'd swallowed a concrete block. What was I going to do? Where would I live? I bought a local newspaper, got a load of ten pence pieces and stood in a phone box, dialling up landlords from the small ads section. I had to find somewhere for the night at least, and I didn't have much cash. After a day of phoning I eventually got a tiny room in a grotty shared house with a very dodgy, rough-looking landlord. I didn't understand what I was getting myself into, but I was desperate. I made up a bed and cried and cried and cried.

I didn't phone Tim; I didn't let him know where I was – I'd sort that out later. I felt lonelier and more desolate than I had in the whole of my life, but I had to survive. Luckily, I still had my jobs, but I'd relied on Tim's family money and grant to make life work. So I had to get more jobs, and I worked and worked. I took anything I could get, in different cafés and bars. Plus I still did ironing, gardening, washing people's cars; anything to earn a fiver. It was incredibly tough. I lived on lentils, beans and pasta and little else. It was hard to eat well after the rent was paid. I got so poor and thin that I would scavenge vegetables from shops and supermarkets at the end of the day and boil them into a curry and live on it for days. I tried to nourish myself but it was hard.

When I met friends in pubs and cafes, I said I'd just eaten or drunk, so I didn't spend, and I didn't let on how tough things were. I never wanted to be a sob story – I was too proud. If I visited someone's house to eat, that was fantastic, but on the whole without Tim I was very alone. The friends we'd had from the time we lived together were now mostly drifting away from Portsmouth. Their degrees over, there was no longer any reason for them to stay.

As time went on I began to see that I had landed in a pretty hairy household. There were heroin addicts and drunks and the place was really a bug-ridden flophouse. No wonder it was so cheap. The landlord turned out to be a local gangster, driving a flash fast car and dealing drugs. At certain low points I even found myself accepting some of his drugs, which he made out was a freebie and then, in the months when I was low on cash, he made it clear I could pay in another way – with sexual favours. Just like the horrible men on the Cowley Road had demanded from my friend Sandy.

I was habituated to this kind of abuse from my years with Kevin and Mark and the various social workers, so sometimes, to my disgust, I complied, as there was no other way to pay the rent. Being stoned or drunk helped me get through it. I didn't care. I had learnt to disconnect from my body through years of abuse. I occupied my mind. It was ghastly but I did it and tried not to think about it afterwards. It was a means to an end, although it made me feel totally sick.

To distract myself further I decorated my room as well as I could using paper, paint, drawings, collage, pictures, anything to give it some colour and life. I picked up a couple of stray animals, a pretty little cat and a pup, who kept me company, but this was a horrible, lonely, terrible time in my life and my health began to suffer badly. All this time I'd had no real contact with Barbara. She was always venomous and vindictive the minute I got in touch with her while I was with Tim, so I tended to steer a wide berth.

I had, from time to time, over the two years I was with Tim, tried to explore something more with Julie. Part of me still hoped she would turn out to be a real mum to me. However, she inevitably disappointed. She didn't turn up, or whatever we planned somehow went wrong. She always put herself first, and I was always forgiving her and then trying again, hoping desperately that she would change. I did find out some of her story, however, which was important for me to know.

I discovered that my father had been a Jewish taxi driver in his thirties who had formed a relationship with Julie when she was only a teenager, around fourteen. They had sex in the back of his taxi and, bingo, that's how I came about. Julie herself wasn't Jewish, so I wasn't technically Jewish, as it follows the matrilineal line. However, I had my father's dark hair and olive skin, which is why Barbara was always taunting me. This put me in a difficult position: I'd always been told I was Jewish, in a nasty way, and rejected by Gentiles (like Barbara), and yet I was now not Jewish, so I couldn't belong to that community either. I was in a difficult place socially and culturally. What was I exactly? Where did I belong? Who wanted me? I didn't have a proper pedigree; I was a real outcast, a mongrel, like some of Barbara's poor dogs.

I also found out that when Julie got pregnant her parents gave her an ultimatum: give up the baby for adoption or never come home again. They were very religious people, but not at all compassionate. She had no choice and was forced to give me up in the strict nursing home where she gave birth, aged fifteen. She was also banned from seeing my father again. It turned out he was a married man, already with children, and that he completely ditched Julie once she'd got pregnant, although he had broken the law due to her being under age. She never saw him again and he didn't contribute to my upbringing.

Julie's own father was a bigamist, she discovered later, which caused her all sorts of emotional problems. She was a confused and rejected woman who had never really grown up emotionally. Her childlike behaviour meant she had husband after husband, but was never really able or willing to be a mother to her own children (including me, who was an embarrassment). I was an uncomfortable reminder to her of that time in the back of the taxi with my wayward abandoning father.

I eventually found out his name and where he lived, and even got his phone number. One day I got up the courage to phone him and explain who I was. He sounded very surprised and uncomfortable, but we agreed to meet on a bench in the University Parks, one of my favourite places, but he never turned up. I suppose it was one step too far for him to take. I was devastated, as I was never to meet him before he died. I was incredibly sad and hurt about this, which all happened while I was living with Tim, and continued once I had left and was surviving the best I could in my grotty bedsit.

I was hell-bent on trying to keep myself afloat and get into college. I was used to no one wanting me; it seemed like my default position. I was getting thinner and thinner, and got far too interested in drink and drugs for my health and sanity. I was in such pain. I was so lonely, desperate and rejected, and trying to create a successful persona for the world to see, that I was abusing myself and the stress began to wear me into the ground.

By this time Tim was long gone, taking a gap year before beginning his MA elsewhere. We were no longer in touch. One day I was feeling very desperate. I had a packet of seeds and I went out to the scrubby patch of yard at the back of the flats. It was unkempt and untended, with old furniture and bricks strewn about. There was one corner that got a bit of sun, though, and it had a bit of earth. I cleared a patch with a kitchen fork, opened the packet and scattered the seeds on the ground. I thought to myself, *If these seeds come up, I'll go on, but if they don't, that's it. Finito.* I felt my life was hanging by a thin thread, and something as simple as seeds not flowering would be a sign that the struggle to survive was too great for me to continue bothering with.

Deep down I was exhausted. I was drowning in pain and rejection and yet I was trying to keep afloat. I started pulling out hair again – eyelashes, clumps from my head. I counted as much as I could, when I could remember to. I watched those seeds avidly over the next weeks and months, willing them to come up. It felt a slow and difficult time waiting, as there didn't seem much to see yet. Meanwhile, my health was failing and I began to get feverish. I got very sick and took to bed for days. In the end I was ulcerated and in agony all over my mouth, my face, my lips, my guts and my windpipe. Eventually I felt so bad I took myself to a local GP, who took one look at me and called an ambulance. I was whisked into the local hospital, where I was told I might have AIDS. I was put in isolation, as AIDS was a big deal at that time, called 'the gay plague', and everyone was terrified of it as a killer.

Word got back to my flat and the landlord burned my bedding, believing AIDS was infectious. After more blood tests the hospital worked out I had a rare viral infection called Stevens–Johnson Syndrome, which is an extremely serious stress-related breakdown of the immune system. I lay in bed for about three weeks then, sweating and shaking, in agony.

This is an illness you can die from, and a lot of the time I didn't care if I lived or died. A couple of friends visited and I asked them to look after my rescue pets. I had to give Barbara's number to the hospital as next of kin and, indeed, she did visit once. She stared at me down her pointy nose and didn't touch me, didn't comfort me at all, and then left.

Barbara must have told Julie, who turned up briefly, took one look at me and said, 'Is it catching?' and then left, holding her nose. The only help I got was from one of my friend's mums, who would bring me bits of tasty food she had cooked – some quiche or fruit or jelly. She took pity on me, as she could see I was alone, suffering and fading away. I wasn't sure if I wanted to get better, if there was anything to live for any more. Life was too tough and I was weary of struggling.

Eventually, after a few weeks, I turned the corner and did recover, gradually. Julie popped in towards the end of my hospital stay and I gathered up the courage to ask her to lend me £10. I'd been in hospital for about six weeks and hadn't been able to get any money from anywhere. She looked at me, really put out.

'Oh no, I haven't got it – I'm short this month,' she said, examining her pink nails. 'Didn't Barbara give you anything?'

She was wearing new shoes, clothes and jewellery, as usual. I didn't ask again. So when I eventually got home, thanks to a lift from my friend's mum, there was nothing in the fridge and I had literally no money to buy anything. I was incredibly thin and pale, fragile and delicate. I lived on crackers and herb tea and whatever I could scavenge, or on the kindness of friends.

Soon after I came home there was a knock at the door and a policeman handed me a cat collar: my lovely puss had been run over. Could things have got any worse? I was dodging the advances of the landlord, who was straight round for his rent 'payment' in kind. It was clear I couldn't deliver, as I was exhausted, and didn't even have bedding, as he'd burned it. It was a horrendous, disastrous mess, and I had no idea how I was going to get out of it and get my life on track. I was at the lowest possible point and I had no idea how to raise myself up again. It would be a long, slow haul back to health, and I would have to do it alone. Would I survive a day longer?

~⋇~

A few days after I got home from hospital, I ventured out into the back yard, wrapped in loads of layers. There, in the corner, to my surprise, was a beautiful sight: an array of stunning flowers swaying in the breeze. They looked like magic; like they were sprinkled with sparkling fairy dust. I could pick out bright blue cornflowers and pretty pink and purple sweet peas; there were poppies, campion and forget-me-nots – my favourite little blue flowers with the black centres. My wild 'mixed seeds' from dear old Sean and Iris and John, who I used to visit with Ian and William as a child in Oxford. 'Don't forget-me-not,' John had quipped. I hadn't. Now they had finally bloomed. And saved my life.

At the lowest of my low points I had thought there was nothing to live for. I felt, as I swayed there with weak knees like Bambi, that the flowers were speaking to me: 'Go on, Louise. Go on, you can do it. You can make it. Keep going.' They had actually bloomed just for me. There was hope. Life went on. My life could go on. Spring did always follow winter, no matter how bleak. The flowers were a revelation to me. I drank in their beauty and stared at them, and thanked them for being there. They were a sign that in my darkest of dark hours I simply had to go on. They were a blooming beacon of the power of hope.

Every day from then on I watered the flowers and thinned them out and tended them. I remembered tending Sean's little garden with him when I was a child. I would scatter the seeds and he would water them with his big silver watering can. Then he would show me how to thin them out and say, 'Well done, girlie' to me. He also had vegetables: carrots, cabbages, lettuces and onions. I thought it was magic then – seeds turning into beautiful, living things – and I still did now.

So, despite living in a total grot-hole, I cleared a little bit of garden, just like Sean had taught me, and I began to feel better and recover. I managed to get back to a couple of cleaning jobs, which kept the money coming in. I also succeeded in getting some benefits, so I could pay the landlord his rent and keep him at bay for a while. I was determined to get myself straight. And as I tended my beautiful corner of colourful flowers, I began to learn to tend to myself, too. I realised I needed to look after myself as, if I didn't, I would simply die.

I cut down on the drink and drugs and gave myself herb tea and better food. I needed to move out of that place, and I soon did, to a better room with nicer people and no evil landlord. I also decided to focus on getting into art school again and, this time, despite my poor education, I managed it. It was a total turning point: I was going to go to Portsmouth School of Art and I was getting a grant to go there. I was completely over the moon. They were persuaded by my work and, despite not being able to spell properly or having any qualifications, I was able to present myself well at interview. My art – of which there was a lot by now – spoke for me, and luckily it was good enough to get me a place.

It was the beginning of my new life. A lifeline. I was on my way: wanted at last.

And Finally...

I t took me a long time to get back on my feet but I was determined to succeed. I understood I had to work hard and save every penny. I was used to deprivation and could endure a huge amount of discomfort, and my eye was firmly on the goal of succeeding, no matter what. When I finally got my place on the Foundation course, I was ecstatic and worked incredibly hard. I wanted to go on to do fine art, but my lack of education and qualifications got in the way. It was before there were 'Access' courses, and they were simply not willing for me to proceed. Undeterred, I managed to get onto an HND in environmental design. I got scholarships to go to Berlin and New York. It was a great time.

After this course, I worked as an illustrator and got jobs in fashion, in magazines and window dressing, just about anything I could do that involved art. I painted all the time and continued to work on portraits. I was artist in residence with deprived children, I taught art in prison, and also got work at Portsmouth Art School as an art teacher, so I was in a creative, artistic environment for over twenty years.

I scrimped and scraped and decided very early on that I needed to save money to buy a property, and that is exactly what

I did. A girl with absolutely nothing, and nothing behind her, had to get something and make something of herself – and that was me. It took a long time for me to earn enough, but I was able to get myself into all sorts of amazing jobs by sheer force of my personality and drive. I had a lot of energy and determination. I was short on paper qualifications (except for my HND), but I was driven to make things work. For this I needed inspiration to keep going, so I made any place I lived look as beautiful, artistic and wacky as a modern-day Blenheim Palace.

❧

I did go back to see Barbara once I was at college, and then when working, although I needed to distance myself at first. The bond I had with her from my side was strong, as she was the only mother I knew, albeit a damaging one. I could have walked away completely many times, but there was something about her that kept me in touch. I had seen her in pain: hugging her dolls and rocking back and forth on her bed, crying in the forest when she dumped me. The constant cry of 'rape' and her mask of misery made me feel that she was deeply unhappy, and it was hard for me to let go.

Ian died shortly after he retired, of cancer, at sixty-seven years old, but Barbara lived on until she was over eighty. She moved to a smaller property in Oxford but she didn't look after herself well. I visited a few times a year, taking her nice food or helping her with things in her little house, and although she was never warm and I nearly always left in tears, due to something nasty she'd said, I couldn't walk away.

Later in my life I looked after her, visiting regularly, helping her physically. She was never kind, she never said sorry, but

I could sense she was pleased I was there. Barbara began to get dementia, and I could tell on one of my visits that she was struggling. Amazingly, Barbara fell out with Kevin, who started bullying her once I'd left home and Ian died. She became frightened of him. Then he married and moved away, ignoring her in her old age. She was very bitter about this.

Eventually she was moved into a local hospital by a concerned neighbour, and as I walked into the ward I saw her sitting up in bed, her hands over her face, crying. I sat down next to her and said, 'What is it?' She was doing a kind of dry crying, without tears, but she whispered in a husky voice, 'The baby was mine, the baby was mine.'

Barbara was clearly very distressed, and said this as if she was sharing a terrible secret. I leant in and sat quietly beside her. 'Which baby was yours?' She peeked out of her cupped hands and looked up and down the ward to see if anyone was watching. 'Shush,' she said. 'Don't tell anyone, my mum will be angry.' Then she paused. 'It's Tony. He's mine.'

Tony was Barbara's brother. Her father was an impoverished musician and heavy drinker, and she was brought up in Harlesden, London, in the 1920s (she was born in '26, just as the Great Depression hit). Her mother was a cleaner. They had a wild and wandering life, moving all the time, paying rent, picking up odd work here and there. Then they ended up in the workhouse. Barbara had told me over the years, bit by bit, that her father was a violent, abusive drunk. She feared him deeply.

That afternoon, sitting up in bed, she went back to being a child, rocking back and forth. She spoke through her hands, covering her face in shame, about the men her father had taken her to for sex as a small child: the father and son next door, the local policeman, other men from the pub. Barbara had been her father's 'nice little earner'. She had been raped over and over. She had got pregnant, probably around the age of eleven or twelve, and she had given birth to Tony, her so-called 'brother', who was taken in by the family as if he was their son.

She gave birth in an outside 'lavvy' and the doctor sewed her up too tightly, possibly as a punishment to keep her on the straight and narrow. She was in agony. Barbara breathed out this story: 'It hurt, oh, it hurt so much – it was too tight.' I could see now why Barbara said 'all men are rapists', as she had actually been raped: by the next-door neighbours, the local policeman, men from the pub, perhaps even her own father or brother, or other men in the workhouse.

Her mother must have known, as did her father, but it was never spoken about. She whispered about the violence, the harshness, being made to eat dog poo by one of the workhouse warders as punishment one day. There had also been a warder who tied the children to their beds – exactly as she had done to William and I.

'It was horrible, terrible,' whispered Barbara on and on, telling me things she had never spoken of before. She 'confessed' all this to me in her demented state, in a childlike voice, and I began to understand why she had done what she did. She had been abused and raped as a child, treated inhumanely, and knew no other way to be. After the workhouse, she was sent to a convent in the 1930s, which was also harsh and tough with cruel nuns who made her scrub floors with carbolic and make beds with hospital corners. Again, her love of making me clean everything, of carbolic and the constant random slaps and attacks had their root in her own terrifying early experiences. I understood now that she had deep mental and emotional problems from her own childhood. It had been a nightmare. This didn't condone what she had done, but it explained it to me, as she had never received any mental help.

Sex was always painful for the rest of her life, so when Ian tried she hated it. She felt she was being raped all over again, as she had been as a child. Her unnatural interest in Kevin was also a re-enactment of her relationship with her brothers and other boys and men, possibly the only comfort she had had as a child. It was all very twisted but somehow, despite everything, my heart went out to her. Later, when I saw my own records, I discovered that many of the social workers had wondered about getting Barbara to see a psychiatrist during the months when I was fostered, and then adopted, in 1967 and 1968 and then later. Some questioned her ability, but there was a shortage of fosterers and a large amount of unwanted babies. There were many notes about her 'not coping' and 'needing support' but nothing was ever done.

Barbara herself had questioned if she was able to look after me, and my notes showed that twice I could have been given to someone else during that first crucial year before she legally adopted me in 1968. And yet each time the system failed to protect me or to give her the help or support she needed. No one asked her about her own childhood or her fitness to look after children. The system was under pressure to suck up the unwanted children as a result of the huge glut of illegitimate pregnancies that occurred after the 'summer of love' in 1967. I was the product of that, and Barbara's early traumas were completely ignored, unchecked and untreated. If only…

It may sound strange, but during the years of her decline I visited her as often as I could, and I even made sure she eventually went to a good care home. She became increasingly confused and, as she lost her powers, I felt more tenderness for her. One day I took her out for a walk in her wheelchair and her face slumped on one side: she'd had a stroke. After that she quickly deteriorated. She ended up in a hospital at the end. Luckily I had organised a green burial site for her on the South Downs, which she knew about and approved of. I felt protective of Barbara; I could see she was vulnerable and alone and, despite all that she had done to me – and to William – I could not personally operate from hate or revenge. I didn't want to hand on the pain. I wanted to be a better person. For my own satisfaction and sense of what was right.

The day she died I had been to see her in the evening, and I could see her breathing was shallow. She was propped up on pillows and was quite out of touch. I looked down at the pinched, pale and pointed face – the one I had stared at all my childhood in terror. Now she was tiny, reduced, fading. I tussled with myself for a moment: should I stay or should I go? I realised that although I genuinely loved her out of some deep human compassion for her own suffering in her childhood (that no one but me knew about), I nonetheless could not sit with her and see her out of this life.

Before I left I put a film on for her on the TV and left it running. Then I looked down at Barbara for the last time, touched her hand and said, 'I'm off now, bye.' She raised a hand weakly from the bed, and mumbled, 'Bye.'

I didn't say, 'See you later,' as I knew I wouldn't. I went home and made a cup of tea and got on with my household chores.

I had forgiven her for so many things, but she had done some really terrible things to William and I and had left big bruises and deep wounds on our lives. I understood now what had happened to her, and I empathised, truly, but it did not make me want to be there when she died. It was too intimate, too much about unconditional love. I spent so much of my childhood scared and crying that I felt I couldn't comfort her on her very last stage of her journey, despite having been there as much as I could be in her last years and months.

I felt that after throwing me away as a child she had to go alone into her next life, whatever or wherever it was. I had also learnt to look after myself now, and being there at the very end was simply one step too far.

❧

Luckily, Kevin had married and moved away to another city, so I was able to avoid him completely. Also Julie moved on again to yet another man. Vernon died an early death (to Julie's obvious relief: 'He was a bit boring and moaned about my spending – men!') and her two children emigrated. Julie often tried to get money from me once I was earning. I discovered she too had a very confusing and hurtful childhood. As her own father had turned out to be a bigamist, when he died, two families turned up for the funeral with no warning and Julie discovered she had brothers and sisters she had never seen or known. It was so hypocritical for him not to allow her to keep her own child when he was cheating all the while. What a mess! It was no wonder she was unreal.

Amazingly, I eventually also managed to track down dear William, after a lot of dead-end leads, through a notice of his marriage in a local newspaper cutting in Barbara's papers. I found the cutting when I was clearing out her house, finally. We eventually met after thirty-seven years apart. It was an amazing moment. We sat together on one of my favourite University Parks benches and cried and cried and cried. We could hardly speak. We just held hands and sobbed. He repeatedly said, 'Why didn't anyone help us?'

Today we are still piecing together the mad story of our broken childhoods. William's story should also be told, as I think there must be many Williams and Louises who got lost in the system in the free-love era of the 1960s baby boom. Hopefully they didn't get put into a family that was already being investigated for child cruelty like we were, and then ignored and abused – that was something I wouldn't wish on my worst enemy. I still can't understand to this day how that happened. And I would like to find out more, and make sure it never happens to any other so-called 'unwanted' children.

In the end I was lucky enough to meet a lovely man at art college who I was eventually to marry years later and with whom I am still incredibly happy. We have two children of our own, and we also foster children together. It is a joy and a challenge, and I feel incredibly blessed and grateful on that front. But that's another long story, for another place.

As for dear old Irish Sean – the man who saved my life and gave me some lovely childhood memories – I loved him dearly until he died. I still do. He was my real family – generous and kind. I continued to see him as often as I could. He always welcomed me back with a warm 'Hello, girlie, come in,' until the very last. He would always get the whisky out, or some Guinness, and pour me a huge glass ('Down the hatch, girlie'). He continued in his caravan as long as he could, and carried on betting on the horses, growing his veg and flowers and walking his dog, Frida.

One time I visited him towards the end of his life, when I had finished art school. There were several older men sitting on seats outside his caravan. The sky was glowing warm and orange in the summer evening, and the air smelt of jasmine and honeysuckle. As I got nearer to the caravan I could hear gravelly talk and raucous laughter and music. The men on the seats in caps and tweeds, belts and braces, all had instruments with them: a fiddle, a drum, a tambour, a penny whistle and a squeeze box. There was a crate of Guinness and brown ale by the side of the caravan and most were smoking ciggies or pipes.

'Oh, there you are, come here, girlie,' rasped Sean, laughing. He introduced me to his gang, all ex-navvies from his past. I was handed a bottle of Guinness and some crisps and then the men tuned up and suddenly struck up a wonderful Irish jig. I sat on the step of Sean's caravan, listening to the fantastic bouncy music. My foot was tapping and my heart was full to bursting as I watched Sean tooting on his penny whistle, as all the players made the jig ring out through the orchard into the night air. As I watched Sean's rosy cheeks fill as he blew, and listened to the wonderful sound, I thanked him with all my heart for the happy times and care he had given me in my childhood. I knew absolutely that I would not have survived without him. I could see the road ahead of me was going to be a long and winding one, just like the Beatles song I loved. But that along the way there were significant people, like Tim and Sean, and later my wonderful husband, who had simply made all the difference between me living and dying.

That was certainly something to be thankful for, after all.

Afterword

C hild abuse is not a comfortable subject to think about. I will be honest with you: I was scared about writing this. Scared for all the reasons you can imagine and some you can't.

There are four types of abuse: sexual, physical, emotional and neglect. The easiest one to prove is physical abuse, as long as the marks are still showing. Neglect can also be easy to detect, but not all neglect presents itself as a snotty face or dirty tangled hair full of head lice. Emotional neglect is the most recently legally acknowledged form of child abuse, but I suspect it plays a big role in all the other kinds.

As a stand-alone abuse, I wonder how many adults are doing this to children every day without any awareness that their behaviour is even abusive or that it will have long-term effects on that child's mental health? I believe children are abused because they are young and vulnerable. I believe adults abuse because they can.

After reading my story you may be surprised to know that I think my educational neglect was the worst part of all the abuses I suffered. It has been my life sentence. I have managed to live with the other abuses, which have somehow settled into my form, and I think I've been good at hiding them; most people would never know and I have never told. But poor literacy skills, no basic maths and a narrow awareness of the world has been a terrible cage to be trapped in and impossible to hide. I have felt ashamed and humiliated as I have observed people thinking I'm thick.

In all subjects except art I was labelled remedial and, as an adult, I was diagnosed with dyslexia and dyscalculia. When I did go to school my head was fizzing with fear and hurt; there was no room to learn and I was not encouraged to do so. I've had to work hard to try and catch up, and I'm aware that my thoughts, ideas and approaches can be a little unconventional, but I put that down to a non-formulaic learning experience – or creativity: depends who's asking!

❦

Young Louise is part of me now; I keep her safe and make sure she has everything she needs. We get along well and she makes me smile. I know she will never leave me; our child-hoods never do. These days I spend my time looking after other people's children, as well as two stepchildren and two of my own. But when I began fostering with my husband a few years ago, we found a world that was far removed from what we had hoped.

We see social workers struggling to manage huge case-loads and it has become harder for them to spend time with the children and young people in their care, as they feed the hungry machine of legislation and data collection and so on. This stifling bureaucracy takes them away from the reason most of them came into social work – to make a difference in children's lives.

We began our fostering journey via an independent

agency – the first one that popped up when we typed 'fostering' into the search engine – and we naively believed their marketing. These agencies are a mix of charitable, not-for-profit and private companies, and it can be difficult to tell the difference from their websites, but we soon learnt that most are owned by bankers and venture capitalists who make millions from the agencies recruiting foster carers to look after local authority children. It feels like capitalism has been allowed to run amok in children's social care.

We responded to the national call for more foster carers but, after successfully going through a rigorous assessment process, the agency we were with still couldn't find us a placement after more than a year. We began to wonder if there were any children who needed a foster home.

Millions of pounds of public money is somehow lost to tax havens while carers like me have to fight to get even the basic resources and therapeutic support for our foster children. In 2014, £3 billion went to the looked-after children's budget and £1 billion of that went to the independent fostering agencies.* I shiver at the thought of shareholders feeling happy that more children are going into care – it feels like children's misery has become a commodity.

I think we all agree that the best outcome for a child going into care is a good foster placement that offers a safe and secure home for as long as is needed. But so many good foster carers are leaving; tired of being bullied and disregarded, they say it simply isn't worth it. Unfortunately, carers have no rights

---

*Statistics from https://www.gov.uk/government/collections/childrens-social-care-statistics

or protection. They are often subjected to malicious and mischievous allegations from foster children, their families and sometimes even social workers. I have seen foster carers and their families destroyed as allegations go forward without good evidence or a decent hearing, and this takes time and money away from the work and results in the loss of more foster homes.

If governments genuinely want to improve children's lives then they need to look after the people who look after the children; they should divert the money back into children's social care, improve these children's life chances, and stop lining the pockets of people who want to develop their own wealth portfolios.

❧

Abuse isn't particular to any one social group. It is found freely among the whole social strata – which is why we need carers from a wider reach of backgrounds. Foster carers have traditionally been a husband and wife, with the wife being the primary carer. I believe we need to attract a more modern fostering workforce that represents all the backgrounds of children in care. When social workers threatened me with foster care if I didn't behave (and as a foster carer I would hate to feel that we are a punishment for behaviour caused by trauma), I would have willingly packed my own suitcase if they'd told me I was going to live with a gay couple who loved the Arts and shopped at Liberty. But I know I didn't want to live with another family. I didn't like my own family and the thought of living in someone else's would have been awful.

Teenagers are the hardest to place. For many, their experiences of family life have been harmful and chaotic, so the traditional family model may be too much for them. Someone else's family unit can feel like a foreign country: new smells, different food and rules. Teenagers may work better with adults who are not trying to be a parent but a friend who takes responsibility for them and does right by them.

I would love to see a new attitude in fostering and adoption. My drive is to know that vulnerable children will get a fair chance in life and learn how to free themselves from a traumatic childhood. Perhaps all young people should be educated in what the consequences are for children, parents and society if a child is abused or neglected. We should collectively join up and teach them about the responsibilities of having children. Cycles of abuse can be stopped through good education and the necessary support being there for vulnerable people. If we cannot get this right, then we are simply behaving like undertakers sending out assassins. We have to tackle all the cycles of abuse. But we also need to be sure that foster carers – who are so important to these processes – are treated with respect.

The true character of a society is revealed in how it treats its children.

Nelson Mandela, 1997

You can contact Louise at:
Louise-Allen.com

Acknowledgements

Louise would like to thank: all the people whose acts of kindness have given me the strength to go on. The friends along the way with whom I have laughed and danced, and the people whose warmth and compassion made it possible for me to learn to hug. My lecturers from art school, who gave me that chance: Ian Hunter, Mark Harrington, Howard Mason, Brian Lunn and Dave Jenkins. You truly opened my eyes to art, design, culture, friendship and the pub!

William, for answering my letter. My cousins, who after so many years have come back into my life. Lyn and Mike, who know more than most. Sue, George, Laura and Jack for showing me what a good family looked like.

Jane, my special agent from Graham Maw Christie, for having faith and making that call. Corinne Sweet, for sitting with me and displaying such kindness and insight. Kerri Sharp, for her editing wizardry and to Simon & Schuster for giving me a chance.

And finally, all my children, who made me understand what childhood is all about, you are so important; and my husband Lloyd who understands and keeps these matters light.

~❧~

Corinne Sweet gives heartfelt thanks to Jane Graham Maw of Graham Maw Christie, Kerri Sharp of Simon & Schuster, Susanne Torok, Katie Smith, Olamiju Fajemesin, Vicky Abram, Tim Davis, Gill Doust and the WSEG, Johnnie McKeown, Clara Potter-Sweet and the Keedees.